D0803638

PLAYING NO-LIMIT HOLD'EM
AS A
BUSINESS

ABOUT
ROB TUCKER

Rob Tucker moved from New York City to Toronto to earn his M.B.A. from the Schulich School Of Business. It was while earning his degree that he discovered what a great city Toronto is for poker players. Rob quickly took to the no-limit hold'em games in the five casinos in and around the city, in the host of Toronto's live private games, and online. He soon realized that his decision to move to Toronto was a wise one.

Rob has been a regular winner in cash games for years and has at last written this book on his unique approach to winning no-limit hold'em cash games. His next book focuses on how to win no-limit hold'em sit 'n go tournaments online and in live action.

PLAYING NO-LIMIT HOLD'EM AS A BUSINESS

ROB TUCKER

CARDOZA PUBLISHING

Cardoza Publishing is the foremost gaming and gambling publisher in the world with a library of more than 200 up-to-date and easy-to-read books and strategies. These authoritative works are written by the top experts in their fields and with more than 10,000,000 books in print, represent the best-selling and most popular gaming books anywhere.

FIRST EDITION
Second Printing 2014
Copyright © 2010 by Rob Tucker

Library of Congress Catalog Number: 2010932984
ISBN 10:   1-58042-263-2
ISBN 13: 978-1-58042-263-5

Visit our website or write for a full list of Cardoza Publishing books and advanced strategies.

CARDOZA PUBLISHING

P.O. Box 98115, Las Vegas, NV 89193
Toll-Free Phone (800)577-WINS
email: cardozabooks@aol.com
www.cardozabooks.com

TABLE OF CONTENTS

4. EVALUATING YOUR OPPONENTS   51

5. AVOIDING TROUBLE HANDS 61

6. FINDING THE RIGHT GAME   99

1 INTRODUCTION

You hold in your hands a proven and profitable game plan for winning day in and day out in no-limit hold'em cash games. This is how I make my living and I'm going to reveal those secrets to you. You too can make money at poker. Lots of it. That is, if you employ the tried and true plan I show you in this book—and faithfully follow it.

Playing No-limit Hold'em as a Business gives you a powerful moneymaking game plan. It is not based on the hotshot play of those overly aggressive tournament players you see featured on television. In fact, the strategies in this book show you how to take advantage of the flaws in their play when they sit down with you in no-limit hold'em cash games. Unlike tournament specialists, you're not a hit 'n run player who takes unnecessary risks and strikes out in the third inning—you're a cash game specialist who stays in the game for a full nine innings, hitting homeruns with the bases full.

I've included numerous real-life cash game situations that take you beyond elementary preflop play and skillfully lead you through the flop to the river with detailed explanations of how to analyze and how to act each step of the way.

You'll learn how to play your strong hands expertly to win big pots, as well as how to avoid the cash game pitfalls that cause players to lose too much money in marginal situations. You'll learn a disciplined approach that consists of waiting patiently for big hands, and playing intelligently in all your other hands to maximize your wins and minimize your losses. You'll also gain successful strategies for controlling the size of the pot to your advantage, playing shorthanded games, and mixing up your game just enough to deceive your opponents, as well as managing your financial risk to grow your profits at poker.

Playing No-limit Hold'em as a Business just might be one of the best investments you've made in a long time. Follow my advice, and you may be in for a lifetime of profit playing poker.

2 THE WINNING APPROACH

"How's your game going? Been winning?" When you ask a poker player this question, you often get an answer such as, "I've been running bad for months. My game's good but I just keep getting unlucky."

Despite what losing players tell you, their problems are not rooted in bad luck. Their main problem is that their risk tolerance is way too high to play regularly in cash games. Even many experienced players use a faulty strategy and take on too much risk. You don't have to join their ranks. This book gives you a tried and true game plan for winning big and winning consistently in no-limit hold'em cash games.

A lot of poker books—particularly tournament poker books—claim that playing aggressively is the only way to win at poker. The patient, disciplined method in this book is specifically designed for you to take advantage of opponents who mistakenly think it's wrong to play no-limit hold'em conservatively. Of course, you should play some of your strong hands aggressively, but if you believe that "Attack!" is the only mode to use, you are unwisely dismissing a more profitable approach. Winning professional players take a far more disciplined approach to capitalize on the loose, high-risk playing styles so predominant in online and live cash games.

Poker rewards players who know how to yield points to their opponents when the circumstances call for it. You don't have to play a hand of no-limit hold'em like a gunslinger from the Wild West simply because you've already put some chips in the pot. You don't need to get involved in a hand with J-7 offsuit just because you're sitting on the button. You don't have to shove all your chips in the middle to play a flush draw with a straight draw just because you've seen pros do it on TV. Sometimes you need to back down—simply because your goal is to get great results in cash games, not to win every pot. Avoidance is an art form in no-limit hold'em. Some of the most profitable plays in poker come from your ability to show restraint.

ARE YOU NATURALLY AGGRESSIVE OR CONSERVATIVE?

Aggressive poker isn't a style that all players feel comfortable playing. Of course, if you are a natural gambler and risk taker, you cannot change your innate tendencies—but you can learn how to temper your basic style by playing an at-times aggressive, yet always intelligent, style of poker. If you prefer a more conservative approach to playing poker, you will benefit in a big way from using the proven game plan presented in this book. This book's patient and disciplined strategy is designed to refine and perfect your game, showing you when and how to take calculated risks without going overboard outside your comfort level.

Or maybe you haven't yet decided which style of poker is better for you. Not to worry!

Playing No-Limit Hold'em as a Business gives you a moneymaking method for playing poker—even if you're still trying to figure out what type of player you want to be. If you have the discipline to wait for big hands and avoid the high-risk situations that too many players embrace these days, you can win a lot of money at poker with the profitable and easy to learn strategies in this book.

WHY IS MASTERING CASH GAME STRATEGY SO IMPORTANT?

Making money on a regular basis playing poker has become increasingly challenging because the pool of players is more competitive than ever. The growth in home games, online play, and casino poker rooms has produced more and more educated and experienced players, although online poker still offers a lot of opportunity to play against weak players. In short, there are still plenty of fish in the sea, but more sharks are lurking out there than ever before.

The proliferation of how-to information and opportunities to practice poker skills online and in live games has made it harder than ever to make a living playing poker. Keep in mind that I'm saying "challenging" and "harder," but certainly not impossible. In fact, making a lot of money playing poker is a realistic and attainable goal if you use the right approach. The increase in the skill level of poker players and the fact that many players continue to use a loose-aggressive style have made the world of cash games highly complex. Therefore, you need to use an effective game plan to be successful in the long run, a game plan that gives you a reliable way to deal with all the complexities of the game. In this book, I introduce you to a proven and profitable plan for making money at poker.

WHY PLAY CASH GAMES RATHER THAN TOURNAMENTS?

We are currently experiencing an era of poker that is heavily influenced by tournament philosophy, which espouses a loose-aggressive style of play. Since tournaments are constantly aired on TV and so many poker books have been written about tournaments, aggressive play has become so embedded in the minds of hold'em players that it is almost considered shameful to play a different style.

Many poker books teach tournament play. This is good, of course, because the upside of finishing deep in a big one makes it worth the investment of time and money to improve one's tournament game. Most superstars in the game became famous by winning at least one big-league professional tournament, and that is the main area of expertise they share with the public through their books. However, it has become increasingly difficult to win a big tournament.

Here is a list of all the things that need to go your way in order to win a tournament:

1. **Getting lucky.** You have to get lucky at least a few times by hitting a big flop, being on the right end of a set-up hand, and drawing out on someone when you are behind in a hand.

2. **Not getting unlucky.** Flopping two pair when someone else flops a set is usually a recipe for disaster in a tournament, and these are hands you must avoid if you want to win. You also have to avoid an opponent's drawing to a straight or flush and getting there when you have been betting the hand correctly the whole way. Of course, you also

need to avoid the infamous suck-out when most of your chips are committed in a big pot.

3. **Winning coin flips.** When the blinds reach a level where many players are short stacked, you will be involved in a number of key situations where you only have about a 50 percent to 60 percent chance to win the hand. You have to win more than your fair share of coin flips to win a tournament.

4. **Not getting outplayed.** Most tournaments have a fair number of quality players who are adept at finding just the right moment to bet you off the better hand. It is difficult to win a tournament if you fold the best hand numerous times against tricky opponents.

5. **Bluffing successfully.** To win a big tournament you not only need luck on your side, you need to pull off a fair number of bluffs. And you have to succeed with your continuation bets most of the time.

6. **Playing at the right table.** Sometimes things go your way in a tournament. You get strong cards, you don't get unlucky, you have a relatively big chip stack at your table, you have a good read on your opponents, and many of your opponents are weak players. Suddenly the tables get rebalanced and you are moved to another table where you are fifth in chips and the caliber of players is much stronger. To win a large tournament, you need to be fortunate enough to play at the right table most of the time.

Most poker players, including some who have made an occasional appearance on TV, do not make a great living playing tournaments. Many players go through long periods of time, even years, before they make a huge score. Some never do. It is just too difficult to make a decent living playing strictly tournaments—and that is why learning to win at cash games is so important.

WHAT'S THE DIFFERENCE BETWEEN TV POKER AND REAL POKER?

The difference between the poker you see on TV and the poker played in real life, day in and day out, is dramatic. When you compare the cash game strategy you will learn to play in this book—in other words, "real" poker—with TV poker, you will find that they are in fact polar opposites.

What you see on television is usually the final table of a large tournament. The players on TV are not playing with chips that are actually worth real money. How much money they earn is based on how high they place compared to their opponents. They have already gone deep enough in the tournament to earn a healthy paycheck. This influences their play and causes many of them to play fast and gamble more. After all, everybody at the final table is going to get paid and make a profit no matter what.

Their chip stacks are often small relative to the size of the blinds and antes, so the finalists can't afford to play patient poker. They need to play aggressively and make moves to avoid getting blinded out. And some final-table players don't want to get bluffed out of a pot on TV, so they call and raise with marginal holdings far more often than is necessary to win in cash games. In the world of cash games and real money, you are under far less pressure to play fast and loose.

The tournament prize structure further motivates players to play aggressively to accumulate chips. In tournaments there is often a very large difference in prize money between first place and all other places. This difference motivates players to play more aggressively to win pots instead of waiting around for big hands. They often make high-risk moves to accumulate chips to have a shot at winning the tournament.

This book arms you with a game plan that empowers you to take advantage of players who fail to understand these basic differences between poker on the tube and poker in real life.

HOW DOES CASH GAME STRATEGY DIFFER FROM TOURNAMENT STRATEGY?

Cash game and tournament formats are quite different—they require vastly different strategies and playing styles. In a tournament, you are assigned a table and seat number so you have no idea who you will be playing against. More importantly, blinds and antes increase at regular intervals and eat away at your chip stack. Therefore, many players and a lot of pros use an effective approach for tournaments that includes getting involved in a lot of pots in order to accumulate chips.

When blinds and antes are very high, many players cannot afford to fold even marginal hands. For those who prefer a proactive approach in tournaments, good play means being aggressive, gambling for big payoffs, and bluffing or semi-bluffing in order to take down as many pots as possible. With a bit of luck, you will hit a big hand along the way and get paid off since your opponents won't put you on anything strong because of your relentlessly aggressive play. In short, you play a tournament with one objective in mind: Win a lot of chips before your opponents do. To meet this objective, some players choose to take on a lot of risk. Certainly, tournament poker on TV has influenced many players to play this way.

The nature of a cash game is very different from that of a tournament. You don't need to accept a lot of risk to make money regularly in cash games. Since blinds don't rise and there are no antes, you can afford to be patient. You hope that weak, mistake-prone players accumulate chips in a cash game. Why? You want them to stick around long enough for you to eventually win their chips. You also can choose your opponents in cash games. You can run searches for players that you often beat online, or play at casinos or clubs that weaker players visit.

WHY PLAY CONSERVATIVELY IN CASH GAMES?

This book's approach to winning in cash games is conservative—for a very good reason. In cash games you are constantly facing situations that appear to offer good opportunities to gamble, situations that entice you to bet all your chips with a solid yet still vulnerable hand. You need a solid strategy that prevents you from unnecessarily leaping into a big pot. In tournaments many of these same situations become easier to confront since there is a limited number of opportunities for you to win a big pot. Therefore, the decision you arrive at more often than not in a tournament is to go ahead and put your money in the pot.

This book shows you how to get a handle on the cash game pitfalls that cause most players to drain their chip stacks with weak hands, as well as how to recognize situations that cause many players to lose all their money, even with strong hands. To be successful in cash games, you need to wait patiently for big hands; play your strong hands well so that you almost always win in big pots; and play intelligently enough in all the other hands you are involved in so that you don't lose a lot of money unnecessarily.

THE WINNING APPROACH

While the patient, disciplined method outlined in this book is relatively easy to implement, you still need to be in the right physical and mental state to play well because failing to account for one or two small factors as you think your way through a hand can lead to disastrous results. The next chapter outlines what it takes to play no-limit hold'em cash games profitably.

3 THE KEYS TO SUCCESS IN CASH GAMES

The basic building block of your new approach to playing cash games is simple. You make your money by winning just a few big pots with big hands. Sometimes you might win only one big pot in an entire session.

WINNING A FEW BIG POTS WITH BIG HANDS

In limit hold'em the convention for measuring success is showing a profit of one big bet per hour, whereas in no-limit hold'em, many players believe they need to win one big *pot* every hour on average to remain in the profit column. Do not accept this assumption for no-limit hold'em. Since there aren't a lot of opportunities to hold a monster hand, you cannot expect to win a big pot every hour on average; therefore you shouldn't be concerned with your hourly rate of earnings. You should only care about winning one big pot in a session that allows you to meet your profit objective, and winning a few small pots along the way to help you avoid falling well behind that objective.

When some players think about winning one big pot per hour, they begin to press and play too aggressively in an effort to make it happen. In fact, some players just assume that their medium-strength hands are winning because they believe they are due to win a big pot. That is faulty logic. Any player can easily get beaten at any time or go card dead for hours. Even though you haven't seen a hand as good as top pair for over an hour, it is still preposterous to fight the laws of nature so ferociously as to be blind to the fact that your top pair can still be crushed by an opponent's set.

You never need to start feeling anxious or overly eager to win a pot. Don't stray from your game plan and play differently just because it has been a long time since you've scooped a big pot. One or two big hands might be all it takes for you to hit or surpass your profit objective, so always remain patient and you will be rewarded eventually.

BIG HANDS

This approach means that you rarely bluff—and you do not bluff in big pots. You need to be extremely patient and disciplined as you wait for a flop that makes you a monster hand. You might not accept this approach right away because you may be used to playing a lot of pots and constantly working to outthink and outdo your opponents. However, winning a few big pots with big hands is all you need to make a lot of money. It is the basic tenet here, and the foundation upon which your future success in cash games will be built.

What I mean by big hands is at least top two pair (using both of your hole cards). However, a big hand isn't only defined by what you are holding. When opponents also have hands that they like (such as top pair/top kicker or a smaller two pair), your big hands become even more valuable because your opponents will pay you off on every street even though they have few outs, if any, to beat you. These are situations that are worth waiting for.

Other examples of big hands are flopping a set when an opponent has an overpair, and turning a full house when a weak opponent turns a flush and gives you his stack despite the paired board. Another is holding the nut flush when your opponent is holding a baby flush. That's right, even holding a small flush isn't good enough to justify playing a monster pot.

BENEFITS OF "BIG-HAND POKER"

Here are the main benefits to adopting this style of play:

1. THERE IS LITTLE CHANCE THAT SOMEONE HAS YOU BEATEN WITH A BETTER HAND.

You will be playing truly premium hands so you will rarely lose a big pot. It will happen on rare occasions that you lose with bottom set when someone has a higher set or your top two pair will get beat by a set. However, the message here is that you will be the one holding the dominating hand almost all the time.

2. YOU CAN'T GET OUTPLAYED IN A BIG POT.

There are quality players that have learned how to outplay their opponents. While you should try to play at tables with at least one or two good customers (weaker players whom you routinely beat), there might still be a couple of strong, aggressive players at your table who will try to take a large pot away from you by representing a really big hand. Suffice it to say, you won't often be fooled into folding the hands that I recommend you play in big pots.

3. YOU WILL CONSERVE CHIPS FOR MONSTER POTS.

When you don't bluff off your money, get caught in a big pot with a dominated hand, or drain your chip stack chasing flush draws and straight draws, you will ensure that you have enough chips in front of you to do a lot of damage when you hit a big hand without having to rebuy. When you win a big pot, you would prefer that it help you meet your profit objective, not merely help overcome a large deficit in the session.

4. IT WORKS EQUALLY WELL FOR ONLINE AND LIVE GAMES.

The world of online play exposes you to the newest generation of young, aggressive poker players as well as many weak players. While aggressive online players love pulling off shrewd bluffs, bullying conservative players and outplaying other quality players, weak online players will often play unpredictably by calling with just about any two cards preflop and even after the flop. The game plan you will learn in this book will render all of these players virtually powerless.

The *Playing No-Limit Hold'em as a Business* method is also designed for you to play more than one table online. Since you will need to be patient and wait for big hands, playing multiple tables allows you to get involved in bigger pots more often. Just be sure that you stick to the game plan and that you don't start loosening up or you will be exposing yourself to unnecessary risk at numerous tables at once. You must stay in control and try to study at least some of your opponents so you can take advantage of them when you do play big pots. If you are able to do this well, you can make a lot of money.

5. YOUR OPPONENTS WILL PERCEIVE YOU AS A WINNER.

Players often start playing a lot of pots with someone who has been losing because they see the losing player as being very unlucky or they think he is making poor decisions. But when you've been winning, fewer opponents are eager to play pots with you. This can be a good thing because you will have less competition on the flop. The problem with getting more than two callers when you have a good hand is that you run the risk that your opponents might hit their outs on the turn and river to beat you. While an opponent might miss a straight draw, someone else with second pair may hit his kicker and hold a higher two pair. Maybe a player with bottom pair will hit trips. Although these events seem unlikely, they are not uncommon in multiway pots.

To illustrate this point, let's say that you are holding top two pair with 10♠ 8 ♥ on a flop of 10♦ 8♣ 6♠, and you are up against three opponents. While you could be losing to a straight or a set, you are still holding a strong hand that you will want to protect to make sure nobody draws out on you.

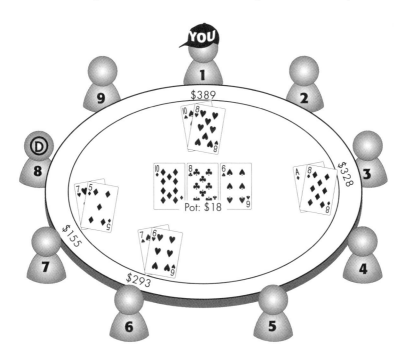

One of your opponents is holding A♦ 8♦, so he has three outs (three aces) to make a higher two pair. Another player is holding 7♠ 6♥, so he has six outs to beat you (two sixes for trips and four nines for a straight). A third opponent is holding 7♥ 5♦, so on top of the four nines that we've already counted, he also needs one of four fours to complete his open-ended-straight draw. While you have each player beaten on the flop, you still have to dodge a total of thirteen outs, which is a lot. If you are perceived as a winner and you make a large bet of about two-thirds the pot or more, your opponents will be more likely to lose heart and fold instead of calling and potentially drawing out on you. At worst you will play the pot heads-up after the turn. Being seen as a winner allows you to win your fair share of small and medium-sized pots, and allows you to protect your big hands from draw outs in big pots.

6. YOUR HANDS ARE MORE DECEPTIVE THAN YOU THINK.

Although you won't fool anyone into thinking that you are a loose player who is capable of playing a pot with any two cards, your holdings will be so strong that people might read you wrong. Opponents will often think your hand is weaker than it really is, especially when they don't know you well. Unless your online opponents keep good notes on you, or unless you always play with the same people at live games, opponents will often underestimate how dangerous you can be in big pots.

7. THE GAME PLAN IS EASY TO EXECUTE.

You don't need to be a highly experienced player or a rocket scientist to win because this book's basic approach to playing hold'em is simple. The *Playing No-Limit Hold'em as a Business* method is a ready-to-play strategy that enables you to win immediately. To execute your new game plan, all you need is patience and an understanding of the types of players you are up against, skills that you will learn in later chapters.

8. YOU WILL HAVE FUN.

Enjoyment is an underrated part of playing poker. Simply by knowing that you have a powerful game plan, you will have a positive outlook that will help you make better decisions. And since you won't take on as much risk as others do, you won't experience frequent large swings in your chip count. Therefore, you will not feel the stress and anxiety that other players do. You will confidently look forward to the fun of playing poker.

You now know that winning with big hands is your mantra, but you will need to master all the components of the *Playing No-Limit Hold'em as a Business* method before you can successfully put your new strategy into action. You must still learn which starting hands to play, what types of hands can get you into trouble, how to play after the flop, and how to keep some pots small even when you are holding a strong hand. Also, since you will still be involved in numerous smaller pots (albeit less frequently than your opponents), you will need to understand the role that these situations play within the broader context of your game plan.

CORRECTLY DETERMINING THE STRENGTH OF YOUR HAND

You may be accustomed to thinking that top pair or an overpair are hands that are strong enough to make it worthwhile for you to risk all your chips after the flop. However, to be successful in the long run, you must avoid playing big pots with only one pair, especially in multiway pots. Playing A-K and hitting an ace-high or king-high flop is always nice, but you shouldn't go to war with it. A lot of the time when you flop top pair, you make a bet and get one caller with a weaker pair who then folds when you bet the turn. Only on rare occasions will you be able to win a few bets from an opponent who is holding top pair with a weaker kicker; the rest of the time you probably will be beaten by two pair or a set. An opponent will let you bet your stack away by smooth calling all the way to the river, or he may raise you on the turn and entice you to move in. In short, you either win a little or lose a lot with one pair.

This is precisely why you hear many players say they dislike pocket aces. They tend to get married to them, so they become willing to bet all their chips with them even when they suspect they might be beat. One pair is often a weak hand after the flop, so you must not get carried away.

KEY TAKEAWAY

Your job in cash games is to wait for a monster hand to play a big pot. Avoid losing a lot of money with just one pair, which often is a weak hand.

While you will usually hold at least top two pair in big pots, occasionally there will be situations in which you will need to play a big pot with only a marginally strong hand such as bottom two pair or sometimes just top pair. Despite the fact that you will need to stubbornly stick to your game plan in order to make big money in the long run, you don't live and play in a vacuum. No two poker sessions are ever the same, so sometimes you will find that you won't need to wait for a monster hand in order to win a big pot. This will mostly depend on the caliber of your opponents and on how loose the table is playing.

In a no-limit $1/$2 game, let's say that you raise to $8 with A♦ K♣ in middle position. One player calls from the cutoff position and the flop comes A♠ Q♥ 3♦.

YOUR HAND

THE FLOP

You have flopped top pair/top kicker, so you bet. Your opponent calls. Your notes on your opponent say that he is a weak-loose player who overvalues any ace. Based on how you've seen him play during the last twenty minutes, you feel strongly that he also has top pair but with a weaker kicker. Your best play is to keep betting and building the pot because, if you are correct, he only has three outs to make two pair and beat you, so you have him crushed. As you master the *Playing No-Limit Hold'em as a Business* method you will learn to distinguish between high risk and low risk situations such as this. Just know that once or twice per session you may need to be flexible and deviate slightly from your game plan by playing a big pot with weaker holdings than top two pair when you are confident that your hand is way ahead.

Although you don't want to develop the habit of playing big pots with one pair, if you think it is necessary to put someone all-in preflop when you are holding pocket aces, by all means, do that. With A-A you will have someone dominated by at least 3.3 to 1 (pair over pair is about 4.5 to 1) and that's a pretty strong advantage if your opponent calls. Moving in preflop with A-A (or K-K if you are certain your opponent does not have A-A) will also prevent you from getting outplayed after the flop. However, even after moving in preflop with A-A or K-K, you want your opponents to fold when the pot is sufficiently large. You would avoid facing the possibility of losing a huge pot if they call, and you would take down a medium-sized pot if they fold. After all, if you move in with K-K and someone holding A-Q suited calls, you will only be ahead by about 2 to 1 with all your chips on the line. Even 4.5 to 1 aren't insurmountable odds, and this type of domination is still not as strong as holding a set against an opponent who is holding top pair or two pair.

THE RULE OF FOUR AND TWO

With two cards to come, multiply the number of outs by 4 to get the approximate percent chance to improve. For example, 2 outs x 4 = 8 percent.

With one card to come, multiply the number of outs by 2. For example, 2 outs x 2 = 4 percent.

To illustrate the previous point, if you flop a set of eights on a board of A♦ 8♣ 7♥ and your opponent is holding A♠ 7♠, he only has two outs to beat you (two aces), and he will be holding a big enough hand for you to win all his chips. Even another 7 will give you a higher full house (eights full of sevens versus sevens full of aces).

YOU

OPPONENT

THE FLOP

Using the **Rule of Four and Two**—a shorthand method to calculate the probability of improving a poker hand—your opponent has only about an 8 percent chance to win, or about 11.5 to 1. That is a much larger advantage for you than the 4.5 to 1 advantage if you move in preflop with a dominating pair. Large mathematical edges such as this make it worthwhile to wait for big hands after the flop and to avoid playing big pots with one pair.

KEY TAKEAWAY

You will make the hands you've been waiting for after the flop, and they can be even stronger than holding A-A pre-flop.

GIVING UP SMALL POTS

You will not hold a big hand most of the time, so you will often need to fold after the flop when there is a lot of action in a multiway pot. To avoid getting involved in big pots without big hands, you must often let your opponents succeed in winning small pots from you by folding marginal or medium-strength hands. Giving up small pots will help you conserve chips for when you hit a big hand. It will also help ensure that when you get paid off, your win will put you in the profit column rather than just erasing previous losses.

Using this approach will also help to prevent you from bluffing away your chips in medium-sized multiway pots, a tendency that is a terrible flaw in the games of many amateur poker players. Surrendering pots might be the most difficult concept for you to accept, but it is a necessary part of abiding by your new game plan.

Approaching the action in a way that best suits the quality of your hand and the level of risk you face is an integral part of your game plan. This often means taking measures to keep the pot small even when you suspect that you are holding the best hand. If you don't believe the time is right to risk getting involved in a big pot, you will sometimes need to fold a made hand. Of course, you shouldn't instantly muck top pair when an opponent makes a bet. Certainly you should feel free to call or raise if you think that is the right play. And if you are first to act with top pair, feel free to bet for value or to discourage a player from drawing to a better hand. Your willingness to surrender small pots doesn't mean you should play poorly on purpose. You will still aim to win the majority of those pots, assuming you have at least a medium-strength hand. Just be aware that when you do so, you may be creating a larger pot. There is only so much action that top pair can withstand, so you should have a plan as to what you want the action to look like after the flop. Sometimes this plan will involve playing your hand passively by checking or check-calling on the turn or river in order to avoid playing a big pot.

Another benefit of using this approach is that you usually will not need to make large raises preflop. The strategy in this book emphasizes playing big pots with big hands *after* the flop. More often than not, you won't be dealt aces or kings—the only big preflop hands in no-limit hold'em—so you usually should try to keep the pot small before the flop with all other starting hands. By taking the lead preflop, you can control the size of the pot and the size of the opening bet on the flop.

When you raise just three or four times the big blind, you give yourself a chance to win a small or medium-sized pot without risking a lot of chips. Why? Because there won't be as much money in the pot after the flop. This is important because your game plan still allows you to defend your preflop raises with continuation bets. However, you don't want to get involved in a big pot without a strong hand just to defend your preflop raise. Of course, if you are playing in a game where raising three or four times the big blind invites five callers, you probably will have to mix up your preflop betting. At a table like that, you will often want to raise big enough—perhaps seven or eight times the big blind—to play a pot heads-up, or just limp in to see if you flop a big hand.

PLAYING PATIENTLY ONLINE

Getting involved in numerous pots with marginal hands is one of the most common ways that amateur poker players lose money online. They see that online play is loose so they believe they too should loosen up. However, they mostly end up losing money by getting into battles that they shouldn't be involved in at all.

Playing online is different from playing in most live games. It is a trickier game. Here's why: Online players always pounce on perceived weakness. As soon as they see an opportunity to win a pot, they bet; and quite often they bet with the weaker hand. If everyone limps in preflop, the blinds raise it almost every time. If someone raises preflop from the cutoff position or the button, players give the raiser action because they think he is making a positional bet with nothing. If a player just calls a bet after the flop, the preflop bettor usually bets again; and if a player checks, you can expect someone else to bet.

Why do online players play this way? It might be because of the anonymity of playing alone in front of a computer. Perhaps online players feel more comfortable playing aggressively and bluffing when they don't have to worry about giving away physical tells. Many people believe the influence of final-table tournament poker on TV is the main culprit, as watching these TV shows might be the main way that many online players learned to play the game. Regardless of why online play is so aggressive, you must understand how to approach it so that you can win consistently.

The *Playing No-Limit Hold'em as a Business* method is designed for you to be able to win online since it discourages you from playing a lot of pots with marginal hands. You have to stubbornly stick to your game plan because many online players have a sneaky way of luring their opponents into playing medium-sized pots, only to win most of those pots with large bets on fourth and fifth streets.

Let's look at an example. In a nine-handed online $2/$4 no-limit game, you raise to $12 with A♦ Q♥ in the cutoff position. The small blind calls, the big blind folds and the only limper folds, so you are heads-up. Your opponent is a loose player who plays a lot of pots and is pretty aggressive when he plays a hand. However, you believe that he has a decent hand since he is voluntarily playing a raised pot out of position. You have $456 in chips and he has $478. The flop comes 9♠ 5♠ 5♥. He checks, you make a continuation bet of $18 into a $32 pot, and he raises to $48.

YOU

THE FLOP

You might be tempted to call his raise because you think your ace high is winning. You may think he is putting you on a weak hand since your preflop raise in the cutoff position signaled a steal bet, so he doesn't require a strong hand to play back at you. Also, the odds of his actually hitting this flop seem pretty long. Even if he hit the 9, you still have two overcards with possibly six outs to make a higher two pair. Since you think he is just trying to move you off your hand, you decide to call and see what happens on the turn.

The turn card is the 3♣, which you don't think helped him. Your opponent bets $60, a little less than half the pot. You still think you might be winning so you call, hoping to check it down on the river and possibly win with ace-high. The river is the 10♦ and your opponent bets the pot, which is $248. Now you no longer know whether you are winning. Perhaps he paired the 10 or maybe he was winning the whole way with a pocket pair and he believes you missed the board since you never raised after the flop. It's a big bet and you don't want to lose a big pot with just ace high, so you decide to fold.

The problem in this hand is that your opponent was correct in assuming that you missed the flop. You knew that your starting hand was stronger than he thought, which is why you continued playing with him. However, you never took control so you never gave him a reason to think that he couldn't bet you off your hand. As a result you had to fold after investing $120 in the pot. In fact, if you thought you were winning, it could be argued that the correct play was for you to reraise on the flop. However, you don't need to take on that kind of risk to win in cash games.

You can clearly see how getting involved in online battles without strong hands can cause you to lose money. You should have cut your losses in this hand by folding your A♦ Q♥ when your opponent check-raised on the flop. Remember that to implement your new game plan successfully online, you must avoid confrontations with weak hands and wait to get your money in with strong, made hands.

GETTING PAID OFF

You may wonder how players will pay you off since applying your new strategy means that they will perceive you as one of the tightest players at the table. There are two key reasons you will still make money. First, you will be playing with at least some weak, undisciplined players, especially if you play online. I don't recommend that you routinely sit at tables filled with quality players if you want to make a lot of money in the long run. You need to seek out good games with players that make mistakes and pay people off on their big hands. These games are not that hard to find; you will always recognize who the weak players are. They overvalue any ace in the hole, gamble too much with draws, and overvalue marginal made hands. When they hit a half-decent hand, they fail to utilize any type of radar to discover whether they have fallen into a trap against a bigger hand. Of course, even quality players can make mistakes, so there is still money to be made from them. Surprisingly, there always seems to be someone who puts you on a flush draw when you are holding a set, even after you've waited patiently for over an hour to play a big pot.

The second reason you will get paid off is that sometimes your looser opponents will try to crack your strong hands. Although opponents often will fear getting into a big pot with you, sometimes they will just want to try to outflop you, outdraw you, or just outplay you. They will call your preflop raise with 6-5 suited when you are holding pocket aces. They will overpay for their draws to try to beat your set or two pair. They will wait for a scare card on the turn or river and try to bluff you. Since you will be trained to understand how your opponents play and how to think your way through a hand— and since you will be holding a big hand—their attempts to win big pots from you will fail most of the time.

KNOWING WHEN YOU ARE POT COMMITTED

Throughout this book you will read about situations in which you try to build a big pot with a monster hand, avoid playing a big pot with a marginal hand, or avoid losing a big pot with a strong hand against an opponent who wants to draw to an even better hand. To make the best possible decisions in these situations, you need to know what qualifies as a big pot. A big pot is a pot that is worth more than 50 percent of your starting stack, where your starting stack is your original buy-in of 100 big blinds (or the maximum buy-in if it is less than 100 big blinds). For example, suppose you are in a four-way pot in an online $5/$10 no-limit game where each player has invested $150. There is $600 in the pot before the flop, so it qualifies as a big pot because it is 60 percent of your $1,000 buy-in. Make sure that you have a big hand before you put any more money into this pot because it will probably cost you at least another $300 to make an effective bet or to call a bet—and you never want to lose a hand in which you have invested that much of your chip stack. Keep in mind that a big pot remains 50 percent of your 100 big-blind starting stack even after you top up (add more chips to your stack) or rebuy into a game.

You are also playing a big pot when the value of the pot would increase to at least 50 percent of your starting stack if you call or raise. For example, let's say that you are holding Q♠ Q♣ preflop in an online $5/$10 no-limit game. You raise to $30, an opponent reraises to $90, a second opponent reraises to $250, and the action is back on you. The value of the pot is $385 (including the blinds), only 38.5 percent of your $1,000 buy-in. However, if you decide to call or come over the top, the pot will increase in value to more than 50 percent of your buy-in, so the pot already qualifies as a big one. Therefore, you will need to be very confident that you are holding the winning hand before you decide to reraise or even just call. Folding is your best play in this situation.

When do you know you are **pot committed**? You are often committed to investing all of your remaining chips when you have already invested more than one-third of your live chip stack in a pot. Measure your pot commitment by the chips you currently have in play on the table, not by your starting stack of 100 big blinds. The basic idea behind pot commitment is that when a lot of your chips are already invested in a pot, you don't want to risk folding the best hand. Also, if you get the rest of your chips in the middle and you are losing, you might still get an opportunity to hit one of your outs to win the pot.

> ## KEY TAKEAWAY
>
> You are often committed to investing all of your remaining chips when you have already invested more than one-third of your live chip stack in a pot.

Thinking about pot commitment can be a useful way to protect your investment in a big hand since you can avoid getting outplayed and folding the best hand in a big pot, and it can prevent you from investing heavily in a marginal hand or a drawing hand. However, not all situations require that you throw the rest of your chips in the middle even after investing more than one-third of your live stack. Sometimes you will use your best judgment and decide to fold because you strongly believe your hand is crushed, regardless of what you have invested in the pot up to that point.

Here are the most common situations in which you need to consider that you are pot committed, or that you are at risk of becoming pot committed.

1. YOU BET WITH A BIG HAND. YOU ARE ALMOST CERTAIN YOU ARE WINNING.

Let's say that you start a hand with $600 in chips in a ten-handed live $5/$5 no-limit game. You are holding Q♠ J♠ in the big blind, a tight player in middle position raises to $25, and a loose player on the button calls. You are getting 3 to 1 on your money. Although you don't think you are winning, you decide to pay another $20 to see if you can outflop the raiser. The flop comes Q♣ J♦ 7♥, so you are holding a big hand with top two pair. You check, the original raiser bets $60, and the other player calls.

SITUATION

You Have: Q♠ J♠
The Board: Q♣ J♦ 7♥
Money in the Pot: $200
Bet for You to Call: $60
Number of Players: Three

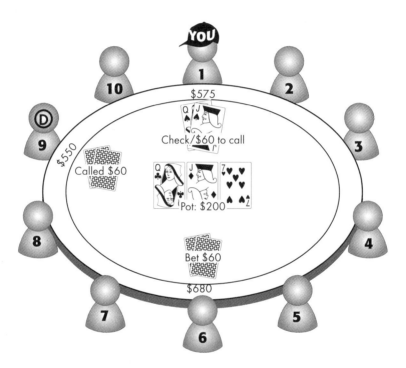

It is possible that the preflop raiser in Seat 6 is holding A-A, K-K, A-Q or K-Q, so you think you have a chance to win a nice pot from him. The other player might be on a straight draw but he also might have just a pair of jacks, so you decide not to raise him yet because a check-raise might scare the preflop raiser into believing that he is beaten. You are taking on a little risk here by smooth calling instead of raising to protect your hand, as your looser opponent sitting to your right in Seat 9 could be holding 10-9, so a king or an 8 on the turn would give him a straight. However, the risk is small, so you decide to stick to your plan of keeping the preflop raiser in the hand.

You just call. The turn card is the 6♠, so the board is Q♣ J♦ 7♥ 6♠. You come out betting $140 into the $260 pot to entice your opponent in Seat 6 to come over the top, so you have now spent a total of $225 in the hand. You have more than one-third of your $600 live stack in the pot, so even if someone moves in, you will have to call because you cannot risk folding a big hand like this after investing so much in it, even though the raiser could have a set. Assuming an opponent moves in, he will have you covered, so you will be getting better than 2.4 to 1 on your money to call ($915 in the pot divided by $375 that you have left), and that is probably too good a price to risk folding what is likely to be the best hand.

As it turns out, Seat 6 moves in and the other player folds. You call and he turns over A♣ Q♦. Your hand holds up and you win a big pot. This was pretty standard play without any tough decisions to make because you were holding a big hand in a situation where you thought you could win an opponent's entire chip stack. When you made a strong bet on the turn, you were willing to commit the rest of your chips to the pot because you believed you were winning.

2. YOU BET WITH A MEDIUM STRENGTH HAND, AN OPPONENT PLAYS BACK AT YOU, AND YOU ARE ALMOST CERTAIN YOU ARE LOSING.

In a nine-handed online $2/$4 no-limit game, let's say that you start a hand with $370. You are holding A♣ Q♥ under the gun, you raise to $15 and you get three callers. The flop comes A♠ 8♣ 6♦. You have top pair with a strong kicker. The big blind checks, you bet $50 into a pot of $62, and the only caller is the player sitting to your immediate left.

SITUATION

You Have: A♣ Q♥
The Board: A♠ 8♣ 6♦
Money in the Pot: $162
Number of Players: Two

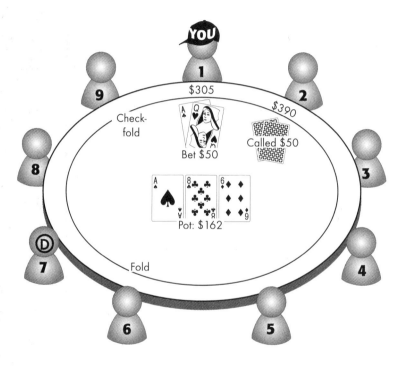

Anytime you are holding only one pair after the flop and you get a caller in a multiway pot, you're in danger. Why? Because when numerous players get to look at the flop, there is a greater chance that someone has made a big hand. Also, your opponent in Seat 2 is a very tight player who usually has a strong hand when he plays a pot after the flop.

The turn is the J♣, so the board is A♠ 8♣ 6♦ J♣. You decide to come out betting $90 into the $162 pot to find out where you stand. Your opponent moves in and he has you covered. You have spent $155 already and you have $215 left, so you have committed well over one-third of your stack to the pot. You are quite certain that your opponent has you beaten with either A-K, a set of eights or sixes, or maybe top two pair. You have never seen him make a move in a big pot, especially after one of his opponents shows strength like you did under the gun. Also, you don't think he is holding A♣ 10♣ or A♣ 9♣, which would give him top pair with a nut flush draw. This means that there are almost no hands he could reasonably be holding that you are beating. You decide to save the rest of your chips and fold instead of calling just to satisfy your curiosity.

Many players in your situation would have gone ahead and called with your hand after committing so many chips to the pot. However, based mostly on your knowledge of your opponent, you felt strongly that you were beaten, drawing very slim with only one card to come, if not drawing dead. Since you never want to lose all your chips with only one pair after the flop, folding and saving the rest of your chips was the right play despite the fact that you were mathematically pot committed. This example illustrates one of the few situations in which you would have a legitimate reason to fold your hand even after committing more than one-third of your live stack to the pot.

3. YOU SEMI-BLUFF, AN OPPONENT PLAYS BACK AT YOU, AND YOU ARE CERTAIN YOU ARE LOSING.

You start a hand with $420 in a ten-handed live $5/$5 no-limit game. You are holding J♦ 10♦ and limp in under the gun. A player in middle position raises to $25, four players call in front of you and you decide to call since you are getting 6.5 to 1 on your money. The flop comes Q♦ 5♦ 4♣, so you have flopped a flush draw. The blinds check to you and you also check hoping for a free look at the turn, but the preflop raiser bets $80 into a pot of $150. The other players fold and you raise to $180 to see if you can move him off his hand in case he was just making a continuation bet. You also have nine outs to hit your flush in case he calls. However, your opponent moves in and he has you covered.

SITUATION

You Have: J♦ 10♦
The Board: Q♦ 5♦ 4♣
Money in the Pot: $725
Bet for You to Call: $215
Number of Players: Two

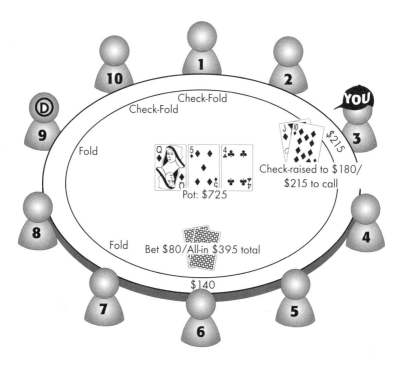

You have $205, almost half of your stack, invested in the pot so you will probably have to call because your flush draw should at least give you a chance to win. You decide to consider the pot odds anyway. There is now $725 in the pot and it will cost your remaining $215 to call, so you are getting about 3.4 to 1 on your money. With your flush draw and two cards to come, you only need about 1.8 to 1 on your money (you have about a 36 percent chance to make your flush) so you are getting the right price, even though you realize the danger in continuing with a flush draw that is not a draw to the nuts. You call even though you know you are drawing against a made hand. Your opponent turns over Q♠ Q♥ giving him top set. You miss your flush on the turn and river, and lose all your money.

This hand is an excellent example of how playing drawing hands aggressively can get you into trouble. While calling your opponent's all-in bet was correct based on pot commitment and pot odds calculations, you should never have found yourself in that position by making a high risk raise that committed you to the pot. When you have trained yourself to eliminate these types of plays from your cash game repertoire, your cumulative profit will start to grow.

4. YOU BET WITH A MONSTER HAND AND YOU THINK AN OPPONENT MAY BE ON A DRAW.

In a nine-handed online $5/$10 no-limit game, you raise to $40 preflop on the button with the A♣ A♥. Two players call. The flop comes A♠ 7♦ 4♦ so you are holding the nuts. You recently got unlucky in a medium-sized pot so you only have $640 left, and both of your opponents have you covered. There is $135 in the pot. An opponent leads with a $70 bet, the other folds, and the action is on you.

SITUATION

You Have: A♣ A♥
The Board: A♠ 7♦ 4♦
Money in the Pot: $205
Bet for You to Call: $70
Number of Players: Two

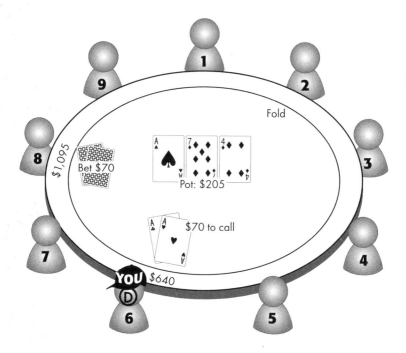

Your opponent in Seat 8 is a very loose player whose chip stack has yo-yoed up and down the entire session. He has shown that he is willing to play just about any two cards preflop, and has played his drawing hands aggressively. As you try to hide your excitement about a loose player giving you action, you realize that you need to play your hand in such a way as to prevent him from drawing out on you in a big pot when you are pot committed.

You started the hand with $680, so if you raise to about $190 or more, you will be pot committed. This means that if your opponent calls a normal sized raise and a diamond comes off on the turn, you would still be obliged to put the rest of your chips in the pot, even if you are losing.

Raising can be a good play on the flop because if your opponent is on a draw, he will pay to see the next card. However, it also gives your hand away. Of course, he won't know you're as strong as you are (with trip aces) but he will think you have A-K or A-Q. By just calling his bet on the flop, you might trick him into thinking you're playing K-K or Q-Q and you're nervous about the ace on the flop. It could win you another bet on the turn.

The problem with raising is that if your opponent is on a flush draw, he is the type of player who will not lay it down unless you move all-in. In fact, considering the way he's been playing, you wouldn't put it past him to call an all-in bet since he would have two cards to come to hit his flush, and he knows he has you covered. Also, if he calls a normal raise and a diamond comes off on the turn, you might feel obliged to put the rest of your chips in the pot when you are losing.

You decide to just call his $70 bet to disguise the strength of your hand and to see if the turn looks like a safe card. If it is, he might check, at which point you can bet big and even move in to shut him out so that he doesn't get to see the river. Alternatively, you could make a value bet and again hope you don't see a diamond on the river. However, making a small value bet on the turn would be the riskier play because your opponent could have a lot of outs to beat you. Your best play on the turn is to bet big and make your opponent pay through the nose to see the river card.

The turn is the 9♥, so the board is A♠ 7♦ 4♦ 9♥. There is $275 in the pot, he bets $100, and you move in for a total of $570. After going into the think tank, he folds. He types "gb" into the chat box, which is short for 'good bet', indicating he was probably on a draw.

You might think that if I'm suggesting to check-call on the flop and push on the turn to shut him out then I might as well shut him out on the flop. That makes sense. However, the purpose of playing the hand the way I recommend is to avoid losing a big pot against a very loose player. If he is the type of player who can't lay down a drawing hand then let's at least get all the money in with only one card to come (after pushing on the turn) as opposed to giving him two cards to come (after pushing on the flop).

This is a very important part of managing risk against strong-loose players. Even when I'm holding a big hand, I will consider giving up a small pot on the turn if a scare card comes as opposed to giving my opponent an opportunity to draw out on me in a huge pot with two cards to come on the flop.

The point of this example is to demonstrate pot commitment when an opponent is on a draw and you start a hand short stacked, which limits your options for how to play the hand.

Understanding the concepts of pot size and pot commitment is vital in the development of your risk management skills. The concept of pot commitment is designed to encourage you to protect your investments. Always be mindful of the size of your bets relative to your chip stack and to the quality of your hand so that you know whether you are willing to commit all your chips even before your opponents act. In addition, you must consider whether the relative quality of your hand is worthy of playing for a pot that is equivalent to half your starting stack because the secret to your success will be winning those large pots. What you need to avoid is committing to a big multiway pot and finding out that you are beaten after all your chips are in the middle. That is why you will often need to find ways to keep the pot small when you are holding a vulnerable hand.

THE KEYS TO SUCCESS IN CASH GAMES

Correctly evaluating your opponents is another major key to your success in cash games. It is so important, in fact, that the next chapter is devoted to categorizing opponents so that you can successfully determine how to play profitably against them.

EVALUATING YOUR OPPONENTS

Knowing your opponents is an integral part of the *Playing No-Limit Hold'em as a Business* method. Although in the past you may have relied more on great cards to win than on your ability to outthink other players, your new game plan requires a reliable approach to evaluating your opponents. Here are some key reasons why:

1. **You will get paid off more often on your big hands.** The last thing you want to do is fail to extract chips from your opponents when you hit a big hand. You need to understand the people you are playing against to figure out what cards they are holding in order to figure out the best way to maximize value for your monster hands.

2. **The "science" of tells is too unreliable.** I don't mean to say that online or live tells aren't useful in some cases, because they certainly can be. However, if you will be playing regularly in cash games you will need a reliable way to evaluate how people think and play their hands, not how fast they click the check button or whether they twitch when they are bluffing. There is too much guesswork in detecting and correctly reading tells, a risk that you don't need to take to do well in cash games. The

approach you are learning to use here will help you think through hands and make better decisions based mostly on how your opponents have bet in certain situations in the past.

3. **You can more easily avert disaster.** You will save your stack in these and other tough situations if you understand the hands that your opponents are capable of playing. This will only happen by carefully considering the hands you can beat, the hands you cannot beat, and whether your opponents might be holding those hands based on the decisions you have seen them make in the past.

4. **You can win more small pots.** Although winning big pots with big hands is your mantra, you don't want to play your small pots poorly. You still need to win some small pots with marginal or medium-strength hands, especially in heads-up or three-way pots, so that you don't drain your chip stack unnecessarily. To accomplish this, you need an understanding of your opponents so that you don't get outplayed and repeatedly lay down the best hand.

5. **You will gain more respect.** A lot of players don't really fear tight opponents because they think they are predictable (which is true in many cases). As a result they might feel comfortable playing hands against them, and in some cases they will try to run over them in an attempt to get them to fold the best hand. Therefore, it can be very important to let others know that you know what you are doing. By showing that you know how to make good decisions based largely on knowledge of your opponents, players will respect you. Once opponents respect you, you will be able to take

control of the hands you play and put them on the defensive. You won't have a monster hand every single hand you play, so it can be helpful if players are less willing to mess with you, even in small and medium-sized pots.

6. **You can successfully pick off bluffs.** This will be necessary in a few of the small pots you play, and even in a big pot once in a while. If you are up against a player on a draw, and he attempts to bluff you after missing his draw, you don't want to muck your hand instantly merely because you only have top pair. You especially don't want to quickly throw away a big hand like a set just because a scare card comes off on the river. You need to think about how the hand was played, figure out the possible range of hands your opponent is holding, and then make the right decision.

GROUPING YOUR OPPONENTS

The best type of hand analysis comes from thinking about the types of players you are up against and what kinds of plays and bets you've seen them make. This is a function of staying aware at the table and utilizing your memory skills so that you can put your opponents on a hand. These skills become vital when playing after the flop. Memory skill in poker only develops if you work at it, so you need to be proactive rather than passive. You cannot afford to become one of those people who play poker while reading a magazine. Observe players while you are not involved in a hand, making an effort to commit important information to memory.

The best way to start leveraging your memory skills is to group your opponents, since thinking in detail about eight or nine separate players can be difficult. Studies in cognitive psychology have shown that people can remember very long strings of numbers if they chunk the numbers into smaller groups. This approach is useful when trying to learn how opponents play.

WEAK VERSUS STRONG

One type of grouping is weak players versus strong players. Weak players overvalue marginal starting hands. They also overplay and overpay for draws. And when they hit a decent hand, they often do not stop to consider whether they are beaten. You can win a lot of money from weak players. Strong players are pretty much the opposite. They don't do anything rash, they know how to sense weakness in their opponents in order to win a pot with a weak hand, and they back off a good hand when they recognize they are up against a monster.

LOOSE VERSUS TIGHT

Another grouping is loose players versus tight players. If a player plays a lot of pots, plays just about any type of hand preflop, and in general does not shy away from high-risk situations, he is loose. Loose players like to play a lot of hands with connectors and gaps, and are willing to raise a multiway pot with a drawing hand. A loose player might also play every street when he's on the button and try to use his position to outplay opponents. He might even be willing to get involved in a multiway pot with only a second-best pair even when he is out of position. Conversely, if a player's range of starting hands is pretty narrow and conventional, he is probably tight. Tight players frequently fold in multiway pots even after hitting a piece of the flop, rarely bluff, and can sit through hours or even an entire session without playing a big pot.

Combining these categories gives you a total of four groups that you can reliably use to classify players. They are:

- Weak-loose
- Weak-tight
- Strong-loose
- Strong-tight

Thinking in these terms will help you remember the types of cards your opponents are playing, the degree of risk they can tolerate, and the plays they are capable of making. Grouping all the players at the table this way can only come from watching them play pots. If you see an opponent pay someone off with a weak or medium-strength hand on the river, and you classify that player as weak-loose, you will need to remember specifically how he played his hand. Online, you can simply take notes on players. A good way to do this in a live game is to review what you have just seen as soon as the hand is over.

Here are some things you might find yourself thinking:

a. "That guy called a bet on the flop in a multiway pot with second pair, called a raise on the turn with second pair and a gutshot draw, and then paid off the winner's value bet on the river after failing to improve his hand. Once he decided to play a weak hand like that, then he probably should have raised to give himself a better shot at winning the hand. Just calling was really poor play. He is weak-loose. I will not slowplay this guy. I will keep betting if I hit a big hand against him."

b. "That guy shows some patience preflop as he hasn't played many hands. But all of a sudden he loses a lot of chips with an overpair of pocket tens when it was obvious he was beat. In a four-way pot on a flop of 9♣ 9♥ 7♦, the preflop raiser leads out at the pot, another guy raises, a third player smooth calls, and then this guy calls with just an overpair. Are you kidding me? He shouldn't be getting involved at all. Not only is he beat, but he also has the preflop raiser to act after him who might reraise with a bigger overpair. This guy is weak-tight. I can put him on strong starting hands, but he's not skillful, especially when playing after the flop."

c. "That was a very nice bluff. On a flop of 8♦ Q♠ 8♠, a tight player who raised preflop bet two-thirds of the pot. This guy called. The preflop raiser seemed to have something like A-Q, K-Q or maybe even A-A or K-K. The turn was the J♦, and the preflop raiser again bet two-thirds of the pot. This guy called again. The river was the 10♠ so the board was 8♦ Q♠ 8♠ J♦ 10♠. The preflop raiser checked and this guy bet the pot. After his opponent folded, he turned over 2-2. He's a strong-loose player. He knew his opponent well enough to know he could represent trip eights by making bluff-calls on the flop and turn, and then waiting for another scare card on the river to move him off his hand. I'll remember that he's capable of making that play. I probably don't want to play a lot of pots with him."

d. "This guy waits for solid starting hands and knows where he's at in the hand. He called an early position raise with A♠ Q♣ in the cutoff seat after another guy called before him. It was three-way and the flop was A♥ 5♠ 3♥. The preflop raiser bet out, the other guy called, and this guy raised. Both of his opponents called, but he knew he was up against a couple of loose players. The turn was the Q♠ so he hit top two pair and the preflop raiser bet out again. The second player folded and this guy pushed all-in and announced that his opponent couldn't call with his J-10 of hearts. His opponent called anyway (out of spite, I think) with the Q-10 of hearts, almost the exact hand the cutoff seat had put him on, and failed to improve on the river. This guy is strong-tight."

Keep in mind that some strong players are capable of playing either tight or loose, as they know how to mix up their game. For your purposes, you should classify a player as loose when you repeatedly see him take on significant risk with a draw, or when you believe he has attempted a few bluffs in good-sized pots. A strong-tight player will make moves less often, especially in big pots.

You can add "average" player to the weak and strong player groupings if you think certain players fall somewhere in between. This would give you six groups in which to classify your opponents: weak-loose, weak-tight, average-loose, average-tight, strong-loose, and strong-tight. Since you will have specific reasons to classify players into four (or six) groups, you should be able to remember the specific hands they play. Be proactive and keep your energy level high. It isn't easy to constantly take in information, but doing this type of work at the poker table will pay off. If you use this information well when playing a hand, it will unleash the full potential of your game plan.

PASSIVE VERSUS AGGRESSIVE PLAYERS

Sometimes you will notice that an opponent rarely drives the action after the flop. He mostly just hangs around and keeps calling, which you might find surprising or confusing. This means he is using a passive approach to playing after the flop and it is useful to keep this in mind because he won't often reveal the strength of his hand by raising. Both loose and tight players are capable of playing passively. Loose-passive players will often hang around with top pair or sometimes just second pair, and possibly long enough to improve on the river. These players are most commonly referred to as "calling stations." A tight-passive player might hold a hand as strong as two pair but he will prefer to keep the pot small, see what develops on later streets and hope his hand holds up.

The playing style you are learning in this book will incorporate some tight-passive elements because it can sometimes be the appropriate way to manage risk against loose opponents on dangerous boards. The opposite of a passive player is an aggressive player, who habitually bets out or raises. Identifying someone as an aggressive player will help you to avoid getting fooled into folding the best hand when he is merely doing his usual betting with just a marginal hand or with a drawing hand.

OTHER BEHAVIORS TO LOOK FOR

Sometimes the range of personalities at a table is wider than these groupings. Human beings are vastly complex. As a result, there may be other personality traits or behaviors that you will want to pick up on because they might reveal something about how your opponents play.

Players show up to a cash game with different objectives. A couple of players might be there just for fun. Sure they want to make money, but they don't really work on their game, read books, or analyze their play in order to improve. You like those players! Others might be aggressive players who are willing to go to war to accomplish what they believe is "playing the game correctly," which really means embracing risk in most of the hands they play. There might be a young player whose objective is making moves. For him, it is just as important to pull off a few great bluffs or advanced plays, as it is to actually make money.

Another opponent's objective might be to play speculative hands so that he can outflop an opponent who is playing a big pocket pair and win a huge pot from him. I knew a young man in Toronto named Dave who showed up to games "to make people puke," as he so eloquently put it. He was a gambler who played a lot of baccarat and he liked trying to crack an opponent's big pair with starting hands that added to nine such as 6-3 or 5-4 offsuit. Dave frequently called large preflop reraises with these hands. He knew he was behind and he lost big pots most of the time, but he just wanted to experience the thrill of beating someone's pocket aces with two pair or trips, or by drawing to a straight.

People also react to losing in different ways. Some players tighten up when they have lost a few pots while others loosen up. This is something you also want to pay attention to. Some tight players become looser to try to win a few pots and make up for their losses. You need to readjust and think through the hands you play with them differently because their range of starting hands might open up, or they might start to play top pair or their draws more aggressively. Other tight players become even tighter, waiting very patiently to pounce on someone who gives them action in a big hand. Less common is seeing a loose player tighten up. When they are losing, they usually will play even looser and play more pots. What loose players often look to do when they are stuck is to build pots by making big raises preflop and then making a big continuation bet to steal pots.

Paying attention to these sorts of objectives and attitudes toward the game can help you pick up important information which, when combined with your player groupings, will improve your decisions. Never think that just showing up to a game and waiting for big hands is all you need to do to win. You will always have work to do whether during a hand or in between hands you play. The effort you put into studying your opponents will be worthwhile, as your down-to-business approach will make it very difficult for your opponents to beat you.

Avoiding hands that cause you trouble and finding the right game are two other very important keys to your success in no-limit hold'em cash games. The next chapter defines trouble hands that can lure you into losing pots, followed by Chapter 6 which shows you how to find cash games that will increase your potential for making money.

AVOIDING TROUBLE HANDS

Trouble hands are those that appear to be strong but can cause you to lose big pots to better hands. Your basis for success in cash games is playing big pots with monster hands, so it's important that you recognize the ones that look like giants when they are really midgets. Many players think that some of these trouble hands are so strong that they wouldn't dream of folding them. However, even some of the highest-ranking hands can lure you into situations where you lose all your chips. To avoid disaster you need to become aware of these dangers.

TOP PAIR OR AN OVERPAIR

You already know that you should avoid losing big pots with only one pair, but it is worth looking at that concept again because one pair is the most common trouble hand with which players lose a lot of money every day. Have you ever heard someone talk about how they hate A-K because it always misses the board? Players hate A-K because they commit too much money to the pot by making preflop reraises or sometimes even all-in bets with it and then losing. You've probably even heard people say they hate pocket aces because too often their aces get cracked "forcing" them to pay off an opponent and lose a big pot. The sad part is that most players continue to play these hands the same way and keep putting themselves at risk of losing big pots. What eludes them is the will power and discipline to play big pots only with monster hands. With one pair you are always vulnerable, especially in multiway pots. You should be willing to risk folding the best hand in a small pot so you can avoid losing a potentially big pot with a weak hand.

Suppose you're in a raised pot where you are heads-up holding A♥ A♣ on a flop such as K♠ 8♣ 2♦.

YOU

THE FLOP

The range of hands you need to be concerned about is very small—pocket eights, pocket twos or maybe K-8 if your opponent is a loose player or is in the big blind—so you should feel comfortable, though you shouldn't start salivating like Pavlov's dog at a chance to move all your chips to the middle. You should instead look to take down a small to medium-sized pot.

The real danger in playing an overpair is that you won't know you are beaten until you have committed a large portion of your stack, maybe even all of it. Although you will often have your opponent crushed heads-up, sometimes you can lose all your chips if he outflops you. That is why you should play big pairs carefully by trying to keep the pot size small and to avoid committing all your chips if you can. However, sometimes it just can't be helped that you end up playing a bigger pot than you would like to with an overpair. This usually happens when there are multiple raises preflop, you play the flop heads-up, and you strongly believe your opponent is holding a lower overpair to the flop. You may need to commit all your chips at that point because you won't be able to check or get away with small bets to keep the pot small (and you wouldn't want to in that situation).

Here is an example of how it can be difficult to play pocket aces after the flop. Let's say you are holding A♥ A♣ on the button in a live $5/$5 no-limit game that has been playing pretty fast and aggressive. You raise to $35 after a few players limp in, and you get three callers. The flop comes J♥ 10♠ 7♠.

SITUATION

You Have: A♥ A♣
The Board: J♥ 10♠ 7♠
Money in the Pot: $145
Number of Players: Four

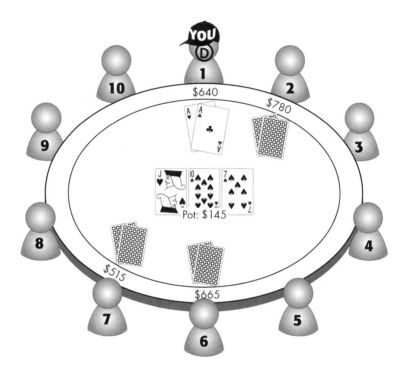

The first word that comes to mind is "yuck." This is the kind of board that interests a lot of players, especially when they are holding limping hands that they couldn't raise or reraise with preflop. A lot of people like to play J-10 and that hand has you beat. The same goes for 9-8 suited, which makes the nut straight on this flop. Assuming that nobody flopped a big, made hand and you are still holding the best hand right now, do you think you will be able to play a small pot with your one pair? That is doubtful.

On a flop of J♥ 10♠ 7♠ your opponents could be on a wide range of suited connectors and one or two-gappers that give them flush draws, straight draws, or maybe a pair with a flush draw or straight draw. Hands like 9♠ 6♠ or 8♠ 6♠ give them an inside straight flush draw, a big drawing hand that most players love. The same can be said about suited or even offsuit hands like J-9, J-8, 10-9, 10-8, 9-7 and 8-7. Why do people play hands like these? To hit a flop like this. You will have little chance of playing a small pot here because players love raising with these types of drawing hands.

If you bet the flop, a player check-raises and another one calls, you will have to bail. Assuming your hand isn't already beaten, so many turn cards could help your opponents that the safe play is to get out before you get involved in a big pot with just one pair, and when you feel that you have no real sense of control over the hand. No matter what card comes off on the turn, you will likely face another big bet when you're holding a vulnerable hand. If you bet the flop and even one player calls, you might have to give it up if the turn is a spade. If you get a caller and the turn is a K, Q, 9 or 8, you will have to be concerned about:

1. Your opponent hitting **a double belly buster draw** with K-9.
2. Your opponent hitting **an open-ended straight draw** with Q-9.
3. Your opponent hitting **any gutshot draw**.
4. Your opponent picking up **an open-ended straight draw with a flush draw.**
5. Your opponent making **a pair with an open-ended straight draw or flush draw.**

Even against some of the hands that you are still beating on the turn, you wouldn't have a huge edge; more importantly, you wouldn't really know where you stand. Also, even if you turn an ace for a seemingly monster set, you could conceivably be losing to someone holding K-Q for the nut straight. You would have no choice but to try to keep the pot small in these situations, although that would be hard to do if you turn top set.

Suppose you bet the flop after everyone checks to you and you get one caller. The turn card doesn't seem to have helped him (let's say it's the 3♥) and he checks. In that case, you can throw out one more bet and hope he folds. If he calls, you won't know whether you are already beat or he is still on a draw. After all, he might be able to put you on a big overpair or maybe A-J, so he would have no reason to raise to protect his two pair, set or straight from a flush draw. You will have to hope that your opponent checks the river. If he does, you will have to use your best judgment as to whether or not he missed a draw or is holding a jack and would pay off a value bet. Still, you're probably better off checking behind. Just be aware that he might throw out a steal bet and put you to a decision if he did miss a draw. Hopefully, the pot would still only be a medium-sized pot. These are always tricky situations when you are holding one pair. We'll look at more circumstances like this in greater detail later on.

In general, with a dangerous flop such as J♥ 10♠ 7♠, if everyone checks to you, your best play with pocket aces might be to throw out one bet to see if you can take it down right there. If you get too much action, you should consider giving it up and losing a small pot. This wasn't a great flop for you anyway, especially since it was played four-way.

Now let's change this scenario: What should you do if an opponent bets into you? First, let's discuss just calling. Again, you would need to be concerned for all of the same reasons that we have discussed. You might be winning, but your opponent could have a lot of outs to beat you. When you consider the added complexity of a second opponent possibly check-raising behind you, you can see that this option isn't ideal as you would have no control over the hand if you just call. If the first player in seat 2 bets into you and the other two players fold, then you might decide to call since there is no danger of an opponent check-raising behind you. You will have to hope the turn is a blank, like the 4♦, and you can check the hand down from there in order to keep the pot small. Assuming you both check on the turn, what if the river also seems like a safe card, like the 3♣, but your opponent bets two-thirds of the pot? Unfortunately, you will probably have to call because he could have missed a draw and has decided to buy the pot. Or he could be value betting a pair of jacks with a hand like K♦ J♦. If you are wrong and he was slowplaying a straight or he was cautiously playing two pair, at least you minimized your losses because you didn't do anything foolish like move in on the flop.

The next option to consider is raising. The main benefit of raising is that you would make an opponent who is on a draw pay a lot of money to see the next card, and he might choose to fold if he is a tight player.

Now let's look at the downsides of raising in this situation. If the bettor is a loose player, he might come over the top and move in. This would put you in the position of having to decide whether to play a huge pot with only one pair, a situation you would prefer to avoid in this spot. If he is a tight player, you couldn't be sure that he didn't out-flop you. That there are four players in the hand makes it riskier for him to bet, so he is more likely to be holding a strong hand. Therefore, raising him would seem unnecessarily risky. Also, sometimes even a tight player might choose to play a big draw—for example, if he were holding the K♠ Q♠—so there is no guarantee that you would make him fold by raising.

Finally, if you raise, it would look like you were playing a big pair or maybe A-J, so you might not scare away your other opponents. Someone else might be on a draw that he can't lay down; for example, a hand like 10-8 would give an opponent middle pair with a straight draw. So, you wouldn't necessarily guarantee yourself a chance to play the hand out heads-up against the first opponent who bet into you. Raising is not the right play in this situation as there are too many opponents in the hand and the board is just too dangerous.

To summarize, both calling and raising are weak options, so folding is your best play here.

This hand also highlights a key difference between you and your opponents. They love creating big pots with drawing hands that may or may not come to fruition, whereas you create big pots only when you have a really big, made hand. Your opponents might have won this small battle, but in the long run you will win the war by showing great profit while many of them will lose or break even at best.

KEY TAKEAWAY

One pair is often a weak hand that can cause you to lose a lot of money. Be willing to risk folding the best hand in a small pot to avoid losing a big pot with a weak hand.

BOTTOM TWO PAIR

The best way to think about bottom two pair is that it is only one hand ranking higher than one pair. Let's say that you are holding 8♠ 6♠ in middle position in a live $5/$5 no-limit game. You get to see the flop for the minimum and there are six players in the hand. You started with $550 in chips. The flop comes K♥ 8♥ 6♣.

The first thing that should come to mind is that while you are probably holding the best hand, it's possible you are already crushed by K-8, K-6, 8-8 or 6-6, so play accordingly. The action gets checked to you, and you bet $25 into a pot of $30. A tight player to your left raises to $75, a loose player on the button calls, and the big blind reraises to $160. You are familiar with the big blind. He is a moderately tight player who usually has a solid hand in big pots. The action is back on you.

SITUATION

You Have: 8♠ 6♠
The Board: K♥ 8♥ 6♣
Money in the Pot: $365
Bet for You to Call: $135
Number of Players: Four

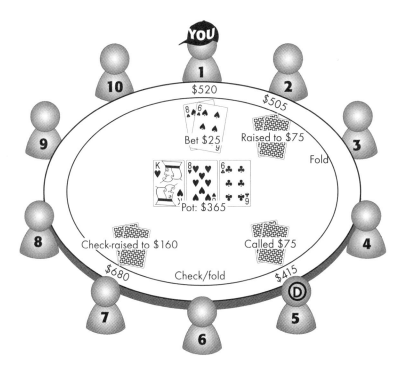

You don't like this at all because the pot is big, a tight player came over the top by check-raising in a multiway pot, and you don't have a monster hand. Since this was an unraised pot preflop, someone could easily be holding one of the hands that can beat you. The first raiser in Seat 2 could simply have a king with K-Q or K-J although you aren't sure yet. You think the button might only have a flush draw or an open-ended straight draw, since he is loose enough to flat call a raise with a draw. However, you have to take the reraise by Seat 7 (the big blind) seriously since he could be beating you with a higher two pair or a set; and perhaps when the button called the raise, he decided to reraise simply to protect his hand.

One of your options is to just call to see what your opponents do on the turn and to see if a scary card like a heart comes off. However, you might not get to see the turn card because if you call and then Seat 2 (directly to your left) moves in, you will probably have to fold, especially if Seat 7 in the big blind calls in front of you. Also, it seems likely that you will face another big bet on the turn, meaning that you will have the exact same tough decision you are facing now but in a bigger pot with almost one-third of your live stack committed. Therefore, calling is not a great option.

Another option is to reraise to find out where you really stand. However, you would be committing all your chips and that is too much risk to take on. All signs are pointing to the conclusion that you are either already beaten or you're up against a big flush or straight draw, and you don't hold a big edge against a hand like that. Also, some players are willing to call off all their chips with a big draw, so you might not get everyone to fold even if you are holding the best hand. Reraising is a very high-risk option.

Your last option is to fold, which is a very reasonable play against this much action, even though it means you might be folding the best hand. However, you should be willing to take that chance because your objective is to win big pots with monster hands, not to lose big pots with vulnerable trouble hands. In this situation, you simply have to ask yourself whether the big blind is bluffing or would make this play with A-K, K-Q or K-J, which are the only decent hands you can beat on the flop. If the answer is no, you have to fold. If he happened to be semi-bluffing with a big drawing hand, then kudos to him for making a strong play. However, he rarely makes those plays and you still wouldn't be a big favorite against an opponent with twelve or more outs.

So you fold, as does Seat 2. Seat 5 calls. The turn is the A♦. Seat 7 moves in from the blind and Seat 5 folds. Seat 7 shows K♦ 8♣ to the table to reinforce his tight image. He flopped top two pair. You should pat yourself on the back for losing only $30 in that hand when many other players would have lost their whole stack. Too many players would have thrown caution to the wind in your situation by moving in. That is why bottom two pair is a trouble hand. It can fool players into thinking they are holding the best hand, so they allow themselves to get trapped and lose all their chips.

Another very big problem with bottom two pair that we didn't discuss in this example is the possibility of getting counterfeited. This can happen when your opponent has top pair or an overpair, the board pairs, and you lose to a higher two pair. In the example above where you were holding 8♠ 6♠ and the flop was K♥ 8♥ 6♣, suppose an opponent was holding K♦ J♣. The turn was the 5♠ followed by 5♦ on the river. You would lose to a higher two pair, K-K-5-5-8 over your 8-8-6-6-K.

Here's another example of getting counterfeited. You are holding 5♣ 4♣ against an opponent's pocket queens on a board of J♣ 5♠ 4♦ 9♦.

YOU

OPPONENT

THE BOARD

Your opponent has eight outs to beat you (three jacks, three nines, two queens). If the river brings a jack or 9, you wouldn't put any more money into the pot because your hand would lose all its value.

Bottom two pair isn't a hand you should fold instantly all of the time, of course. It depends on the circumstances. In the example above where you were holding 8♠ 6♠ with the K♥ 8♥ 6♣ flop, if there had been a preflop raise and you were playing the pot heads-up, you might put the raiser on A-K or A-A. Then you could consider getting your money in a bit more liberally. At least that situation would more closely resemble the ones you want to wait for. In general, however, when you consider that bottom two pair can trail a bigger two pair, a set, or better, and that bottom two pair can get counterfeited, it is often a good idea to keep the pot small.

SMALL FLUSHES

One of the worst ways to lose a big pot is with a baby flush. When your 5♦ 2♦ gets crushed by K♦ Q♦ on a board of J♦ 3♦ 4♥ 10♦, everyone at the table will acknowledge that they also would have lost all their money in that situation. However, since your approach to making money at cash games is different from other players, their consolation should mean little to you. While it might seem impossible to fold a flush, remember that many opponents play carefully when there is a three-flush on board. Therefore, if they keep betting, it could mean they have a higher flush. When you also consider that an opponent continues to give you action even though you usually show down monster hands in big pots, you will sometimes be able to get off your hand. At the very least, you shouldn't be the one to drive the action in multiway pots or look for opportunities to get all your money in, even heads-up, with a small flush. Instead, you should try to keep the pot small. If you don't use a careful approach to playing baby flushes, you simply won't know whether you are beaten until you have committed all your money to the pot.

Here is an example. In a live $5/$10 no-limit game, a moderately loose player raises from early position to $70. Two players call in front of you. You are holding 5♣ 3♣ on the button and decide to gamble and call. The big blind also calls, so you are five-handed with $355 in the pot. You all started the hand with about $1,500 in chips. The flop comes Q♣ 10♣ 4♠, so you have flopped a flush draw. The big blind and the preflop raiser check. Seat 7 in middle position bets $140. The next player folds and the action comes to you.

SITUATION

You Have: 5♣ 3♣
The Board: Q♣ 10♣ 4♠
Money in the Pot: $495
Bet for You to Call: $140
Number of Players: Four

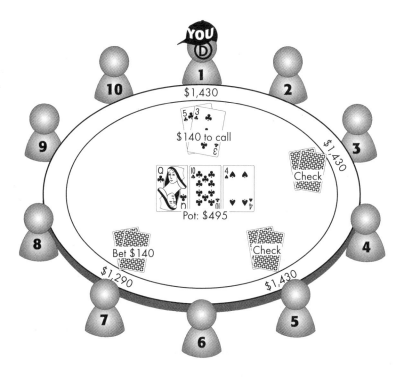

With nine outs to make your flush on the turn, you need about 4.5 to 1 on your money. Since you are getting about 3.5 to 1, you decide it is close enough, so you call. Seat 3 folds. The preflop raiser in Seat 5 raises the minimum to $280. Seat 7 calls and the action is on you again.

SITUATION

You Have: 5♣ 3♣
The Board: Q♣ 10♣ 4♠
Money in the Pot: $1,055
Bet for You to Call: $140
Number of Players: Three

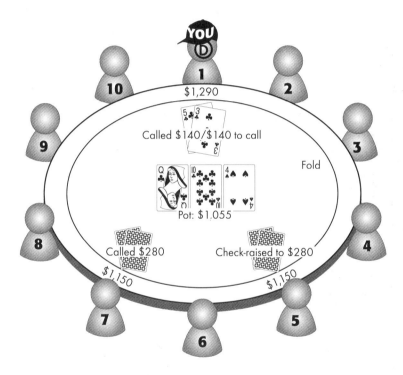

Now it's costing you only $140 more with $1,055 in the pot, so you are getting about 7.5 to 1 on your money. The minimum raise is scary since it looks like Seat 5 wants callers, but you figure that you have to call because you are getting such a good price; further, if you hit your flush, you might take down a huge pot. So you call. The turn is the 8♣, so you just hit your money card. Both players check to you.

SITUATION

You Have: 5♣ 3♣
The Board: Q♣ 10♣ 4♠ 8♣
Money in the Pot: $1,195
Number of Players: Three

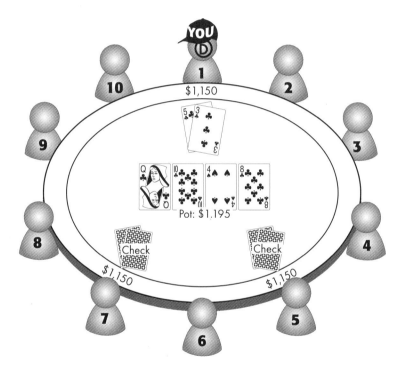

You decide to bet $500 to get some value for your hand and to push your opponents off a bigger flush draw just in case someone has the A♣ or K♣. Seat 5 moves in. The player in Seat 7 shakes his head, shows his cards to the player sitting next to him to elicit sympathy, and mucks his hand. You call, turn over your hand, and Seat 5 shows an ace-high flush with A♣ K♣. No cards can help you on the river so you lose all your money.

Seat 7 proudly announces he had J-9 with the J♣, so he made a straight on the turn but he couldn't call with that much action in front of him and a flush seemingly already made. Seat 7 played his hand very well on the turn. He didn't want to risk betting big into a made flush, and he didn't want to risk throwing a small feeler bet out there because that bet wouldn't have pushed someone with a big club off a flush draw. He was probably hoping you would check behind on the turn and that the river would be a safe card. In that case, he probably would have checked it down, just called, or check-called a modest bet on the river.

What happened in this hand poses a few big problems. One problem is being willing to lose all your chips with a baby flush. It wasn't as if you flopped a flush and got crushed by someone who flopped a higher flush, as that would be both unlucky and unfortunate. In this case you got your money in the pot drawing extremely slim on the flop (you needed to make a pair with a non-club 5 or 3 to pull ahead in the hand), and drawing dead on the turn. Another big problem is spending money chasing a draw, especially when it isn't even close to a nut draw. You should not have overpaid that first time on the flop (when you were getting 3.5 to 1 on your money) to draw to a potential trouble hand.

Chasing draws is a losing play in cash games. You almost never get a good price to call, and even your implied odds are often unattractive. The reason your implied odds are often unfavorable is that if you make your draw, and especially if you make a flush, it could scare your opponent and prevent you from winning a huge pot. However, you should note that double belly buster straight draws offer more attractive implied odds since they are more deceptive; and if you hit your draw, your opponent won't necessarily slow down.

Another problem in this hand is that you ignored the warning signs of the minimum check-raise. When the preflop raiser in Seat 5 made a small check-raise against two other players who showed interest in that kind of flop, it was unlikely that he was protecting a hand such as A-Q or an overpair. Even with two pair or a set, many players would raise bigger in that situation to take their opponents off a possible draw. Considering the vulnerability of your hand, you needed to make a highly unconventional play by mucking it on the flop. Just look at the action: Seat 7 bet and after you called, the preflop raiser check-raised and Seat 7 called. If Seat 7 had just a pair of tens, fours, or a middle pocket pair such as sevens, eights or nines, he probably would have mucked it after the check-raise. Therefore, he was most likely holding a pair of queens or he was on a draw. The action on the flop signaled that there could have been a bigger draw out there. You should have picked up on that.

Nevertheless, mucking your flush draw is not an easy choice to make, which is precisely why baby flushes are so dangerous. You can get seemingly favorable pot odds that lock you into a situation that results in your losing your whole stack. Remember that if you are holding a weak hand like a 5-high flush draw and there is substantial multiway action, you must consider that someone else could be on a flush draw. You either need to get away from it or try to keep the pot small even if your flush card hits.

One last point: Even if you are holding the nut flush, if the board is paired you should try to keep the pot small because someone might have a full house. You should only look to play monster pots when you have a flush if it is the nut flush or maybe the second or third-nut flush, and only on an unpaired board. Settle for nothing less.

KEY TAKEAWAY

Paying money just to look at the next card is bad business because you almost never get a good price.

BIG DRAWING HANDS

Big drawing hands are problematic. While having a large number of outs can entice you to participate in a big pot, you do not yet have a big hand. In many cases, you don't even have a made hand. It makes sense to look for hands like these in tournaments because they give you a pretty good chance to win a big pot, and you might run out of chips by the time you get a chance to hold a hand with so much potential. However, in a cash game you should not invest heavily merely in your hand's potential; you must play big, made hands that already have your opponents beaten. In short, when you hold big drawing hands in a cash game, try to keep the pot small instead of looking to increase it.

Here are some of the big drawing hands with which most players are willing to take on excessive risk. Each hand is listed with the corresponding number of outs to improve the hand, followed by the two hole cards, the flop, the approximate percent chance to improve the hand with one card to come, then with two cards to come, and the cards needed to improve the hand.

BIG DRAWING HANDS

#	TYPE OF HAND	OUTS	HOLE	FLOP	CHANCE TO IMPROVE		CARDS NEEDED TO IMPROVE
					W/1 CARD	W/2 CARDS	
1	Flush draw and open-ended straight draw	15	7♠6♠	A♠8♥5♠	60%	30%	9 spades, 3 nines, 3 fours.
2	One pair and a flush draw	14	A♦4♦	9♦8♦4♥	56%	28%	9 diamonds, 2 fours, 3 aces.
3	Flush draw and open-ended straight draw	15	7♠6♠	A♠8♥5♠	60%	30%	9 spades, 3 nines, 3 fours.
4	One pair and a flush draw	14	A♠4♦	9♦8♠4♥	56%	28%	9 diamonds, 2 fours, 3 aces.
5	Flush draw and a gutshot draw	12	K♥7♥	9c 8♥5♥	48%	24%	9 hearts, 3 sixes.
6	Top pair and open-ended straight draw	10	10♠9♠	10♣8♥7♥	40%	20%	4 jacks, 4 sixes, 2 tens.
7	Two overcards and a flush draw	9	Q♣J♣	9♦6♣3♣	36%	18%	9 clubs
8	Two overcards and open-ended straight draw	8+	Q♥J♠	10♣9♣2♥	32%	16%	4 kings, 4 eights
9	Double belly buster	8	8♥6♠	10♦7♣4♠	32%	16%	4 nines, 4 fives.
10	Open-ended straight draw	8	5♦4♦	Q♥3♣2♠	32%	16%	4 sixes, 4 aces.
11	One pair and a gutshot draw	6	9♦8♠	9♠7♣5♥	24%	12%	4 sixes, 2 nines.

Hand 6. Top pair and open-ended straight draw. Even a loose player might be careful if he hits his 9 kicker, which gives him two pair but creates an open-ended straight draw on board, so he might not consider a 9 as an out.

Hand 7. Two overcards and a flush draw. You have at least nine outs, and possibly 3 queens or 3 jacks if your opponent is holding a lower pair, assuming his kicker isn't a queen or jack.

Hand 8. Two overcards and open-ended straight draw. You need 4 kings or 4 eights, and possibly 3 queens or 3 jacks if your opponent is holding a lower pair, assuming his kicker isn't a queen or jack.

Hand 11. One pair and a gutshot draw. You have at least 6 outs (4 sixes and 2 nines), plus possibly 4 eights.

AVOIDING TROUBLE HANDS

One reason so many players overplay these hands is because they know that with two cards to come, their hand might actually be mathematically ahead by a small margin. This can be true even when an opponent is holding two pair. Look at hand 1 above. Suppose you are the player who is holding 7♠ 6♠ on a flop of A♠ 8♥ 5♠.

YOU　　　　　　　**OPPONENT**

THE FLOP

Your drawing hand could be up against a solid hand such as A♥ K♣ (top pair/top kicker), but with 15 outs and two cards to come, you have almost a 60 percent chance of making your hand.

Unfortunately, when a lot of players think about a 60 percent to 40 percent advantage, they think they are holding a monster hand. Sure, if they push all-in they get the added advantage of their opponents possibly folding. However, if they get called, they have all their chips on the line with only a small edge to win. This is a very high-risk play that isn't necessary to win in cash games. Don't be fooled into thinking the same way that other players think with these hands.

Here are some other problems that big drawing hands pose:

1. **One card to come.** Many players fail to consider that they will see only one card at a time; instead, they think in terms of seeing two cards to make their hand. If a player misses his draw on the turn, the math more heavily favors his opponent with the made hand. In example 1 above, let's say the turn is a card such as the Q♥ that doesn't complete the draw, so the board is A♠ 8♥ 5♠ Q♥.

YOU   **OPPONENT**

THE BOARD

You still have 15 outs with your 7♠ 6♠, but with one card to come you are behind by about 30 percent/70 percent, so you are about a 2.3 to 1 underdog. Therefore, a pot-sized bet, or even a little less, will price you out of the hand. If you think about how many players would call large bets to hit draws with just eight or nine outs on the turn, you begin to see how poorly some cash game players play. With one card to come on either the flop or the turn, you almost never get a good price to call.

2. **Going against a set or two pair.** While a big drawing hand still has a good chance to win against two pair or a set, its entire hand value gets decimated if the board pairs on the turn and makes a full house for an opponent. That is something few players take into account when they play drawing hands in big pots. An opponent with a set on the flop has seven outs or about a 14 percent chance to pair the board on the turn. A player on a big draw might be counting on seeing two cards to make his hand, yet he could be drawing dead on the turn and already have all his money in the pot.

3. **Transparency.** Another serious problem with big drawing hands is that most players these days expect opponents to play big draws aggressively. Sometimes it is so obvious that a raiser is on a draw that an opponent with a made hand will put him all in to shut him out, which he often can do with just one pair. The drawing player wastes his money by raising the flop or turn because he can't call the all-in bet. The transparency of playing drawing hands aggressively also means that you have a higher risk of getting called if you move in, which significantly decreases the long term value of making this play, especially on the turn with only one card to come.

4. **Getting paid off.** A lot of the time when you hit your flush or straight, your opponents slow down because they are afraid of the card that just came out. When you don't get paid off, your investment in these hands proves to have been a poor choice.

Players have only themselves to blame when they lose big pots with drawing hands. Any player who decides to move in with one of these hands, gets called, and misses his outs has no right to walk away cursing the poker gods about his bad luck. Moaners need to be reminded that a 55 or 60 percent edge isn't nearly as good as an 80 or 90 percent advantage. If a player decides to take on the risk, he has to blame his own play, not luck. In short, never assume a small mathematical advantage gives you a license to play really fast. That certainly is not a part of your new winning game plan.

This doesn't mean that you should never play a drawing hand. If you can find a cheap opportunity to turn or river a nut flush in a multiway pot, it might pay off big if someone hits a smaller flush. As you will read later, in some cases you can play the pot very cheaply to try to see the next card. Just remember that you never want to go crazy, even with nut draws.

LOWER STRAIGHT

Losing with a lower straight seems to happen more often than losing with a lower flush. One advantage you have when trying to avoid losing a big pot with a lower straight is that you have all the information you need to make a decision right in front of you. You know 100 percent of the time whether or not you are holding the nuts, but with a baby flush, you won't know whether you are beaten until the showdown. If you are holding a straight that isn't the nut straight, consider keeping the pot small to avoid allowing an opponent to take a big pot from you. Here are a few examples:

1. WEAK ACE.

Any time you are holding a weak ace such as A-4 and you hit a straight, you are vulnerable. If the flop is 5-2-3, you could be losing to a 6-4, a hand that some people like to play. I'm not suggesting that you muck your hand instantly if players bet into you, but be aware of how tight your opponents usually play. This is especially true if it seems as though your opponent turned his money card. If the turn is a 4, you are holding the sucker end of the straight. If your opponent comes out firing, you probably have to fold because he may have turned a better hand with 6-5, turned the nuts with 7-6, or he may have outflopped you with 6-4. Also, if the turn is a 6, he may have made a higher straight if he is playing 7-4 suited. Here is a list of the other weak aces that can get you into trouble with a straight:

- A-2 on a board with 5-4-3. You can lose to 7-6 and 6-2.
- A-3 on a board with 5-4-2. You can lose to 6-3.
- A5 on a board with 4-3-2. You can lose to 6-5.

When holding a weak ace, you must think about what your opponents could be holding. You mustn't carelessly throw all your chips in the middle merely because you are holding what appears to be a strong hand.

2. LEAPFROGGING.

You already know to be very careful when you are holding the sucker straight. You also need to be careful when the board allows opponents to make higher straights than you, which I call **leapfrogging**. For example, let's say you're in a nine-handed, live $2/$5 no-limit game. You are holding 4♦ 3♣ in the big blind in an unraised pot. The flop comes 6♠ 5♥ 2♠, so you have flopped the nuts. Three players are in the hand, $17 is in the pot, and you all have roughly $200. You are first to act, so you bet $10. Both your opponents call. You have to believe that at least one of them is on some kind of draw. The turn is the Q♣. You are still winning, so you make a strong bet of $30 into the $47 pot to protect your hand from a potential spade draw. Again, both opponents call.

SITUATION

You Have: 4♦ 3♣
The Board: 6♠ 5♥ 2♠
Money in the Pot: $167
Number of Players: Three

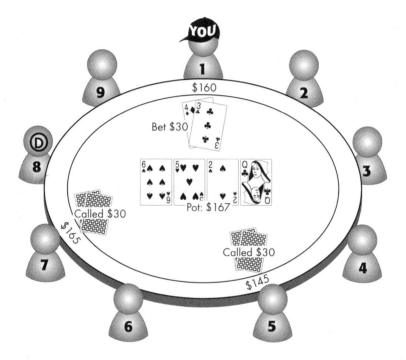

Twice your opponents just called, so you're not putting anyone on a set because most players would raise to protect that hand on a drawing board like this, especially on the turn. You are confident that if the board pairs you will still hold the best hand, but just in case someone is playing two pair carefully and rivers a full house, you will still probably keep the pot small. Mostly, you are hoping you don't see a spade on the river.

The river is the 3♦, so the board is 6♠ 5♥ 2♠ Q♣ 3♦. This seems okay because nobody made a flush and you are still holding a strong hand. You recognize that you might chop the pot if an opponent is also holding a 4, but you decide to bet the river for value just in case someone is holding a hand that can pay you off (perhaps hands like 6-5, 6-3 or 5-2). There is $167 in the pot, you have $160 left, and you bet $60. Seat 5 folds, but Seat 7 calls. He shows 6♥ 4♥, so you chop the pot.

Although betting the river was a decent play, it wasn't a great play. Why? Because there was a chance you were going to just chop the pot, and you were out of position against two opponents. The real risk was that an opponent could have had you crushed if he was playing 7-4, which makes the nut straight. He would have hit his open-ended straight draw and then raised by moving in on the river. Since you had already committed half of your stack to the pot, and since you only had $100 left with what would have been $387 in the pot, assuming your opponent had you covered, you would have had to call and pay him off with the rest of your chips.

What you needed to do was make a defensive check on the river to keep the pot small and to prevent someone with the nuts from winning all your chips. By just check-calling, you would have set yourself up to lose less money. With $167 in the pot, an opponent with the nuts might have bet $100 or less to ensure he got paid, especially after you showed weakness. By betting, you also could have allowed an aggressive player holding merely a 4 to try to raise you off your hand in an effort to avoid chopping the pot. Although in this case you would have called anyway because you were pot committed, it would have been a really tough decision if you both had a lot more chips, in which case you would have had to consider folding.

In general, leapfrogging is dangerous because it usually happens when you are holding a strong hand, which means you can get blindsided and lose your whole stack. Whenever you have a straight, always consider that an opponent could have leapfrogged you, and play accordingly.

RECOGNIZING THE DANGER OF BEING LEAPFROGGED

Here is another example. In a ten-handed live $5/$5 no-limit game, you are holding 10♣ 9♥ in an unraised six-way pot. The flop is Q♥ J♦ 8♠. You have flopped the nut straight. You are first to act and you bet two-thirds of the pot.

YOU

THE FLOP

The button, a moderately tight player who usually makes pretty conventional plays, calls. The turn is the 9♣, so the board reads Q♥ J♦ 8♠ 9♣. You should immediately recognize that you are at risk of losing a big pot: Your opponent could have hit an open-ended straight draw with K-10, which would give him the nut straight, so you should think about trying to keep the pot small.

You decide to bet half the pot on the turn to find out where you really stand. He calls. You now know that he doesn't have a hand such as bottom two pair, he has better than that. You feel strongly that he has a 10 in his hand, so you have to make sure you don't create a monster pot when you could be up against the nuts.

The river is the 4♥, so the board is Q♥ J♦ 8♠ 9♣ 4♥. You check because you've learned that you can lose less money that way when you are up against the nuts. He bets half the pot. You realize that there are still a few hand combinations he could be holding with a 10 that would allow you to chop the pot. He could have A-10 and flopped a double belly buster draw, Q-10, J-10, 10-10, and maybe even 10-8.

YOU   **OPPONENT**

THE BOARD

You call and he turns over K♥ 10♠ for the nut straight to win the pot.

Despite the fact that your opponent got rewarded for playing poorly by overpaying for his draw on the flop, you still played your hand well by recognizing the danger of getting leapfrogged even after flopping the nuts.

3. PLAYING 9-8.

This hand is dangerous because there are many ways in which you can run into a higher straight with it. If the board is Q-J-10 offsuit, you are holding only the third-best hand. You are losing to A-K and to K-9. If the pot was unraised preflop, someone could easily have limped in with K-9 suited or perhaps one of the blinds is holding K-9 offsuit. The worst aspect of holding 9-8 in this situation is when an ace, king or 9 comes off on the turn or river. In that case, you would probably have to fold your hand if someone comes out betting because they could be holding a higher straight.

You especially need to be aware of the danger when the flop comes J-10-rag. While you have an innocent looking up and down straight draw and would like to see the turn card cheaply, you must not get overly excited if you see a queen come off on the turn or river. This is where many players fail to consider the two hands that can beat them, A-K and K-9. Instead, they are thinking about how lucky they are to have made their straight. Consequently, some players lose big pots in this situation because they do not realize that opponents who overvalue A-K might stick around after the flop and pay to see another card, or that someone holding K-9 might call bets with just a gutshot straight draw.

4. PLAYING Q-J.

This sneaky hand has a way of deceiving players into thinking they are holding the nut straight. However, if you are playing Q-J on a flop of K-10-9, and the turn is a queen, you could get blindsided by an opponent holding A-J, a hand that many players like to play. The same goes for a jack coming off when an opponent is holding A-Q. As with any straight that isn't the nut straight, you must refrain from tuning out the possibility that you can get beaten.

TRIPS WITH A LOW KICKER

Most poker players probably never think about three of a kind as being a trouble hand. However, trips can be extremely dangerous hands because they are very hard to get away from when you are beaten. Still, there are times when danger is staring you in the face, so you have to be aware enough to catch it and then fold.

Here is an example. In a ten-handed, live $5/$5 no-limit game, you are in the big blind holding 8♥ 4♠. Four players limp into the pot for the minimum bet and the small blind checks, so you check. With six players in the hand and $30 in the pot, the flop comes 7♦ 4♣ 4♥. You have flopped trip fours. The small blind checks and you decide to check in order to trap someone into betting a 7, a low pocket pair, a draw, or to encourage someone in late position to bluff. A very tight player in middle position bets $20, a couple of players fold, and a loose player on the button raises to $60. The small blind folds and the action comes to you.

SITUATION

You Have:	8♥ 4♠
The Board:	7♦ 4♣ 4♥
Money in the Pot:	$110
Bet for You to Call:	$60
Number of Players:	Three

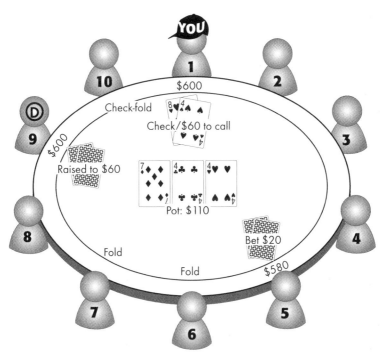

You have to at least consider that someone holding trip fours with a higher kicker has you beaten. You are not yet sure, so you just call the $60 in part to see what Seat 5 will do and in part to keep the pot small. There is no flush draw out there so it's okay to let your opponents look at the turn without reraising because nobody is on a big draw. You also should know that by check-calling a raise, it now looks like you have trip fours so you will gauge your opponents' plays on the turn based on the assumption that they know you have a strong hand. The tight player in Seat 5 also calls.

There is $210 in the pot, and you all have between $500 and $600 in front of you. The turn is the A♦. You bet $100 to see where you stand, and both players call. You take a moment to assess the situation.

SITUATION

You Have: 8♥ 4♠
The Board: 7♦ 4♣ 4♥ A♦
Money in the Pot: $510
Number of Players: Three

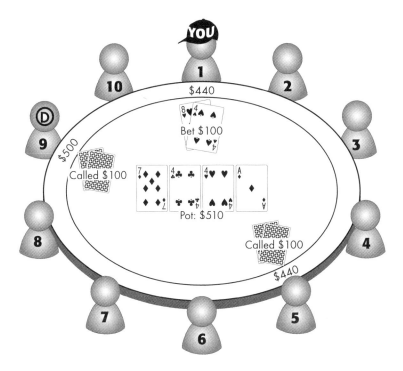

Now you are faced with a real problem. The purpose of your $100 bet was to remind your opponents that you have a hand, to see how they respond, and to decide if you might be beaten. Both of your opponents have to put you on a strong hand by now, so the safe play is to assume that one of them already has you beaten. You think Seat 5 is the most dangerous. But why isn't he raising to protect his hand and take down what is already a pretty nice pot? He is a very tight player who continues to just call on a paired board with a potential flush draw out there, and another player to his left (seat 9) that could catch his money card on the river.

The best answer is that Seat 5 might be holding a monster hand. He probably wouldn't play hands like K-4, Q-4, J-4, and so on, but he could have limped in with A-4 suited, against which you are drawing dead (and the same goes for pocket sevens). It now really feels like he could be holding one of those two hands. However, one possible range of hands that he could be holding and that you are beating is 6-4 suited, 5-4 suited, or 4-3 suited, which give him a lower kicker than yours. If his hand is suited in diamonds, he also has a flush draw, so perhaps he is just calling to see if he rivers a flush. You also should consider 7-4, which would give him a full house. Even though he is a tight player, there is a small chance he limped in with a gap hand just to look at a flop.

The river card is the 9♣, so the board is 7♦ 4♣ 4♥ A♦ 9♣. If someone is holding trip fours with diamonds and a weaker kicker than your 8, they have missed their flush and you have beat them. Still, you remember that your spider sense was really tingling on the turn, and the hands that you were afraid of earlier can still beat you: A-4, 7-4 and pocket sevens. You are satisfied not to make the pot any bigger. You want to avoid betting and putting yourself in a position where, if you get raised, you have to call off the rest of your chips.

You decide to check. If Seat 5 comes out betting, your suspicions will be confirmed.

Seat 5 bets $280 into a pot of $510. The button calls. Now what?

SITUATION

You Have: 8♥ 4♠
The Board: 7♦ 4♣ 4♥ A♦ 9♣
Money in the Pot: $1,070
Bet for You to Call: $280
Number of Players: Three

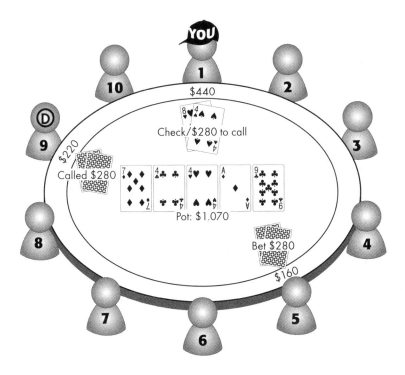

Your fears seem well founded. You decide to make a very tough laydown even though you are getting about 3.8 to 1 on your money. Seat 5 turns over 7♥ 7♠, and the loose player on the button turns over 5♥ 4♦. In last place with his weak kicker during the entire hand, he watches as Seat 5 wins a $1,070 pot with his full house. You made the right fold because you realized you were in danger against a very tight player with your vulnerable trip fours. The button's call on the river gave you more mathematical incentive to call because there was more in the pot for you to win. However, you hadn't committed more than one-third of your stack to the pot, so you stuck to your read on Seat 5 and decided to ignore Seat 9's action.

While the issue for you in this hand didn't turn out to be a kicker problem (although it was a problem for Seat 9), you played your hand intelligently without getting all your chips in with reckless abandon. The lesson here is that when you stop to think things through on each street, and when you think about the types of opponents you are facing, you open yourself up to the possibility that even a hand as strong as trips could lose. And you can save yourself a lot of money.

STRAIGHT, SET OR TOP TWO PAIR ON A SUITED BOARD

When you see a flop that is all the same suit—for example, Q♠ 9♠ 8♠—and you are holding a strong made hand such as Q♣ 9♦, 9♣ 9♥ or J♦ 10♦, you need to play very carefully. Assuming that you aren't already beaten, at the very least you can expect someone holding A♠, K♠, J♠ or 10♠ to be willing to create a big pot as he draws to a flush or straight flush. While you wouldn't really worry about someone's one-outer to make a straight flush, an opponent could still have as many as 12 outs to beat you (with a flush or straight), and so you wouldn't have a big edge in the hand. Therefore, you should try to keep the pot small.

An exception, of course, occurs when you have a set and the board pairs on the turn or river. Your full house should be the winning hand at that point, assuming nobody is holding a straight flush. When the card that pairs the board is the fourth suited card, your full house can prove very profitable. In the example above, let's say that you are holding 9♣ 9♥, the turn is the 2♥, and the river is the 2♠. If an opponent has the A♠, he probably will pay you off.

In general, since you could be up against someone who flopped a flush or who will try to win a big pot from you by drawing to a flush, you will want to play these types of boards very carefully and try to keep the pot small. Don't get angry or disappointed if the fourth suit comes off on the turn or river— the flop wasn't a good one for you anyway.

CONVENTIONAL TROUBLE HANDS

Although the conventional trouble hands don't qualify as big hands that get beaten by even bigger hands, it is still important to be aware of the danger in playing them. The conventional list of trouble hands includes hole cards such as A-J, A-10, A-9, K-Q, K-J, K-10, Q-J, Q-10 and J-10. The basic idea is to avoid getting your one pair outkicked. Therefore, playing A-10 on a board of A-Q-8 in a big pot against a tight player is not a great idea because you are probably losing to at least A-K, A-Q or A-J.

That said, I think there is still some money to be made with top pair/medium kicker as long as you are heads-up or maybe in a three-way pot against a couple of weak players. In the scenario above, there is a big difference between playing your top pair/10 kicker against a strong-tight player and a weak-loose player. Against a weak-loose player in an unraised pot, don't assume that A-10 on a flop of A-Q-8 is beaten. Why? Because he would have raised preflop with A-A, Q-Q, A-K, A-Q, probably A-J, and possibly 8-8. Therefore, you really have only two hands to worry about, A-8 and Q-8. If you've seen your opponent play weak aces such as A-6 before, you should feel confident about playing this pot. Most likely, he will just keep calling your bets and he might even call if all he has made on the flop is just a pair of queens.

6 FINDING THE RIGHT GAME

The types of players you are up against influence many of the decisions you make in a hand. Despite the fact that your strategy is based on playing big hands, you still need to know how to navigate your way through those hands without making a lot of mistakes. Since you will not have the nuts every time you play a big pot, you need to acknowledge that your opponents' playing styles impact the level of risk you face. However, becoming a successful cash game player isn't only about correctly playing your opponents at the tables. It also involves choosing the right game with the right people and a playing atmosphere that is conducive to winning. This chapter is devoted to making sure that you set yourself up for success by making the right decisions before you decide to spend hours playing in a particular game.

PLAYING IN GAMES WITH HEAVY ACTION

Some games are so fast and loose that it becomes challenging for you to execute your game plan. **Fast games** are ones with lots of action and aggressive players who frequently bet and raise. Let's say you want to play in a $5/$5 no-limit game, you want to start with $500 in chips, and your goal is to make a

$300 profit. If the table is playing very fast and the average price to see a flop is around $50, then getting involved in just one raised pot could mean risking your entire chip stack if it is played out. If you call large raises but then miss the flop playing hands such as A-K and A-Q, or if there are overcards when you play J-J or 10-10, you will find yourself bemoaning the size of the preflop action and you will need to repeatedly top up (replenish your chips), even more than you are accustomed to doing.

The real problem you are facing is that a fast $5/$5 no-limit game plays like a $5/$10 no-limit game, which means that you and almost everyone else at the table is short stacked. In a short stacked game like this, most players will be forced to just play high cards or pocket pairs because they can't afford to play speculative hands. They also will look to get all their money in when they hit a hand like top pair. This makes it difficult for you because you usually try to avoid committing all your chips with just top pair. To play in this game you would have to take on a lot more risk than you would like.

Ultimately, you will have two options at a fast table. The first option is to remain in the game but accept that you might lose a little more money than you usually do before you take down a big pot. You will need to start with a higher chip count, let's say $1,000 if you are in a live game with no cap on the amount of your buy-in. Your next step is to make an adjustment in your starting-hand requirements. You only want to play A-A, K-K or Q-Q, and you will have to stop investing in speculative hands in raised pots, although it is okay to try to flop a set with any pair if the price is not unreasonable. By using this approach, you will be able to conserve chips and have enough in front of you to do some damage if you hit a big hand.

With A-A or K-K, you might choose to move in preflop so that you can't get outplayed, and so that you can scoop medium-sized pots by making your opponents fold. If you get lucky, someone holding a lower pair will call your raise and you will win a big pot. Do not move in preflop with Q-Q because you don't want to expose yourself to getting called by someone holding A-K. You never want to be in a coin flip situation with all your chips on the line. Look at the flop first. If there are no overcards, try to take it down by firing at the pot. If you get called, you may have to take on more risk than you are used to accepting by firing another shell, which might mean playing a big pot or committing the rest of your chips to the pot with only an overpair.

The second option is that you leave the game or move to another table, depending on whether you are playing online or a live game. The right type of action at your table is very important, so a table change is easily justified. Being able to quickly change tables is one of the great advantages of online play. There are always other games and you can switch tables or poker sites as many times as you like. The best type of table for your game plan is one that has at least a couple of weak players and is medium-loose but not hyper-loose. Deciding whether to continue playing in a fast game will ultimately depend on your own comfort level.

PLAYING AGAINST OPPONENTS YOU CAN BEAT

Playing at tables against weaker players is important. If you keep sitting in games full of quality players, you will find it harder to get paid off on your monster hands and harder to win small pots with medium-strength hands. While your style of play will be hard for anyone to deal with in big pots, your results will not be as great over the long run if you keep sitting at strong tables. You need to proactively manage this part of your game.

Your daily routine online should not include sitting at a random table with a bunch of strange players, merely hoping they are weak. You need to find out where the weak players are by having them bookmarked or by tracking them on a buddy list. This is a little harder to do for live games. Playing in the right games may mean driving to locations that are farther away than you prefer. Consider this part of the work you need to do to win money; it's well worth it.

If you are playing at a table full of players you are not familiar with, don't get too involved in the action right away. Just observe at first, try to spot the weaker players, and start grouping your opponents. You may want to just limp in with hands like A-K, A-Q or middle pairs to avoid locking horns while you sit back and start memorizing the hands you've seen your opponents play. Once you feel comfortable with the majority of players at the table, and especially once you have identified the weaker players, you can start opening up and raising a little more often preflop with your starting hands.

Position is always important in a poker game but you don't really need to sit to the left of a weak player in order to beat him—a weak player will make mistakes in any seat. Instead choose a seat to the left of a strong player. One exception to this rule is when a weak hyper-loose player is at the table. In a $5/$10 no-limit game I used to play, there was a fellow named Charlie. This man was one of the loosest players in Toronto and poker players would literally leave work early so they could get a seat at the club where he played. Charlie would raise to $110, no more and no less, almost every hand, and sometimes he even raised blind. He would then grossly overplay his hand if he hit any piece of the board or picked up any kind of draw. He routinely loses between $5,000 and $10,000 per night. I took many big pots from Charlie, but I still always tried to sit to his immediate left. It was impossible to play hands cheaply, so I didn't want to limp in with hands like A-10 suited or K-J suited only to have him raise to $110 behind me. I also didn't want to call someone else's raise when I picked up a hand like A-Q or a low pocket pair only to have Charlie reraise behind me, because it would cost too much just to see the flop.

I adjusted my play against Charlie and only played pairs or A-K because I wanted to make sure I always had the best hand before I got involved in a large pot. I started those games with $1,000 or $1,500 and I called his raises looking to flop a set with any pair. I also planned to reraise with A-A or K-K, at which point he would move in if he had A-K, A-Q, K-Q, K-J suited, Q-J suited, J-10 suited, Q-Q, J-J, 10-10, 9-9 or 8-8. I also hoped to flop top pair/top kicker with A-K. I decided to play bigger pots than I usually do if I flopped top pair/top kicker because it is a pretty powerful hand against a guy like Charlie who overplays any piece of the board or any pocket pair. Earlier you read about making a decision to leave or stay in a hyper-loose game. When Charlie was there, it became one of those games, but I decided I was willing to lose $300 or $400 before I hit a big hand; and I once winged a pot that was worth more than $2,000. I also made sure to top up and keep a large chip stack so that I could win a huge pot. The great thing was that when I hit a big hand, I always had Charlie crushed, and he would pay me off every single time, making it worth the risk of sustaining heavier action preflop.

PLAYING AGAINST GOOD PLAYERS

One of the key advantages of applying your new cash game strategy is that highly skilled players are often rendered powerless against you in big pots. Since you will have a big hand every time you play a big pot, they will have a difficult time beating you. Sometimes these sharks will even make a mistake against you and you will win a big pot from them. Eventually, however, good players will adjust and some of them may try a little harder to win small pots from you. While you are usually perfectly okay with this, you still don't want to lose every single small pot you play because it could drain your chip stack too much and make it a little harder for you to reach your profit objective.

The best way to manage this issue is to have position on good players. Having position on strong players will help you manage what I call the "minefield effect."

THE MINEFIELD EFFECT

Just as a person who walks deep into a minefield fears that a mine is due to explode in his face, so a tight poker player fears playing a hand all the way to the river.

The main outcome of the minefield effect is that strong-loose players try to outplay tight players on fourth and fifth streets when they know their opponents are holding a hand that they are capable of folding. Since position will help you deal with strong-loose players who like to take full advantage of the minefield effect, you should bookmark these tough players so that you know who they are and try to sit to their left when you play online. In live games you should also choose a seat to their left. If you are one of the first players to sit down, it is even worth getting up and switching seats once you see where they are sitting.

Here is an example where you are up against a quality player and you have position on him. Let's say you are in a nine-handed online $5/$10 no-limit game. You are in the cutoff position and raise to $50 with Q♣ Q♦. The blinds fold, and the only caller is a strong-loose player who limped in middle position. He likes to play a lot of pots and outplay opponents. Since he just limped in, you don't put him on a strong starting hand. You suspect he might be calling because he feels comfortable playing against you, so you put him on a speculative hand, especially since he is deep enough in chips to be able to gamble a little. You started with $1,100 and he started with $1,000. The flop comes J♦ 7♣ 4♠. He checks.

SITUATION

You Have: Q♣ Q♦
The Board: J♦ 7♣ 4♠
Money in the Pot: $115
Number of Players: Two

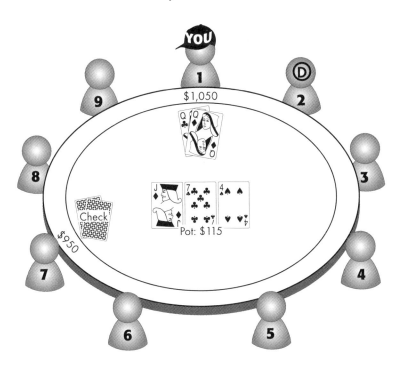

Since you have an overpair and the board doesn't look dangerous, you should bet. If he missed the flop badly, he might lose heart and fold instead of trying to outplay you. Also, you are almost certain that if you show weakness, he will pounce on it and bet or raise big on a later street. You prefer to avoid a big pot if you can since you only have one pair.

You bet $60, about half the pot. He calls. He might see this as a bad flop for you as he might be putting you on A-K or A-Q, so he could be trying a bluff-call to try to steal the pot on a later street. However, you assume for the moment that he at least left himself some outs, so you think about the hands he could be playing. He could have picked up a small draw with a hand like 10-8, 10-9, 9-8, 6-3, or 5-3. Maybe he has an open-ended straight draw with 6-5; however, he might have check-raised rather than just called with that hand, although you can't be sure. If he has a hand such as K-J, Q-J, J-10 or J-9, he might have check-raised you just to see where he was at, but he could also play those hands deceptively by just check-calling, which would help him keep the pot small in case he is up against one of your big hands. While he could have flopped two pair or a set and is slowplaying, you believe you are probably winning. Nevertheless, you are hoping to keep the pot small from here on since he is a tricky player and you don't have a big hand.

The turn pairs the board with the 4♦. There is $235 in the pot. He bets $100.

SITUATION

You Have: Q♣ Q♦
The Board: J♦ 7♣ 4♠ 4♦
Money in the Pot: $335
Bet for You to Call: $100
Number of Players: Two

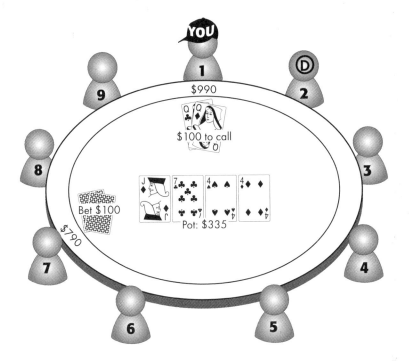

By representing a made hand and possibly a hand that has improved on the turn, this could be his chance to test you to see if you missed the flop. He might simply believe that if you missed the flop, you have to fold regardless of what he is holding. This is a play you see strong players make. They do it to take advantage of the minefield effect. Instead of raising on the flop and potentially getting shut out with a reraise by an opponent holding top pair, or by an opponent who might be restealing with ace-high, they prefer to see another card hoping it scares their opponent and makes their bet tougher to call. This is called the stop-and-go play. It even costs less for your opponent to play this way as opposed to raising on the flop. So far, he has spent $160 after the flop, but if he had raised on the flop, he might have spent $180 or $200 or possibly more.

Assuming he isn't totally bluffing, it is possible that he picked up a diamond draw with a straight draw if he is playing a suited connector, or maybe he actually has a jack and is playing it tricky by betting into you now instead of raising on the flop.

While you think there is a chance he is trying to take the pot away from you, it's still a good idea to avoid creating a big pot by raising at this time. That way you avoid giving him an opportunity to move in, at which point you probably couldn't call. If he has a big draw, you can't be certain you would get rid of him anyway unless you put him all in, which isn't something you want to do without a big hand. Also, there is a remote possibility you are wrong and are being set up if he flopped two pair or a set. If he did and is now betting out with a full house, he might think a bet here disguises the real strength of his hand, so there might be a chance that he will even move in if you raise.

By just calling, you can still let him know that you have a hand and you won't be going away so easily. Maybe he will lose heart on the river, assuming he doesn't make his hand, or maybe he will fear that you flopped a set of jacks if you just call. Notice that because you have position on him, you are the one with all the options even when he is trying to apply pressure on you. You call.

The river is the 9♣, making the board J♦ 7♣ 4♠ 4♦ 9♣. There is $435 in the pot. He checks. You also check. You show your pair of queens and he shows 5♦ 3♦.

YOU	OPPONENT

THE BOARD

It is clear that on the flop he was trying to set you up for a move, and then he picked up a bigger draw on the turn. However, after missing his draw on the river, he lost heart and didn't want to make another play at the pot. Having picked up a flush draw on the turn with his gutshot straight draw, he might have been very aggressive if you had raised him—he might even have moved in hoping you couldn't call with just one pair.

It is also clear that it would have been more difficult for you to win the pot if he had had position on you. He would have had the advantage of letting you act first and he would have applied pressure on you, probably by raising any chance you gave him on the flop and the turn, and possibly by making a large bet on the river if you had checked to him.

KEY TAKEAWAY

Having position on good players discourages them from trying to outplay you. It allows you to win almost all of your big pots and win more of the small pots.

One last point about playing against strong-loose opponents: Make sure you don't try to emulate the way they play. Far too often I've seen a tight player become too comfortable in a game, and start loosening up his play to try some of the fancy moves he's seen strong-loose players make. In the end he loses some big pots. The problem with doing this is that you end up getting off strategy, which usually results in an extended losing streak. You don't need to do this because you don't need to take on a lot of risk to be a big winner in cash games. If you feel the need to try some new plays, try playing in online tournaments where the most money you risk is your entry fee. Do not experiment too much in cash games. The purpose of playing cash games is to win money—and you have a great game plan with which to do that.

PLAYING AGAINST UNINTENTIONALLY TRICKY PLAYERS

Sometimes you will run into a player who can't be easily classified at first. You might observe someone make a tough call on the river with just second pair and winning the pot. He might play another hand aggressively and push everyone out of a pot. You might start to think he is a strong-loose player. Then in his next hand he calls off half his stack hoping to hit a flush on the river and he loses a huge pot. What gives? Is he weak or strong? Most likely what you are observing is a player who is unintentionally tricky. These players are weak-loose, but they can be tricky to play against because when they play a hand, you cannot always be sure whether you are ahead or behind.

An unintentionally tricky player often overvalues his hands. He will often behave like a calling station, so he can win good pots from players who try to bluff him. Also, he often will have only top pair with a medium kicker (or just second pair) and play it like it was the nuts, even in a large multiway pot, simply because he doesn't know any better. And yet, he will sometimes chase everyone off the pot. Of course, all you need to do to beat this player is to wait for a strong hand and avoid bluffing him.

FINDING THE RIGHT GAME

The only real problem with playing against an unintentionally tricky player is that he might call a pot-sized bet on a draw and hit his card when you have a big hand. These players have a tendency to just keep hanging around, so they might occasionally catch up with you in a hand. Unintentionally tricky players can be rather tough to figure out. Although other players may prefer to not play against them because they are so stubborn and somewhat unpredictable, you should feel good playing with them. Just make sure to keep the pots small if you think they might have a decent number of outs to beat you because they will almost always call. Let's look at an example.

In a ten-handed live $2/$5 no-limit game, you are holding A♦ Q♦ in the cutoff seat. After two players limp in, you raise to $30 and get only one caller, an unintentionally tricky player in the small blind. You both started the hand with $500. There is $75 in the pot. The flop comes Q♠ 10♥ 6♦. Your opponent checks.

SITUATION

You Have: A♦ Q♦
The Board: Q♠ 10♥ 6♦
Money in the Pot: $75
Number of Players: Two

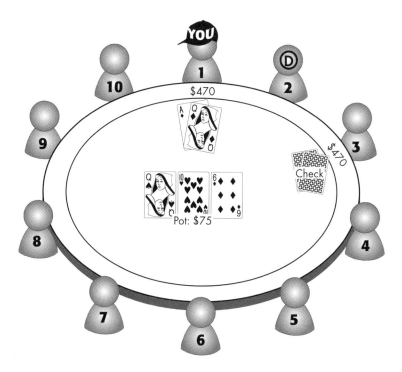

You hit a pretty good flop, so you bet $60. He calls. You are pretty sure you are ahead. Considering the way he plays, he could have a queen with a lower kicker—K-Q, Q-J, Q-10 or Q-9 suited—or he could have second pair with A-10, K-10, J-10 or maybe 10-9 suited. He could also just have 8-8 or 9-9. Further, K-J and J-9 would give him an open-ended straight draw, and A-J, K-9, J-8, 9-7 and 8-7 would give him a gutshot straight draw. In short, there are a lot of hands you are beating, but there are also some hands with drawing potential.

Therefore, you should consider keeping the pot small since you only have one pair and he is likely to keep calling.

The turn is the A♥, giving you top two pair. There is $195 in the pot. He checks. You bet $100. He moves all-in. Now what?

SITUATION

You Have: A♦ Q♦
The Board: Q♠ 10♥ 6♦ A♥
Money in the Pot: $705
Bet for You to Call: $310
Number of Players: Two

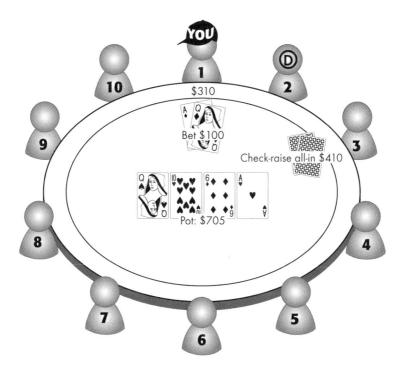

You are holding one of the hands you like to wait for to play a big pot, and you are up against a weak-loose player, so this seems to be a great situation for you. He might have turned a weaker two pair with A-10 or maybe even A-6. And if he flopped two pair with Q-10 and slowplayed them, you again have him crushed. There is also a chance he is holding A-K or maybe A-J because he is weak enough to overvalue those hands by calling on the flop with just a gutshot draw. After all, you did raise six times the big blind preflop, so it should take solid hands like these to call. There is also a remote possibility that he is on a big draw with a hand like Q♥ with another flush card, or any of the aforementioned hole cards that give him a straight draw or a gutshot draw but with suited hearts.

With only one card to come, you are a solid favorite against any of these drawing hands. Although he could have flopped a set of sixes, you don't think he is holding pocket queens or tens because he probably would have reraised preflop with those hands. You are also pot committed, and you are getting a decent price to call, about 2.3 to 1, so you're not in a pot where you have little invested with a marginal hand. You decide there is a high likelihood that you have him beat.

You call. He turns over K♣ J♥, which gives him the nut straight. You still have four outs to make a full house, but you miss on the river and lose all your chips.

If you had more seriously considered that he could have been on a draw on the flop and that he might have turned a straight, you could have checked behind him on the turn and kept the pot smaller just in case you were beat. He would have bet the river, let's say $150 (or maybe less) into a pot of $195, which would have saved you $260 or more if you had just called. You still would have lost a large pot, but you wouldn't have lost all your chips.

The toughest part about playing against a player who is unintentionally tricky is that you don't think like he does, so you aren't always able to correctly put him on a hand. You wouldn't call a preflop raise that was six times the big blind with K-J offsuit, especially in the small blind, and you wouldn't call a bet that is four-fifths of the pot on a straight draw, but it is obvious that he would. As a result, the only hand you took seriously when considering the hands that could beat you was pocket sixes. While you made a terrible mistake and you might start kicking yourself for calling too quickly without more systematically thinking through the range of hands that could beat you, realize that this was a rare, unfortunate hand. He just happened to turn the perfect card that made his straight and improved your hand.

Considering the types of hands that this player overvalues and overplays (such as A-K, A-J, A-10, A-6, top pair with any kicker, and flush draws with gutshot draws), you really didn't want to risk folding a big hand against an opponent who was capable of making mistakes in big pots. Just consider this hand a fluke, and wait to go up against him again when you most likely will come out on top. Very few times will you get all your money in bad like you did against this unintentionally tricky opponent.

Now it's time to move on to the deal, the time when you must make the correct decision in deciding whether you should fold or play. The next chapter goes into extensive detail about selecting the best hands to start with, and how to play them to your best advantage before the flop.

7 MAKING CORRECT PREFLOP DECISIONS

Since you are going to adopt a patient style of play where you wait to hit big hands after the flop, you might be wondering how you should play your hands preflop and what you are trying to accomplish. The answers are simple and follow logically from the fundamental premise of your game plan.

AVOIDING BIG POTS

You almost never want to get involved in a big pot before the flop. You want to play carefully preflop because with any hand other than A-A or K-K, you could potentially be a big underdog, or you might have only a small edge over your opponent's hand; for example, Q-Q versus A-K, or A-Q versus K-J. With the exception of holding A-A and sometimes K-K, the best hand you can hold preflop is one vulnerable pair, so there is almost no hand you could hold that you consider a big hand with which you are willing to play a big pot.

Your objective as preflop raiser is to thin the field without creating a big pot so that you can win a small or medium sized pot after the flop. Make your raises three times the big blind all of the time. There are two main benefits of raising that amount.

1. You will keep the pot relatively small, which will help you avoid playing a big pot after the flop when you aren't holding a big hand. Most of the time you won't hit a big flop, so you don't need to consistently build the pot preflop.
2. You will prevent your opponents from being able to read your hand. By making the same size of raise all of the time, you avoid giving away betting tells, which usually occur when you vary your bets according to the strength of your hand.

There are exceptions to raising three times the big blind, and that occurs when you are reraising. Also, when numerous limpers are in the pot and you want to protect pocket aces, kings or queens—regardless of your position—you should raise a larger amount than three times the big blind to prevent numerous players from seeing the flop.

After you make a raise preflop, if you get one caller and you miss the flop you should bet out about 50% of the time and hope to take it down right there. If you are three-way then make a continuation bet about 30% of the time, and if you are playing the hand four-way then you should look to give it up almost all of the time. If you vary the number of times you make a continuation bet as suggested, your opponents won't know when they should try to resteal the pot from you, and quite often they will fold. Making intermittent continuation bets heads-up or three-way will help keep you closer to your profit objective without taking on a lot of risk.

The degree to which you vary your continuation bets also depends on how tight your opponents are playing, so you should use these recommendations only as a guideline. If you are in a hand against players that you know are capable of folding, you can increase the frequency of your continuation bets. When you play online, you probably will find that softer players are harder to come by; therefore, you will get called a lot more often than in live games. Online players are known for betting or raising when they perceive weakness. They often give action to players who raise preflop because they assume that the raiser will miss the flop most of the time. They also attack players who raise in position because they seem to think that the raiser is trying to steal the pot with a weak hand.

When you play online, don't get involved in wars when you miss the flop simply because you think your opponent is trying to resteal with a weak hand. That is one of the most common ways that amateur players lose money online. In general, you should make continuation bets when you think it is appropriate, but look to give up the pot almost all the time if you get called or raised. Some of the time, of course, you will connect with the flop so you shouldn't feel as though your preflop strategy is all about setting up a bluff after the flop. Just know that when you raise and don't connect with the flop, you can sometimes win the pot with one bet on the flop.

As the preflop raiser with pocket aces, you are hoping an opponent is holding a lower pair such as K-K or Q-Q, so you can get all his chips in the middle. As the preflop raiser with pocket kings or queens, you want to make most opponents fold so that you can either end the hand right there or play the flop heads-up. You should usually raise three or four times the big blind although, on a table that is playing fast and loose, you may need to raise more than that to push most players out of the pot. It is justifiable to play Q-Q aggressively preflop because, if you make a raise or reraise, you might end the hand right there. If not, you will certainly narrow the field significantly, especially given your tight image at the table. You might get one caller, and hopefully take down a small pot with one bet on the flop, assuming there are no overcards.

AVOIDING GOING ALL-IN PREFLOP

Always avoid going all in preflop unless you are holding A-A or possibly K-K if you feel certain that your opponent isn't holding A-A. If you do not feel certain, you must consider that your K-K could be beat. You could also come over the top with a third raise with K-K to see if your opponent goes all in after you. If he does, you should consider yourself beaten by A-A, and you should fold unless you are getting 4.5 to 1 on your money to call. When you are holding K-K against a weak-loose or average-loose player who is capable of overplaying A-K, Q-Q, J-J or 10-10, it will be a little safer to get all your money in preflop. However, you shouldn't be thrilled if he turns over A-K since you would only be about a 1.9 to 1 favorite. That is why it can be dangerous to move in preflop. If an ace hits the flop, you will lose all your money whereas if you had just called and looked at the flop, you would have been able to get away from your hand. Alternatively, if an ace comes off on the turn or river, you could have won the pot on the flop with a solid bet. Therefore, merely calling a preflop raise or reraise with K-K or Q-Q is a play that can come in very handy because most of your opponents will overplay a big ace.

There is an important lesson here that will help you save money that you might otherwise lose with one pair. When you are holding K-K or Q-Q and you are facing a fourth raise preflop, you should fold most of the time. A fourth raise often means that your opponent is holding A-A. Since your table image is a tight player, your opponent's aggression is especially dangerous because most players know they should be careful when you reraise. For them to play back at you after you have showed a lot of strength signals that you are beaten.

Once in a while, you will even have to fold pocket kings preflop in a big pot when you are mathematically pot committed. For example, let's say you raise to $20 in a live $5/$5 no-limit game where your live stack is $540. An opponent who has been playing very tight reraises to $80, you reraise to $200, and he goes all in and he has you covered. There is $740 in the pot and it will cost you your remaining $340 to call. You are almost certain your opponent is holding A-A and you are only getting about 2.1 to 1 on your money when you think you need 4.5 to 1. Therefore, even though you have already committed more than one-third of your live stack to the pot, you can fold because you would be shocked if he was holding a hand that justified a call such as Q-Q or A-K. As a general rule when you are holding K-K or Q-Q, it is better to miss an opportunity to take someone's stack if you are really not sure where you stand than it is to give your stack away to someone holding A-A. The best way to think about a big pair is that it is the same as any other middle pocket pair. You want to flop a set—only then should you be willing to get involved for all your chips.

Too many players think it is okay to lose all their chips with pocket kings or queens when an opponent has a higher pair or two overcards. They avoid taking accountability for their actions by considering it really bad luck. You sometimes hear a player say that he was the victim of a set-up hand. A set-up hand is one where a player believes his preflop holding is so strong that he can't consider folding regardless of how heavy the betting is, so he loses all his chips to someone who has a higher pocket pair, or he loses a coin flip against an opponent who hits the board with A-K. You will rarely get caught in a set-up hand preflop because you realize that you should avoid going to war with just one pair. A-A is the only hand you can really feel comfortable going all-in with preflop.

PLAYING SPECIFIC STARTING HANDS

Big pairs are not the only starting hands you will want to play since they don't come around very often. You still need to play some pots preflop to give yourself a chance to hit a monster hand. Let's look at all the different hand groupings that suit your game plan and discuss how to play them preflop.

A-A, K-K, Q-Q

Consider reraising, raising, calling a raise, or limping in. With A-A, you are in control. You should play A-A with the objective of ending the hand preflop or to entice an opponent who is also holding a big pair to move in on you. However, since things don't always work out that way, you will sometimes need to play a flop and hope to take it down with one bet or possibly a second bet on the turn. Ideally you will be playing these pots heads-up. Playing a flop in a multiway pot with just one pair is not a great way to make money in the long run since it is always difficult to know where you stand, especially if you are out of position. That is why it can be useful to shut out your opponents preflop.

If you are holding K-K and an ace hits the flop, or if you have Q-Q and an ace or king hits the flop, you will usually need to slow down and often give up the pot. However, if you are heads-up, you can still fire one bet and hope your opponent folds. The risk of seeing overcards makes it reasonable to reraise preflop with K-K and Q-Q because you prefer not to see a flop at all. When you reraise, opponents holding A-Q, A-J, A-10, K-Q, and pocket pairs such as J-J, 10-10 and 9-9 will have a tough time calling your reraise. Expect some players to call a raise with these hands just to try to hit a nice flop, so you should hope to take the pot down with one bet on the flop.

Depending on the nature of the game and your opponents, it is also reasonable to limp in sometimes with a high pocket pair and hope to flop a set. If you raise with a big pair at a loose table with a few deep-stacked opponents, you might get called by players trying to crack your pair with hands such as J-10 offsuit or 5-3 suited. You might also have to play a multiway pot because once one opponent calls your raise, players with deep stacks will think that it is more worthwhile for them to get involved. Therefore, using the limp as a defensive bet reduces the risk of playing just one pair in a tough situation. Also, if you do flop a set when an opponent hits a flop he likes, you would be holding a deceptively strong hand, and get paid off in a monster pot. Just be prepared to muck your hand if you don't flop a set and there is a lot of action on a dangerous board such as 7♦ 6♦ 5♣, or if there is an overcard and a lot of action after the flop.

YOU

FLOP ONE

FLOP TWO

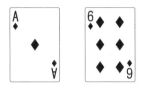

As a rule, you should never lose a lot of money in an unraised pot because your opponents are often playing a wide range of hands and someone could unexpectedly be holding the nuts.

You shouldn't think that by limping in with a big pair you might miss a great opportunity to win a big pot. If you limp in with A-A and someone is holding A-K, A-Q, K-K, Q-Q, J-J or 10-10, he will raise behind you anyway, and then you will have your chance to reraise and maybe entice him to move in. If you don't get raised, you were possibly just going to win a very small pot preflop by making everyone fold. By the way, when players notice that you are limping in with big pairs, you can expect to hear someone say, "Come on, bet your hand. Play a little!" This means that your opponents are having trouble finding a way to beat you and they are getting annoyed. They want you to play more hands so that they can outplay you, and they want you to play your cards the way they would play them. It is a sign that you are doing a great job of staying on strategy and avoiding big pots unless you are holding a big hand.

J-J, 10-10

Consider raising, calling a raise, or limping in. Pocket jacks is a hand you will hear a lot of players say is a hand they despise, usually because they've been playing it poorly, or investing in it too heavily preflop and then getting married to it after the flop. The purpose of raising with J-J or 10-10 is to end the hand right there. If you get a few callers and you see at least one overcard on the flop, it will be easy to get away from your hand so you won't lose a lot of money. If you are heads-up, you should make a continuation bet even with one overcard showing on the board, but do not put any more money into the pot if you get called.

You almost have to expect to see overcards with J-J or 10-10, so you want to play them cautiously preflop, especially in multiway pots. The probability of seeing at least one overcard on the flop with J-J is about 59 percent, and with 10-10 it is about 71 percent. That is why I don't recommend reraising or sometimes even calling a reraise with these hands. The price will usually be too high to try to flop a set or better, an event that occurs only about 1 in 8 times. Further, if the initial raiser comes over the top, you will have to fold and you will have wasted money reraising or calling a reraise. If you do play a raised pot with J-J or 10-10, you are really hoping to flop a set for a reasonable price. However, you need to make sure you are getting the right implied odds, so you need to make sure that your opponents have deep enough chip stacks to make calling a raise worthwhile. The concept of implied odds is discussed in more detail in the next section, "Paying the Right Price."

POCKET PAIRS 9-9 OR LOWER

Consider calling a raise or limping in. You do not need to drive the action by raising since all you want is to flop a set. The probability of seeing at least one overcard on the flop with pocket nines is 81 percent, so you must play this hand and other medium and low pairs cheaply. You should still be willing to call a raise with these hands since flopping a set can make it worth the risk, assuming you are up against players with deep stacks.

A-K, A-Q

Consider raising, calling one raise, or limping in. Since there is only about a 32 percent chance of making just one pair on the flop, you can raise and hope to end the hand right there. However, I recommend you lean toward limping the majority of the time. You are looking to flop top two pair or better and you don't want to spend a lot of money to do this. If your cards are suited, you also hope to hit the nut flush. While flopping a flush is rare, you may still have a chance to hit your money card on the turn, so you hope to get there cheaply if not for free. Just be sure not to overvalue a nut flush draw by playing aggressively against an opponent that you think might have a made hand. That is usually weak play and a danger that many cash game players fail to recognize.

A-K and A-Q can be very profitable when opponents are holding dominated hands. They might get trapped into a big pot against you with a lower two pair or trip aces with a lower kicker (or trip kings or queens with a lower kicker). Sometimes you can win a big pot from a player who is holding K-Q and gets caught with a lower straight when you have the nut straight with A-K. Of course, A-K and A-Q will also allow you to win numerous small and medium-sized pots when you flop top pair and catch someone who also has hit top pair with a lower kicker. Or perhaps an opponent will decide to pay you off with just second pair.

If you raise and someone reraises a large amount (more than triple your bet), you usually should fold. Why? Because, if you are up against a pair, your opponent will have a decided advantage when the flop comes out since you are the one who needs to hit. Chances are you will miss the flop and probably won't get an opportunity to see the turn and river cards for free. In other words, assuming that you would get to see all five community cards, you are in a coin flip situation. But since you probably won't get to see five cards, you are simply behind and shouldn't waste chips by calling and trying to hit your cards.

A-X SUITED

(KICKER IS JACK OR LOWER)

Consider limping in and occasionally calling a raise. Some players avoid this range of hands because they are concerned about their low kicker. Of course, you should not play weak-ace hands just to pair the ace. Any suited ace can be worth investing in cheaply because you have a chance to make the nuts if you flop a flush draw. The odds of flopping a flush are very long, but if you manage to flop a flush draw (about 9 to 1 odds against), you might be able to see the turn card cheaply or perhaps for free. If you hit your flush and catch someone playing a smaller flush, you can take his whole stack.

If your weak ace isn't suited, it is a trouble hand. I realize that being suited only increases your hand's probability of winning by about three percentage points; however, with a suited ace you have something nobody else has—the potential nut flush.

Just remember that playing A-5, A-4, A-3, and A-2 for a straight can get you into trouble if you don't keep an eye out for the nut straight. While you shouldn't get into the habit of folding the wheel when someone bets into you, just consider that perhaps you shouldn't be raising and risking more of your chips if you think there is a decent chance your opponent could be holding the nut straight.

HIGH SUITED CONNECTORS
AND ONE-GAPPERS

(K♠ Q♠, K♥ J♥, Q♦ J♦, OR Q♣ 10♣)

Consider limping in and occasionally calling a raise. With these cards you are looking to hit a flush or a straight either on the flop or the turn, assuming you can see the turn cheaply or for free. If you are holding K♠ Q♠, for example, and you don't flop a big hand, you want to see a flop like A♠ 10♦ 4♠, because this gives you a draw to the nut flush and the nut straight. While you might not always win big pots with these hands, what you are really hoping for is to catch an opponent drawing to a lower flush or straight. For example, suppose you are holding the nuts with K♥ J♥ on a board of 10♥ 9♥ 4♦ Q♠.

YOU

THE BOARD

Here are the ways you could make a lot of money from your opponents:

1. **Smaller straight.** You are beating an opponent who is holding J-8 for a lower straight, and he may pay you off.
2. **Smaller flush draw.** A player holding any low, suited connectors will probably give you action on the turn and then pay you off if the river card is another heart.
3. **Big draws.** A player holding J-10 offsuit will have second pair and an open-ended straight draw, so

he will probably give you a lot of action on this board. If the river is an 8, he will be holding the lower straight. Also, a hand like Q♥ X♥ (where X♥ is not A♥) gives someone top pair and a flush draw so you should get a lot of action from this player on the turn and get paid if the river is a heart. An opponent with Q♥ 8♥ would have top pair, a lower flush draw, and a gutshot draw to a lower straight, so you undoubtedly will get a lot of action while your opponent is drawing dead. Also, a player holding a low suited connector with the 8♥ (8♥ 6♥, 8♥ 5♥, 8♥ 4♥, for example) would have a flush draw and a gutshot draw, so he would give you action on this board. Finally, a player holding 8♥ 7♥ would have an open-ended straight flush draw and would be drawing to only one card to beat you, the 6♥, and you might actually be able to get this player all-in on the turn.

Playing draws is not a key part of your strategy, but the reality is that you won't flop a lot of flushes or straights, so you can play these starting hands hoping to flop a big draw, and then hoping to see the turn or river cheaply, if not for free.

UNSUITED CONNECTORS AND ONE-GAPPERS
(Q-J, Q-10, J-10, J-9, 9-8, 9-7, 8-7, 8-6, 7-6, 7-5, 6-5, 6-4, 5-4, 5-3)

Consider limping in and occasionally calling a raise. The purpose of playing these hands is to flop a straight or better, or to get a cheap or free look at the turn to hit a straight. Considering that your table image is tight, you can deceive opponents with these hands because they will usually put you on high cards. Try not to play too many raised pots with these hands because they are highly speculative, and you can waste a lot of money trying to hit a big hand. Also, you should look to play them in late position. Even if there is a small raise followed by a few callers in front of you, you might consider calling because of the implied odds and the prospect of winning an opponent's entire stack. In early position you won't know if someone will raise behind you or if there will be a reraise, and you often will end up throwing your hand away.

Since you usually will be playing an unraised pot with these hands, be aware that you could be up against the nut straight when you are holding the second-best hand. For example, suppose you hold 7♦ 5♣ and the flop is 9♠ 8♣ 6♥ in a six or seven-way pot, you might need to keep the pot small if a tight player is giving you a lot of action.

YOU

THE FLOP

Your opponent could be holding 10-7, especially if he is sitting in one of the blind positions. If you are playing a three or four-way pot, you can feel less concerned about going up against the nuts and you can play accordingly.

However, always beware leapfrogging. In this case, if the turn or river brings a jack, you want to keep the pot small if you can. You might have to give it up altogether if a 10 or 7 come off and an opponent starts driving the action. Since you are always wary of leapfrogging, you will have far less chance of losing a big pot with connecting cards than you will with low, suited cards. The key difference is that you know whether you are holding the nut straight, whereas with a baby flush you don't know if your opponent has you beaten with a higher flush until the showdown. Be warned that if you have a flush using both of your hole cards, you will be willing to move in almost all of the time when you could be drawing dead against a higher flush.

Except for those times when we have an exceptional read on our opponent, we cannot know if our flush is beaten because we cannot see our opponent's cards until the showdown.

The purpose of playing unsuited connectors is to flop or turn a straight, not hit top two pair. With most of these types of hole cards, making top two pair puts you in a vulnerable position to opponents who are on a straight draw. There is a big difference between holding top two pair on a flop of A♦ J♣ 7♠ and a flop of 7♣ 6♣ 4♥.

EXAMPLE ONE

YOU

THE FLOP

With your A-J, you were hoping to flop top two pair or better, so this is a result that you like and you can play your hand with confidence.

EXAMPLE TWO

YOU

THE FLOP

On the 7♣ 6♣ 4♥ flop, you have to expect that if someone is holding a 5, he will try to draw out on you. And of course, if an opponent has 8-5 (most likely someone in the blind in an unraised pot), he has you beaten already. Also, since someone could be on a flush draw, a lot of cards could come off on the turn that you won't like. Therefore, you should probably keep the pot small.

EXAMPLE THREE

YOU

THE FLOP

While I'm not saying that you should prepare to muck your hand when you are holding J♠ 10♥ on a flop of J♦ 10♣ 7♥, you should be aware that opponents might be drawing to a hand that can beat you, so you should act accordingly. Of course, if an opponent is holding a 9-8, he already has beaten you.

PAYING THE RIGHT PRICE

If someone raises preflop and you're holding pocket sevens, how much should you be willing to pay to try to flop a set? This is an important question since flopping a set certainly qualifies as one of those big hands that can make your night. The odds of flopping a set or better are about 7.5 to 1, which isn't great, so you run the risk of draining your chip stack by making these calls and then missing the flop. However, if you flop a set you have a great chance to take down a big pot, and possibly grab someone's entire stack, so it can be worth the risk. In certain cases you need to make a judgment call, but in others you just need to do a little math to help you make a decision.

You can do a very simple calculation to learn what your implied odds are. Implied odds measure the amount you are risking against the total amount you might win. Notice the difference between implied odds and pot odds, which measure the amount you are risking against what you can win in the current pot. You won't always need to calculate implied odds at the poker table, but understanding this concept will at least help you make some tough judgment calls.

Let's say you're playing a $5/$10 no-limit game. A weak-tight player in early position makes a large raise to $80. One player calls in front of you. You have 9♣ 9♥ in the cutoff seat. You started the hand with $800 in chips, as did the raiser.

YOU

MONEY IN THE POT: $175
BET FOR YOU TO CALL: $80

It will cost you $80 to call the raise when there is already $175 in the pot (two players put in $80 plus $15 from the blinds), so you are getting 2.2 to 1 on your money ($175/$80 = 2.2). Since the odds of flopping a set or better are about 7.5 to 1, it looks like you shouldn't call by regular pot odds calculations. In fact, it's not even close.

However, this weak-tight player raises almost exclusively with A-A, K-K, Q-Q, J-J or A-K. If you hit something like a 10-9-2 flop and he is holding an overpair, you may be able to get a good chunk of his stack and possibly all of it. Therefore, let's assume that the total amount you can win is $895 (the raiser's $720 that he has left plus $175 already in the pot). In that case you are getting implied odds of 11.2 to 1 ($895/$80). When you compare that to the 7.5 to 1 odds of flopping a set or better, you are getting an excellent price to call. It looks like it's worth the risk.

What if the preflop raise were a sizeable $120? You see these kinds of raises more often than you might think in cash games because some players want to protect their starting hands and thin the field. Now your implied odds are 7.8 to 1 ($935/$120), so you are still getting the right implied odds to call. However, this is where some judgment comes in. A bet of $120 means that you are gambling a large portion of your stack (15 percent in this case) for an event that doesn't occur very often. You may prefer to fold in this case and cross your fingers that you don't see a 9 on the flop.

In fact, even folding to that $80 raise is justifiable since it is still eight times the big blind and 10 percent of your stack. As a general guideline, when holding a pocket pair you should be willing to call a raise that is five times the big blind or less, assuming that the risk of an opponent reraising behind you isn't high. You don't want to start laying down pocket pairs on a regular basis because the upside associated with flopping a set is too large. The key lesson here is that if it doesn't cost you a large piece of your stack, and if your opponent has enough money in front of him so that you stand to win a big pot, you can consider gambling.

When you need help making these judgment calls, think about your profit objective for the session. If you are happy walking out with $400-$500 profit, then losing that $120 might feel like you are getting substantially farther away from your objective. Perhaps you just need to tip your cap to a good solid bet and fold. If your profit objective is $600 or more, you may decide that the $120 investment is worth it because of the upside to the hand and the fact that you have to stretch farther to reach your goal.

KEY TAKEAWAY

Although calculated risks can pay off, don't become a reckless gambler. Balance your willingness to gamble with the correct degree of risk to your chips and to your profit objective.

STEALING BLINDS

Stealing blinds is not something you are looking to do because it gets you involved in too many pots with weak hands for very little return. For this same reason you are not interested in defending your blinds unless you have a hand worth investing in to see if you hit a big flop. Be sure that you don't get angry or frustrated by players who appear to be stealing your big blind. Getting emotional can be dangerous. It can throw you off your game plan and cause you to play pots you shouldn't be playing, which is what your opponents want to happen. While they hope to elicit this reaction, don't give them what they want. You are in a cash game, not a tournament, so the blinds stay at their small, insignificant level. Let opponents steal your blinds without allowing it to bother you. Simply move on to the next hand.

Let's say that you are in the small blind holding 8♥ 8♣ in an online $2/$4 no-limit game. An average-loose player on the button raises to $16 after one player has limped in middle position. The player on the button has raised from this position almost every time the pot has been limped around to him, so you are not putting him on a strong hand. You both started the hand with about $300.

YOU

BET FOR YOU TO CALL: $14

Many people believe the correct play is to take him off his hand with a large reraise of $80 or $90, and then make a continuation bet if he calls. While this is a legitimate play since you doubt he is holding a strong enough hand to call, it is not the right play for you. You must choose a course of action that will prevent you from playing a big pot without a big hand.

One important factor that many people dismiss too readily is that the chances are good that a loose player will call after you play back at him. If he calls and you decide to make a continuation bet without having flopped a set of eights, you will be forced to make another big bet because your reraise was so large preflop. With roughly $170 in the pot at that point, you would be forced to bet at least $100 to make your opponent fold when you would have about $120 left. You would become pot-committed in a large pot with a weak hand—and you never want to put yourself in that position.

Your best course of action would be to just call his raise and hope to hit a set on the flop. Even if you don't flop a set, you can still use the stop-and-go play by leading out with a bet of $20 or $25 and hope he folds. If he calls your bet on the flop with overcards on the board, you won't put any more money into the pot. However, you will have at least tried to capitalize on your read that the raiser didn't have a strong starting hand, and you will have done so without risking a lot of chips.

PLAYING THE BLINDS

Most poker pros believe that playing the small blind and big blind well is one of the most difficult things to accomplish in no-limit hold'em. They are right. Why? Because you will be out of position after the flop, which makes it difficult to take control of a pot without taking on significant risk when you are holding a marginal hand. In short, it is difficult to outplay opponents and it is easy to get outplayed. Therefore, when holding a weak starting hand in a raised pot, you will rarely play the small blind and you will mostly fold in the big blind. In limped pots, you can call in the small blind with a wide range of hands and hope to flop a monster; and you should check in the big blind. Avoid the temptation of making a large raise from the big blind with a weak hand in an attempt to steal the pot.

Conventional poker theory suggests that when you are in the blind, you should call a raise with virtually any two cards if you are getting a good price. However, this theory is misleading because it entices players to play small and medium-sized pots regularly from the blinds in poor position.

Here is an example that illustrates the difference between playing in position and playing out of position. Let's say that you are sitting in the cutoff seat with a marginal hand such as J♦ 10♣. You might decide to gamble by calling a small raise and hope to hit a big hand. However, you might also take down a small pot after the flop if you hit top pair or even second pair and bet out after everyone checks around to you. This opportunity makes playing the hand in late position more profitable in the long run.

By comparison, if you connect with the flop out of the small blind, betting out becomes riskier because you have no information about the strength of your opponents' hands. However, if you decide to check and the action gets checked around, you've probably lost your opportunity to win the pot if an overcard or another dangerous card comes off on the turn. In the long run, you lose money playing raised pots in the blinds because it is so difficult to win most of those small and medium-sized pots out of position. Therefore, try to avoid playing from these profit-draining positions.

Here is another example of where many players go wrong. Let's say you're in an online $5/$10 no-limit game holding K♠ 7♥ in the small blind. You have $845 in chips. A strong-tight player sitting under the gun with $620 in chips raises the pot to $40. Two players call and the action comes to you with $135 in the pot.

YOU

MONEY IN THE POT: $135
BET FOR YOU TO CALL: $40

You seem to have enough chips to consider calling the raise without it costing a large portion of your stack, and you are getting almost 4 to 1 on your money, so it looks like calling is a good play. Even if an opponent has you dominated by a hand such as A-K, you are still getting the right pot odds to call.

The problem you are facing is that if you don't flop a monster, there are very few flop combinations with which you can feel comfortable. If you flop top pair with a king, you could get sucked into losing a medium-sized pot against the preflop raiser, who could be holding A-A, A-K, K-Q or maybe K-J. If you hit a 7-high flop, it is going to be difficult to bet confidently since one of the other callers could be looking for a board with low cards. And the preflop raiser could be holding an overpair, in which case he might want to play a big pot. Perhaps you could make one bet with a pair of sevens and pray that everyone folds, but betting is risky since you would be playing a four-way pot, and on a 7-high flop it might look like you are betting a draw. As a result, an opponent might come over the top even if he is holding A-K or A-Q and you cannot call a raise.

Another problem is that the odds of flopping two pair are about 48 to 1 and about 73 to 1 for flopping trips (using one of your hole cards), so you are not getting anywhere near the right pot odds to flop a big hand. The implied odds don't help make up the gap because, even if you can win the preflop raiser's entire stack, you would only be getting about 22 to 1 on your money ($620 + $135/$35). Also worth considering is that the preflop raiser is a quality player. Even if you flop a big hand, he might be able to figure out that you are strong, especially if the flop has two kings or two sevens, so you might not be able to win his whole stack.

Playing this hand seems like throwing money away, as K-7 is not a strong hand and it doesn't even offer as much potential as connecting cards. Although it is only costing you 4 percent of your stack to call, you don't want to throw your money in there and hope for the best. In deep-stacked cash games, gambling with only 1 percent or 2 percent of your chip stack is an excellent strategy. If you repeatedly speculate with larger portions of your stack, you will drain your chip total and end up playing just to get back to your original chip count. Therefore, this is not a good situation in which to make a lot of money. You will more than likely lose your $35 and make it a little more difficult to reach your profit objective. Wait for opportunities to play stronger cards in position.

What if you have a strong hand in the blinds?

When you are holding A-A, K-K or Q-Q and you get raised, you should usually reraise in order to take the pot right there. If you just make a deceptive call, you might end up playing a multiway flop out of position. A good way to play these hands in the blinds is to make a large reraise, even as much as five times the initial raise. Most likely, everyone will fold or you will play a pot heads-up. Then you can hopefully take down the pot with one more bet on the flop. Even moving in preflop with A-A or K-K is justifiable because you don't want to get outplayed after the flop.

PLAYING AGAINST
A SMALL STACK

If your table has a few players with small chip stacks, don't start taking liberties by playing for all their chips just because you don't think they can hurt you. More often than not, if you double up a short stack, it will be a more significant blow to your profit objective than you think. Too often, players holding hands such as pocket nines or lower, A-Q, or A-J look to go all-in heads-up against the short stacks because they think their opponents won't call, or it will be a coin flip if they do call. Remember that playing a big pot in a coin-flip situation is not something you want to do. Also, players often forget that sometimes an overpair or some other dominating hand will crush them. Even a player with few chips is capable of waiting patiently for a strong starting hand. In fact, classic short-stack play calls for avoiding wasting money by speculating and waiting for premium hands with which to double up. Don't deviate from your game plan by taking on extra risk just because you are up against a short stack.

Reiterating an important point, never be content to get into a coin toss in a big pot against opponents with any kind of chip stack. Even if you have A-K and you put an opponent all-in, you could still get called by Q-Q, J-J, 10-10, 9-9 or 8-8, and sometimes even lower pairs. In these cases you would be involved in a big pot with barely a 50 percent chance to win. Your game plan is too effective for you to put that much on the line when so much depends on luck. When you stick to your game plan and avoid situations like these, you will rarely leave the table wondering how you lost money or blaming it on bad luck when it actually was poor play that did you in.

PREFLOP HANDS IN ACTION

Let's look at some examples of hands you might play to crystallize your learning about preflop decisions. In most of these examples, the play will continue postflop so you can see the ramifications of your preflop decisions. Many of these hand examples (as well as those in the postflop section) are designed to show you that, despite implementing a simple and powerful cash game strategy, you will still face tough decisions.

Your game plan is all about waiting for big hands and managing high-risk situations. To be a winning cash game player, you must learn to distinguish between the situations that can make you a lot of money and those that can lose you a lot of money. In addition, you must learn to thoroughly think through the hands you play and think about what your opponents are holding.

Practice, practice, practice is what will get you there.

PREFLOP ACTION HAND 1

In a ten-handed live $5/$10 no-limit game, you are sitting in middle position with $905 in chips. Holding 9♠ 9♣, you limp in hoping to flop a set. The pot is unraised when the action gets to the big blind. When he looks at his cards he makes a knee-jerk move toward his chips, and then decides to just check. That may not be the most reliable tell in the world, but it appears that he either considered making a large raise to steal the pot, or he in fact liked his hand but decided it wasn't strong enough to raise out of position with so many players in the pot.

The flop comes A♠ J♥ 9♦. You flopped bottom set, a very big hand and almost certainly the best hand at this point since nobody raised preflop, although it is possible that the players in early position limped in with A-A or J-J hoping to see a raise behind them. Seven players are in the hand with $70 in the pot. The action is checked to you and you decide to bet $50 instead of slowplaying your hand since you are up against six opponents and a number of straight draws could be made on the turn if you allow your opponents to see a free card. The hands that could beat you with a favorable turn card are K-Q, K-10, Q-10, Q-8, 10-8, 10-7 and 8-7. Everyone folds around to the player in the big blind, who raises to $150.

SITUATION

You Have: 9♠ 9♣
The Board: A♠ J♥ 9♦
Money in the Pot: $270
Bet for You to Call: $100
Number of Players: Two

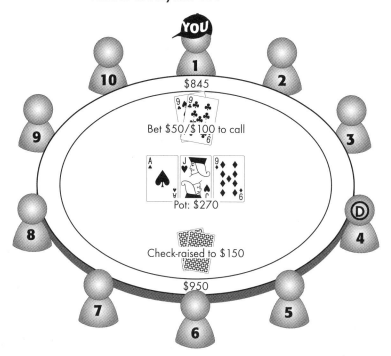

The big blind is an average-loose player, so he could be on an open-ended straight draw with Q-10 or 10-8, but remembering that move toward his chips preflop, you realize that he could have two pair with A-J or A-9, or possibly top pair with a 10-kicker or lower. It would make sense for you to reraise for two reasons. First, he might have a hand such as two pair that he can't fold, and he might not even fold top pair. Second, just in case he is on a straight draw, you will want to put the decision back on him and make him pay to see the turn card.

You reraise to $400. He goes all-in. You call and turn over your set. He shows A♥ J♣. Your hand holds up, and you more than double up.

PREFLOP ACTION HAND 2

In a ten-handed, live $5/$5 no-limit game, you raise to $25 in the cutoff position with A♠ K♠. You get two callers, the big blind in Seat 4 and an early position limper in Seat 6. There is $80 in the pot. The flop is J♠ 7♥ 3♠. The big blind checks and Seat 6 bets $70. You started with $550 in chips and he started with $600.

SITUATION

You Have: A♠ K♠
The Board: J♠ 7♥ 3♠
Money in the Pot: $150
Bet for You to Call: $70
Number of Players: Three

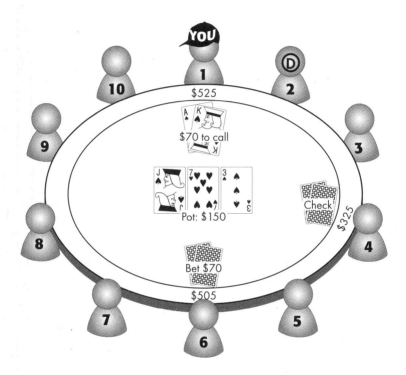

You have two overcards and a nut flush draw but you can no longer see the turn cheaply. Seat 6 is a strong-tight player, so while he could possibly be on a draw himself, he is more likely holding A-J, K-J, Q-J, J-10 or possibly a set of jacks, sevens or threes. Of course, the presence of Seat 4 in the big blind also increases the risk in this situation. Many players would raise to get an opponent to fold if he is only holding one pair.

Further, you would be representing an overpair or maybe even a set of jacks. You also would still have outs to hit the nut flush or maybe an ace or king to win if he calls.

As you continue further into this book, it will become increasingly clear that you often need to do the opposite of what the mainstream playbook says you should do.

Here is the problem with raising in this situation: Seat 6 knows how to play, so if he is holding top pair, you are not only behind in the hand, you also are up against an opponent who might know that he is winning, so he may not fold if you raise. If he calls, you would have to rely on your outs to win the hand in a big pot, which isn't something you want to do. Yet another risk of raising in this situation is that he might choose to vigorously protect his hand and reraise you. His reraise could be an all-in bet, especially if he senses that you are on a draw.

Let's look at why that is a problem.

Let's say that you just couldn't resist the temptation to play your hand aggressively, so you raised to $180 on the flop. The big blind folded and then Seat 6 went all-in. There would be $785 in the pot and you would have $345 left, so you would be getting about 2.3 to 1 on your money. Since your opponent could have A-J or K-J, you could conservatively assume that you have 12 outs to improve (nine spades and either three aces or three kings), instead of 15 outs. With two cards to come, you would have about a 48 percent chance of winning (12 x 4 = 48) or almost 1 to 1 odds, so you are still easily getting the right price to call.

In addition, a raise to $180 would mean that you have invested more than one-third of your live stack in the pot; therefore, you would be committed to investing the rest of your chips. You would then find yourself in a situation where all your money is on the line without a made hand when the correct play is to call. This is one of the dangers of playing a drawing hand aggressively in a big pot. If someone moves in, you either have to fold and waste the money you invested in the hand up to that point, or consider calling off the rest of your chips on a draw.

Another option is to just call his $70 bet, but that doesn't seem like a great play. With one card to come and 12 outs, you would only have about a 24 percent chance of hitting your card on the turn, which means you are behind by about 3 to 1 when the pot is laying you only about 2.1 to 1 on your money ($150/$70). Furthermore, even if you turn an ace or king you would have to risk more money to find out whether you have pulled ahead in the hand or Seat 6 has improved to top two pair. Of course, if he has a set, pairing your ace or king wouldn't even help you. Unless calling frightens your opponent and earns you a free look at the river (which is unlikely against this player), calling isn't a great play in this situation.

Your best decision is to fold on the flop when you face the nearly pot-sized $70 bet. Ideally, you would have gotten to see a free card, but it just didn't work out that way. By either calling or raising you would have taken on too much risk without a made hand against a good player. That is not how you win in cash games.

Clearly, drawing hands get a lot of people into trouble, as they influence players to make poor decisions. You have to fight the urge to gamble in situations like these and wait for a big, made hand before you become involved in a big pot. When we looked at playing starting hands such as A-K and A-Q, we saw that limping preflop can be a good play. Limping prevents you from over-investing, and it discourages you from defending your starting hand too enthusiastically just because you raised preflop.

PREFLOP ACTION HAND 3

In a ten-handed live $5/$5 no-limit game, you are sitting in the big blind with $600. Seat 4 in early position raises to $40.

Four players call, and the action comes around to you. You are holding K♦ K♣. You need to thin the field, so you reraise to $140.

SITUATION

You Have: K♦ K♣
Money in the Pot: $345
Number of Players: Six

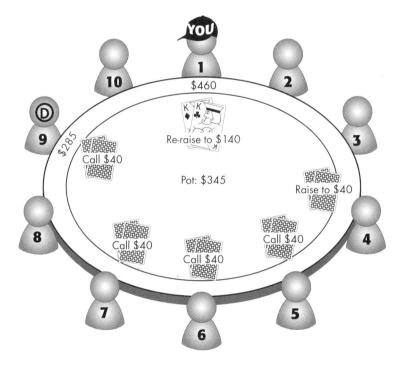

The initial raiser folds, as do the next three players. Unexpectedly, the button goes all in for a total of $325. He is an average-tight player.

SITUATION

You Have: K♦ K♣
Money in the Pot: $630
Bet for You to Call: $185
Number of Players: Two

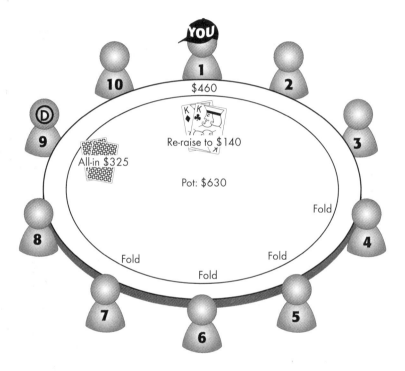

The button had initially only called the raise to $40. If someone is holding pocket aces, they usually want to protect their hand by thinning the field. By just calling on the button, it looked like he was content to play the pot six or seven-handed. It is highly unlikely that he is holding A-A, so it seems that he made a random, instinctual all-in bet, probably with a low pair or maybe with a hand such as A-J, K-Q suited, or K-J suited. He might think that his $325 is a short stack and, with a lot of money already in the pot, he may have decided to gamble, hoping he has live cards. If he is holding a pair, he may be hoping you have A-K and he can double up by winning a coin flip. You call. He turns over 8♦ 8♥. Your pair of kings holds up and you win a big pot.

What would you have done if you were holding Q-Q instead of K-K and the hand occurred exactly as it did above? While you would still think you had the best hand, you would at least have to consider that your opponent could be holding A-K (you don't usually put someone on A-K when you are holding K-K). Perhaps with so many callers in front of him, his initial decision was to merely call to see if he hit the flop before committing more chips to the pot; but after your reraise, he realized he could play a pot heads-up. If he has A-K against your Q-Q, you have less than a 55 percent chance of winning in a big pot, which isn't ideal. So you would do the math. There would be $630 in the pot, and $185 more for you to call. You would be getting 3.4 to 1 on your money when you are about a 1.1 to 1 favorite against A-K. You would easily be getting the right price, so you would call.

PREFLOP ACTION HAND 4

In a nine-handed online $3/$6 no-limit game, you are sitting in late position holding A♣ J♣. With $450 in chips, you have yet to hit a big hand after playing for an hour and a half. Everyone limps around to you. While you could raise knowing that you may very well be holding the best hand, you decide to play it conservatively by playing your hand like a drawing hand, so you also just limp in. The flop is K♦ 9♥ 9♠. A player bets, everyone folds around to you, and you also fold.

Most players in your situation might have been itching to play a pot and would even be tempted to raise preflop with your hand. While nothing is wrong with that play, one problem many players run into is defending their raise too vigorously after the flop, thus getting involved in a big pot without even holding a made hand. For example, some players might have made a bluff-call simply because they felt like playing a flop. They might have tried to represent trip nines hoping the bettor had a king with a medium kicker, and then tried to bluff him off his hand on a later street. The problem with that play is that it would be difficult to convince an opponent with a made hand that you raised preflop with a 9 in your hand and flopped trips. That would be a hard story to sell.

You wisely decided to leave those kinds of plays for other players, and wait patiently for a big hand.

PREFLOP ACTION HAND 5

In a ten-handed, live $5/$5 no-limit game, you are sitting on the button holding A♣ Q♣. You have $450 in chips and you haven't seen a big hand all night. Four players limp in front of you and the action is on you. While a raise could certainly be justified since you are probably holding the best hand, you realize that it would have to be a substantial raise in order to take the pot right there. You decide not to build the pot, so you limp in hoping to hit a nice flop. The blinds check behind you.

The flop comes K♣ 9♣ 9♠. Seven players are in the hand and there is $35 in the pot. Seats 2 and 3 check in the blind positions, Seat 6 bets $25, Seat 7 calls, Seats 8 and 9 fold, and it's your turn to act.

SITUATION

You have: A♣ Q♣
The Board: K♣ 9♣ 9♠
Money in the Pot: $85
Bet for You to Call: $25
Number of Players: Five

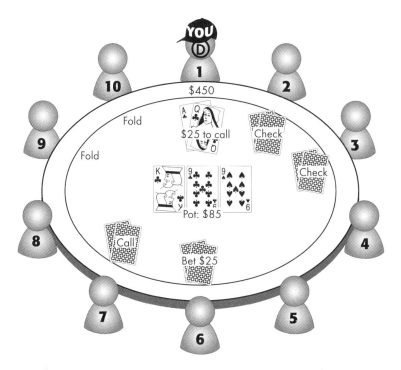

This is a tricky situation. You have flopped the nut flush draw, and if nobody has a 9, you might also win if you pair your ace. However, Seat 7 is an average–tight player who just called a bet on this paired board in what began as an unraised seven-way pot, so he could be holding a 9. He might just have a king and is playing it carefully, but then again, these kinds of trap plays when holding trips are pretty much what he waits for.

It's also possible that Seat 6 is the one holding a 9, or perhaps one of the players in the blinds is trapping with a 9.

This situation is dangerous because drawing to a flush on a paired board could mean you are drawing dead against a full house. Or you might be drawing against trips, which could improve to a full house on a later street. One of the worst situations to be in is when you turn or river your flush and that same card gives an opponent a full house. For example, suppose an opponent has 9♦ 8♥ and the 8♣ drops. Making the flush would lock you into the hand; you would pay off the winner and lose a big pot. That is why you never want to play a big pot holding a flush on a paired board. It is too risky and it is simply bad business. Another thought occurs to you: "I never want to lose a lot of money in an unraised pot." When a pot is unraised preflop, players could be playing all sorts of hands, making it very possible for the better hands preflop to get crushed on the flop.

You decide to think about the math to see whether you are even getting the right pot odds to call. With twelve outs (nine clubs and three aces) and one card to come, the odds are about 3 to 1 against your hand improving, so you are getting the right price to call with better than 3 to 1 on your money ($85/$25). However, if someone has a 9, you are drawing only to your flush, as hitting your ace wouldn't help you. This leaves you with nine outs, so you need to get about 4.5 to 1 on your money, and you're not getting it.

This is not an ideal hand to play. You are merely on a draw against a paired board, so you decide to fold. After you fold, the small blind in Seat 2 raises to $130, Seats 3 and 6 fold, and then Seat 7 moves in. Seat 2 calls and turns over 10♠ 9♥, and Seat 7 turns over A♦ 9♦. When no other clubs hit the board, Seat 7's hand holds up and he wins a big pot.

In your situation, a lot of players would have raised or at least called on the flop, especially since they hadn't seen any big hands. Going card dead tends to cloud a player's judgment and cause him to lose money by taking unnecessary risks. Your fold was an unconventional and conservative play, yet it was the correct play. The situations that will make you a lot of money are ones in which you are holding a very big hand when someone else is also holding a strong hand.

KEY TAKEAWAY

Always avoid drawing to a straight or flush on a paired board. You will lose a big pot if you make your hand and get trapped by an opponent who makes a full house.

PREFLOP ACTION HAND 6

In a ten-handed live $5/$5 no-limit game, a weak-loose player raises under the gun to $30, a strong-tight player in middle position reraises to $100, and after taking some time to think, a strong-loose player calls on the button. The player on the button mixes up her game well and is a tricky player. The small blind folds. You are sitting in the big blind looking down at Q♣ Q♠. You started the hand with $700 in chips.

SITUATION

You Have: Q♣ Q♠
Money in the Pot: $240
Bet for You to Call: $95
Number of Players: Four

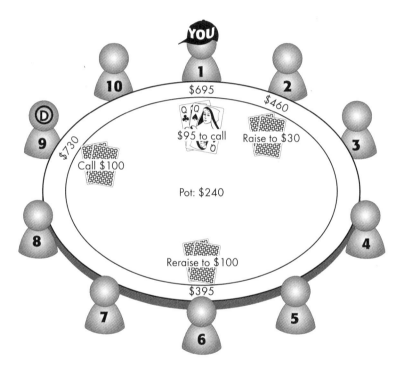

You have a solid starting hand but this is a risky situation, so you need to think about what your opponents could be holding. You are not too worried about the initial raiser because he is loose and you probably have him beat, although he could still move in behind you if you call. He did raise in early position, which means he might be playing a quality hand, so there is some risk though not a lot. You know the reraiser in Seat 6 has a quality hand, but you don't know if he has you beat. Maybe he is holding J-J, 10-10, A-K or A-Q. You can probably reraise him off those hands, but there is certainly some risk of his holding A-A or K-K.

The player on the button worries you the most. She is tricky and enough of a risk taker to flat call with A-A to try to suck in the initial raiser and play a three-way pot, instead of reraising to take it down right there. There is a remote possibility that she called with a weak hand just to outplay the tight player in Seat 6, since she is on the button and playing a deep stack, but that is unlikely.

You realize that just calling the reraise with pocket queens isn't a great play. Even though there is only about a 43 percent chance you will see an overcard on the flop, you could be tempted to play for all your chips if you are holding an overpair on the flop and are beaten by A-A or K-K. In addition, calling could mean playing a three or four-way pot; the pot is already big, so it would cost you a lot of money to find out if an opponent outflopped you. Although you could call just to try to flop a set, the $95 price is 14 percent of your remaining live stack. The call would be expensive, and there is still the possibility that Seat 2 moves in behind you. You also don't want to throw caution to the wind by moving in because you don't feel confident that everyone will fold.

You realize that this situation is too risky for Q-Q. You make a tough fold.

After you fold, the initial raiser in Seat 2 thinks for a while and pushes all in. The next player in Seat 6 curses out loud and folds. The player on the button calls. She has A-A while Seat 2 has J-J. Seat 6 said he folded A-K suited. You averted disaster since no queen hit the board, but luckily for Seat 2, a jack did hit and cracked Seat 9's aces.

PREFLOP ACTION HAND 7

In a nine-handed online $1/$2 no-limit game, you are holding Q♦ Q♣. You raise to $8 from middle position. A weak-tight player reraises to $25 from the cutoff seat, and everyone else folds around to you. The reraiser has been losing and is a little short stacked with only $70 in chips; however, he doesn't come over the top very often. You have $150.

SITUATION

You Have: Q♦ Q♣
Money in the Pot: $36
Bet for You to Call: $17
Number of Players: Two

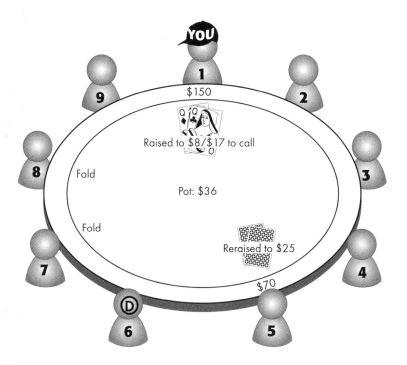

As tempting as it is to throw caution to the wind and move in, especially when you have your opponent covered, you decide to just call and look at the flop. The reason for just calling is very simple and extremely important: If he has A-K he will call an all-in bet and you will be forced to win a coin flip in a big pot. Therefore, you might as well take a look at the flop first to see if an overcard hits. You will be first to act after the flop, so you can bet out and see if he just folds, which he probably would do if he doesn't flop an ace or king. Looking at it from a mathematical standpoint, if he has two unpaired cards such as A-K, he has only about a 33 percent chance to make a pair or better on the flop, so you would be about a 2 to 1 favorite looking only at the flop. Since you would be in a coin flip situation if you saw all five community cards, it would only benefit your opponent if you moved in and allowed him to look at all five cards to see if he makes a pair. The flop comes 7♣ 6♠ 6♥. There is $53 in the pot. You bet $40 and he folds.

Too many players in your situation would choose the high-risk option of moving in preflop. After all, there is no more thinking to do once they are all-in, so it is an easy way out of a stressful situation. Many players would even move in with J-J, 10-10 or 9-9 preflop, which is too reckless when they know their opponent is strong. Remember that you usually want to keep the pot small preflop unless you are holding A-A or K-K.

Notice the difference between your play with Q-Q in this hand and your play with Q-Q in Action Hand 6. In the previous scenario, there was much more action in front of you with a raise, a reraise and a flat call, so you were facing a much stronger possibility that your hand was dominated by A-A or K-K. In this example, you were heads-up against a weak player so you could feel more confident that you were holding the best starting hand, with the possibility that you had him dominated. Still, notice that in both examples you did not just recklessly move all your chips in without first considering the risks you were facing and how to intelligently manage those risks.

PREFLOP ACTION HAND 8

In a ten-handed live $5/$5 no-limit game, you are holding 2♣ 2♦ in the small blind, and you have $620 in chips. An early position player raises to $30 and three people call in front of you. All you need to think about is whether you are willing to pay another $25 to try to flop a set, since you know you will not otherwise have a hand with which to continue.

YOU

BET FOR YOU TO CALL: $25
MONEY IN THE POT: $130

It is costing you another $25 into a pot of $130. You're getting better than 5 to 1 on your money to call, but the odds are about 7.5 to 1 against flopping a set. You also notice that a couple of deep stacks are currently involved in the hand. You don't need to calculate the implied odds, because the pot odds almost seem favorable enough. Further, you know you will have a shot at taking down a very big pot if you flop a set. Calling is the right play. The big blind calls behind you. The flop comes K♦ Q♣ 7♠.

YOU

THE FLOP

You check-fold to any bet.

What if the big blind had reraised to $130 after you called, and two players called in front of you? There would be $480 in the pot and it would cost you $100 more to call, so you would still be getting 4.8 to 1 on your money, and still have a chance to win a monster pot if you flop a set. The problem is that calling means digging deep into your chip stack. You have only $30 invested in the hand with $595 left. Another $100 would be about 17 percent of your remaining chips, which is a lot to gamble to try to flop a set. You knew there was a remote possibility the big blind would reraise when you decided to call the extra $25, and you were willing to take that risk at the time. You should fold.

Now it's time for some action on the flop. The next chapter moves us forward to winning strategies for playing the flop. We'll look at various types of flops you might play against tight, loose, aggressive and passive opponents—and how you can take down pot after pot with the money-making method you are mastering hand by hand.

8 MAKING CORRECT POSTFLOP DECISIONS

Your most important decisions in no-limit hold'em occur on the flop. The flop is where you decide whether you are prepared to play a big pot, you want to keep playing a small pot, or whether to give it up and get out of the way altogether. You need to consider a number of factors to help you make the best decision.

TAKE YOUR TIME

The first important skill you need to develop is the ability to stay calm. You cannot let your emotions take over and cause you to rush. Too many players get excited and leap to a decision when they hit an interesting flop before they've thought about the factors that impact the level of risk they are facing. You must think not only about your hand but also about your opponents' hands. When you attempt to put your opponents on a range of hands, the answers don't always come to you instantly. You need to take some time to think about how you have grouped your opponents and to remember specific hands they have played.

Especially avoid rushing when you are holding a strong hand. You may have the tendency to believe that you don't have to worry about anything, so you might quickly decide to either slowplay your hand or bet for value when in fact you need to do the opposite. However, you must consider a number of things before you act. (The next topic, "Evaluating Risk," details many of these factors.) If you rush and play your big hand poorly, you might allow opponents to catch up and outdraw you in a big pot. Or you could miss opportunities to maximize the pots you win.

When playing online, you must not let the 20-second clock force you to act quickly. On many online poker sites, a beeper sounds after only five seconds to remind you that it is your turn to act. You especially don't want to let it rattle you and make you rush. Often, the pace of online games is very quick. Most of the time, players make a decision before even one half of their time runs out, very often within five seconds. Don't let the speed at your table influence how quickly you act. You can even try to make a game out of it. See if you can become the most level headed player at your table, the one that always takes his time and always ends up making the right decision. Also try to save your bonus time (or "think tank" time) for hands where you might get involved in a big pot.

In a live game someone might call the clock on you if they think you're taking too much time, sometimes even in a big pot. Although calling the clock on you may seem like poor etiquette, don't let it rattle you. Continue your thought process and finish playing your hand. Although it is a player's right to call the clock on other players, consider politely asking afterward that if they do it again, they do it when you are playing a small pot, not a big one.

Also beware of giving away any obvious timing tells either online or in a live game. If you display a tendency to muck a weak hand instantly and take your time only when you hold a big hand, your opponents will pick up on this tell, and they might avoid giving you action when you need it. Some simple tactics you can use to throw your opponents off are occasionally taking your time before mucking a weak hand, and trying to take the same amount of time before betting whether you have a big hand in a big pot or a medium hand in a small pot. A good rule of thumb that helps to avoid giving away timing tells is to always let the clock run down to ten seconds online, or count to ten in a live game, before you act.

EVALUATE RISK

Decisions on the flop will mostly center around whether you are prepared to get involved in a big pot, so you will need to consider the factors that impact the degree of risk to your hand and to your chip stack. The four main factors to consider are the texture of the flop, the number of players in the hand, the quality of your opponents, and the range of hands they could be holding.

1. TEXTURE OF THE FLOP.

The texture of the flop refers to whether the community cards are a good fit or a poor fit for your starting hand and for your opponents' starting hands. Even when you flop a big hand, you might need to play it in a way that won't let players draw out on you in a big pot. That could mean playing aggressively to shut opponents out right away, keeping the pot small if you think an opponent is incapable of folding, or value betting and letting an opponent see one card before moving in to shut him out. A dangerous board is one that interests a lot of players and influences them to play their hands aggressively while they look to draw to a hand that can beat yours.

Let's say that in an unraised six-way pot, you flop a set of threes on a board of 3♣ 4♣ 5♥.

YOU

THE FLOP

You should not jump at the opportunity to make the pot big until you first understand what your opponents are holding, which might be hard to do on the flop. For example, someone who already has you beat with a straight or a higher set could either slowplay his hand, or raise to push out the flush draws. More likely, someone with a big flush or straight draw will look to raise or check-raise, which could put your hand in danger in a big pot if you call or reraise. Many players overplay their draws by raising and calling with them, so you cannot feel comfortable with this flop.

Since the texture of this flop is probably a good fit for a few players, you want to keep the pot small by just calling an opponent's bet or calling one raise. The purpose of playing the hand this way is to look at the turn to see whether it is a dangerous card. If you see an ace, 2, 6, 7, or any club on the turn, you might have to give it up, so you want to make sure that you don't have too much invested in the pot at that point. If the turn is a blank such as the Q♦, you can take the lead and start making opponents really pay to see the river, assuming that you think you are winning on the flop.

YOU

THE BOARD

At that point, players who are on a draw would be in a tough spot because they probably know that you have a strong hand and they will get to look at only one more card to beat you. Keep in mind that if a tight player raises in a multiway pot like this when the turn is a blank, and especially if he moves in, there is a good chance that he has flopped a straight or a higher set. In that case, you would have to consider folding. It is unlikely that he would get that aggressive if he has just two pair on that board, which is the only other strong hand you are beating.

2. NUMBER OF PLAYERS IN THE HAND.

The number of players in the hand also affects the degree of risk you face. Generally, the larger the number of players that look at a flop, the greater the chance of facing an opponent who hits a flop he likes. Let's say that in an unraised pot, you are holding A♦ Q♠ on a board of K♣ J♥ 10♥.

YOU

THE FLOP

You have flopped the nuts but there might be a flush draw out there. Will you keep the pot small for now or start driving the action? The answer probably depends on how many players are in the hand.

In a heads-up or three-way pot, you can consider slowplaying because you may need to let your opponents improve so that you'll get paid off. Slowplaying would be a good play here, as someone with a queen would pay you off with his lower straight if a 9 comes off on the turn or river. Another favorable scenario is for someone holding 9-8 to hit a 7 and make the idiot end of the straight. Or maybe an opponent who improves to two pair will pay you off. However, if you slowplay your nut straight, you would have to keep your fingers crossed that another heart doesn't come off on the turn. Since there is only about an 18 percent chance of that happening, you may decide to take on a little risk in a three-way pot and slowplay, as it is quite possible that neither of your opponents has a flush draw.

If you were playing a five or six-way pot, there would be too much risk of someone drawing to a flush so you would need to protect your hand on the flop. Also, someone else with an ace or queen in his hand could turn the nut straight and you would have to chop the pot with him. Betting out would not only prevent someone on a draw from seeing the turn cheaply, it also might elicit a raise. If an opponent raises and you are playing the pot heads-up, you would have two options. One is to reraise and possibly move in to take down the pot right there, assuming you are up against an opponent who is capable of folding a drawing hand. You might also get called if he has two pair. The other option is to just call to see if the turn is a safe card. If no heart appears on the turn, your opponent might continue betting into you. You can then either raise him off his hand, or just call again to keep the pot small and maybe let him try to bluff on the river if no heart comes.

3. TYPES OF OPPONENTS.

The players you are up against will heavily influence how you play your hands and how you manage risk. If you are getting action on the flop from a strong-loose player, you will need to consider that he could be making a move on you, he could be setting you up for a move on a later street, he could be feeling you out to see if his marginal hand is beat, or he could have a monster hand and is sucking you into a big pot. Weaker players are usually more predictable and more error prone, so you have less risk in facing them.

Let's say that you're playing an online $5/$10 no-limit game. You are holding Q♠ 3♦ in the big blind in an unraised, five-way pot. The flop comes Q♣ 5♦ Q♦.

YOU

THE FLOP

You have made trip queens. The pot contains $50, and you have $1,180 in chips. After the small blind checks, you decide to bet $30 to prevent anyone with a diamond draw from getting a free look at the turn. Betting also allows you to feel out the table to see if someone is also holding a queen, which would likely mean that they have a higher kicker. A weak-loose player calls, and then a strong-loose player raises to $90.

You definitely need to evaluate the risk here. You are out of position against two players, one of who is tricky and just showed a lot of interest in the hand. You are also holding a hand that either has them both beaten, or could get you into a heap of trouble because of your low kicker. Coming over the top might give you some better information about what your opponents are holding, but it seems like a risky play because you could be crushed by an opponent who has made trip queens with a higher kicker. So you start thinking about keeping the pot small by just calling, seeing what the weaker player to your left does, and then seeing what happens on the turn. However, you then realize that the safer approach could create more problems than it solves.

If you just call, the raiser will realize that he might have an opportunity to steal the pot on a later street. His plan could be to make a big bet on the turn or river if a diamond comes off, since he might know that you don't play drawing hands on a paired board. A good player will also know that you could easily have trips with a poor kicker in the big blind, and that you are the type of player who never wants to lose a big pot by getting outkicked. As a result, he might bet big and represent a huge hand, especially if you check the turn.

Another problem if you just call his raise on the flop is that a good player would know how to disguise the strength of his hand if he is in fact holding trips. He would know how to build a false sense of confidence in your own hand and suck you into a big pot. You can never be sure where you're at against this type of player, so you don't often want to play out a hand against him when you are out of position. While the first caller could be the one with the queen, he could also have a hand as weak as a low pocket pair, just a 5, or maybe a diamond draw.

Your best play is to find out right on the flop whether you have the winning hand. You decide to reraise to $300 (you do not go all-in) because only a monster hand can keep playing with you. If someone sticks around, you will know that you are beat and you will not put any more money into the pot since your raise to $300 doesn't commit you to the pot. Also notice that betting $300 increases the pot to $470, which is just short of a big pot of at least $500; therefore, if you get called or raised and you have to give it up, you will not lose a monster pot. By raising you are putting your foot down in a medium-sized pot to find out if you are winning and to avoid getting outplayed. As it turns out, both players fold.

A lot of players make the mistake of only thinking about their own hand in this situation without considering the type of opponents they are up against. Consequently, they put themselves in a position to get outplayed by calling, or they foolishly risk all their chips by moving in. The course of action you chose was based on some foresight and a careful consideration of the ways in which a good player might make playing this hand difficult for you if you had just called.

Another situation in which you need to consider the type of opponents you face is when you need to protect a big hand against an opponent that you are certain is trying to draw out on you. Let's say that you're in a nine-handed online $1/$2 no-limit game. You raise in early position to $7 with A♦ K♠, you get two callers, and the flop comes A♠ K♥ 4♥.

YOU

THE FLOP

The decision to play your hand fast or slow not only depends on how many opponents you are up against but also on how loose your opponents are.

Let's say that you bet $16 on the flop and you get one caller, an average-loose player that you believe is on a flush draw. The turn is a blank, the 5♣. If he is incapable of folding a flush draw, you might elect to bet small or even give him a free look at the river if you are satisfied with winning (or losing) a small pot. Your opponent would be significantly behind with one card to come so either play makes sense, although in the long run, value betting would be the more profitable play for you. However, betting big or check-raising against this opponent could put you in a position where you might lose a big pot.

If your opponent is a more rational thinker (like you), you can consider betting big on the turn to protect your hand because he will not want to overpay to see the river. Betting strong on the turn is an excellent play against a tight player. A big bet will get him to fold a flush draw, which is an outcome you want. And if he has made top pair with an A-Q or A-J, your value bet is the correct move because he will call and pay you off. Either way, a big bet against a tight opponent gets the result you want.

4. RANGE OF HANDS.

Putting your opponents on a hand is important. Specifically, you will put them on a range of hands. If you only think about one hand that your opponent might be holding, you open yourself up to getting caught off guard by a big hand that you didn't seriously consider, or folding the best hand. Thinking about a range of hands your opponents could be holding will keep you well informed and prepared as you choose a specific course of action.

Let's look at an example. In a nine-handed online $1/$2 no-limit game, you are in the big blind with 8♣ 5♥ in an unraised four-way pot. The flop is 8♦ 5♣ 4♠, so you have made top two pair.

YOU

THE FLOP

There is $8 in the pot and you have $225 in chips. The small blind checks, you bet $6, the next player folds, and then an aggressive, average-loose player raises to $15 on the button. The small blind folds and you are now heads-up. Your opponent has $187 in chips.

While your first instinct is to put him on a pair with a straight draw, you need to at least consider that he could be holding the nuts (7-6) or perhaps he has a set and is merely protecting his hand just like you would do on a flop like this. You start thinking about the range of hands you could be up against and gauging the level of risk you face.

If he has the nuts with 7-6, this flop poses little threat to him other than your leapfrogging him or catching up and chopping the pot with him. However, it is doubtful that this guy would raise out of fear of getting leapfrogged because he is not the type of player that would consider that kind of threat. He would almost certainly smooth call with the nuts instead of raise, so you are not inclined to put him on 7-6.

The other hands that are beating you are a set of eights, fives and fours. However, this player probably wouldn't have just limped on the button with 8-8, so perhaps he is holding 5-5 or 4-4. Still, there is a chance he would have raised anyway with those low pairs on the button. Also, the fact that you have 8-5 makes it far less likely he is holding a set of fives. You decide there is only a small chance that he is holding a set.

Perhaps he has a straight draw or a pair with a draw, in which case he could be playing a wide range of hands. These hands are 10-7, 10-6, 9-7, 9-6, 8-7, 8-6, 7-5, 7-4, 7-3, 6-5, 6-4, 6-3, 6-2 and maybe even 3-2. Presumably, some of these hands are suited since they wouldn't look very attractive preflop even to a loose player on the button. You could also have him crushed if he is holding bottom two pair with 5-4 or just top pair with hands such as A-8, K-8, Q-8, J-8, 10-8, and 9-8. Of course, you are also beating a total bluff.

Now that you have considered the range of hands you are facing, you should try to sum it up concisely so that you can come to a decision. You are beating a huge range of hands but only a very small range of hands is beating you. You have virtually eliminated two of the four hands that are beating you (7-6 and 8-8), there is only a very small chance that he is holding 5-5, and a small chance that he has 4-4. You can clearly see that there is a strong likelihood you are winning.

Now you have to decide on a course of action—either raise or call. You are out of position and several turn cards could allow him to put you to a tough decision. Any 7, 6, 3, or 2 would leave you wondering if he turned a straight. Even a 4 could mean that he made trips with 7-4 or 6-4, or a full house with 5-4. Because of the potential ambiguity of the turn card, you decide to reraise to $45 and put the tough decision back on him. He folds.

You will significantly improve your decision making once you get into the habit of thinking about the texture of the flop, the number of players in the hand, the type of players in the hand, and the range of hands your opponents could be holding. After enough practice, thinking about these four key factors on the flop will come instinctively, and you will begin to take your risk management skills to the next level.

AVOID ALL-IN SITUATIONS

When you are holding anything less than top two pair, you don't want to play a big pot. This means that you rarely want to push all-in or call an all-in bet, even if you think you might be winning with top pair, bottom two pair, and sometimes even with top two pair. Here are a few reasons you want to avoid playing a big pot without having at least top two pair:

1. **Big draws.** An opponent on a big draw could call if you go all-in on the flop, putting all your chips on the line with only a narrow advantage, if any at all. When you move in, you will get called more often than you think by a player on a big draw, and sometimes just a flush draw, because many people play that way these days, especially online players. Also, many of your opponents will believe that the only way to beat a tight player like you in a big pot is to draw out on you. Remember that just because you would never make those calls doesn't mean other players aren't willing to take on that risk, so don't give them an opportunity to grab all your chips. They don't deserve it.

2. **Your hand is beat.** Many players know how to mask the strength of their hands. The best part about holding a monster hand like a set is that they are easy hands to play. Checking-raising is a pretty easy tactic to execute, as is smooth calling

a bet and pushing on the next street. While some players don't always move in on the flop with a set because they prefer to slowplay and extract chips, an opponent with two pair could very well move in. In that case, you would need a very strong hand to call.

3. **Opponents adjusting**. Players might realize that they should tighten up in order to play a big pot with you. You shouldn't be surprised to see a strong-loose player try to mix up his game and wait for a big hand to try to beat you in a big pot. He might think that if he pushes, you will interpret it as weakness and call. This is precisely why you want to avoid betting all your chips with anything less than top two pair. Once players start adjusting, the game becomes more complex, which makes it very risky to play big pots without a monster hand. Getting outplayed doesn't only happen when a player bluffs you, it also happens when a bigger hand traps you.

Since you won't want to get involved in a big pot without a very strong hand, especially in all-in situations, you might be concerned that your opponents will realize that the only thing they have to do to win a pot from you is to just move in. The reality is that this almost never happens in cash games. Here are the reasons why:

1. **You aren't always the target**. Players first have to realize that you don't play big pots without a big hand. More often than not, it takes players a while before they pick up on this. Very often they don't think about you at all: They are more concerned about their own cards or about looser players that more habitually drive the action.

2. **You might have a monster.** They can't be sure you don't have a big hand. If you bet out, they will have to guess that you didn't hit the flop really big.
3. **Other players are in the hand.** When a player is considering pulling this move on you, he can only do it if you are heads-up, since he can't always be sure about the strength of the other players' hands.
4. **Losing heart.** After a player pulls off this move once or twice, he may start to fear that either you will finally pick up a monster hand or that you will take a stand and call with an overpair or with top pair. Also, he will fear that other players at the table are picking up on what he is doing, so the likelihood of his getting called increases.

Continuing to move in on you requires a heck of a lot of moxie (or stupidity). It almost never happens that an opponent becomes bold enough or reckless enough to continually do that. Your opponents have to be concerned about some very important factors, which is why they almost never move in on you. Of course, in the very odd event that you run into this type of bold or foolish player online, feel free to just wait him out and trap him with a monster hand. Or you can move to another table if you want to.

EXTRACT THE MOST CHIPS POSSIBLE

You've been playing for two hours, waiting patiently for a big hand. Finally you flop a monster. Now's the time to stay calm and take your time to figure out how to extract the most chips you possibly can from your opponents. Let's look at an example to illustrate some of the things you will need to consider.

Let's say that you are playing a ten-handed live $5/$5 no-limit game that is playing fast and loose. You are holding K♦ K♣ in middle position with $700 in chips, and you raise to $35. Three players call your raise. The flop comes K♥ 10♠ 10♥. You have flopped a full house.

SITUATION

You Have: K♦ K♣
The Board: K♥ 10♠ 10♥
Money in the Pot: $150
Number of Players: Four

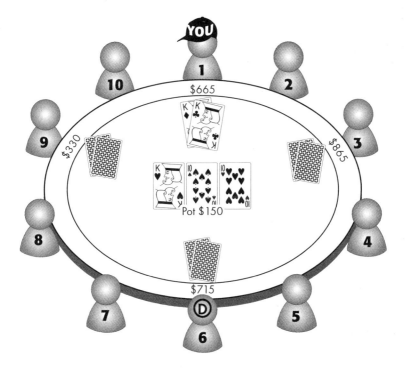

The first thing you want to consider is the range of strong hands or drawing hands that your opponents might have so that you can set them up to pay you off. A reasonable range of hands they could be holding that could stir up some action is A-10, K-10, Q-10, J-10, 10-9 suited, 10-8 suited, A-K, K-Q, K-J, Q-J, middle pocket pairs such as jacks, low pairs such as sixes, and a whole range of flush draw/straight draw hands such A♥ X♥, Q♥ 9♥, J♥ 9♥, 9♥ 8♥, and so on. Wow, you have great potential for getting your opponents involved in the pot.

The action begins with Seat 9, who checks. You are next to act. You need your opponents to either hit their draws or to feel confident if they are already holding strong hands, so you decide to also check. If nobody bets on the flop, the whole table will get a free look at the turn, and you want players to catch up and hit their draws. If you get lucky, an opponent with a 10 will hit his kicker. Seat 3 checks behind and then Seat 6 on the button bets $80 into the $150 pot. Seat 9 folds and you just call. You stick with your strategy by not raising because you don't want to scare anyone away. You want to let players hit their money cards. Your call turns out to be a good idea because Seat 3 also calls. He is strong-tight and the button is weak-loose. You are now in a big three-way pot. The turn card is the 9♣.

SITUATION

You Have: K♦ K♣
The Board: K♥ 10♠ 10♥ 9♣
Money in the Pot: $390
Number of Players: Three

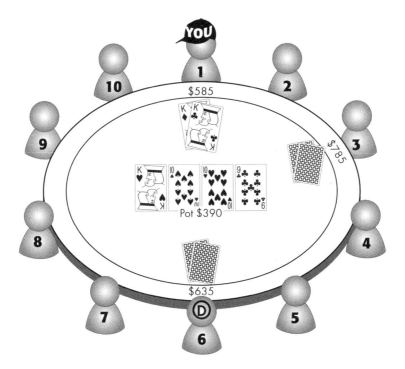

You are first to act and you continue to slowplay by checking. The pot contains $390. Seat 3 bets $140 and the button calls. Things are looking really good. The strong-tight player in Seat 3 bet out, revealing the strength of his hand. Maybe he flopped trip tens and now is driving the action not only to get some value for his hand, but also to protect it from getting rivered by an opponent on a flush draw. The weak-loose player on the button smooth called again, so he could have a hand as weak as a straight or flush draw, or as strong as a boat. Again, you just call.

SITUATION

You Have: K♦ K♣
The Board: K♥ 10♠ 10♥ 9♣
Money in the Pot: $810
Number of Players: Three

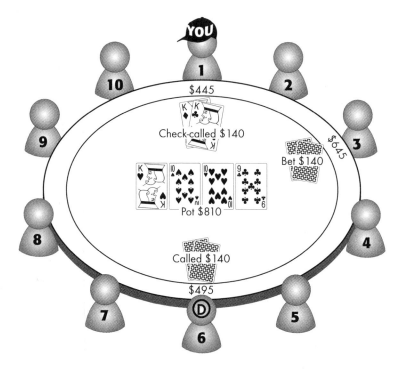

The river card is the 5♦, so the board reads K♥ 10♠ 10♥ 9♣ 5♦ with $810 in the pot. Now you really want to play it right so that you can put someone all-in. That is not a scary river card for anyone, and you believe that Seat 3 has a strong enough hand to raise if you come out betting, or to lead out if you check. If he has trip tens, there aren't a lot of hands you could have to scare him because he probably knows that you wouldn't raise preflop with A-10, K-10, Q-J, 10-9, 10-5 or 5-5. At the worst, he might worry that you are holding K-K, 10-10 or maybe 9-9, but it's much more likely that he puts you on A-A or A-K and thinks that you have been playing it carefully because the board is paired. While any bet other than an all-in bet seems a little coy at this point, you remember that the largest bet so far has been $140. You don't want to shock anyone into folding with a big all-in bet, since you have $445 left. A bet that big might convince your opponents that you've been slowplaying an absolute monster the whole time, or that you turned or rivered a full house; and you don't want to give a player with trip tens and a medium kicker an opportunity to fold. If anything, you want to invite your opponents in and possibly let them hang themselves. Even a small bet of $200 could raise some eyebrows and inhibit the action; it seems like you can get better value for your hand.

You decide to check. Seat 3 bets $275 and the button moves in. You call and Seat 3 reluctantly calls. You turn over your full house, Seat 3 screams an obscenity as he turns over A♣ 10♣, and the button just shakes his head as he shows Q♦ J♠. You win a $2,145 pot. Here are all the good things you did to extract chips and maximize value for your hand:

1. **You thought about** what your opponents were holding and, for the most part, correctly put them on their hands.

2. **You considered** your opponents' playing styles. From that you were able to surmise that Seat 3 bet the turn because he wanted to protect his trip tens. Also, you knew that Seat 6 was capable of playing a drawing hand in a big pot on a paired board.

3. **You stuck to your strategy** by slowplaying without wavering mid-hand. As a result, the button hit a straight on the turn, which locked him into the

hand, and Seat 3 never had reason to think that his trip tens/ace kicker was beat.

4. **You thought about** what your opponents might think you were holding. As a result, you realized that checking the river was a good move because it looked as though you could be holding A-A or A-K. As a result, there was a good chance your opponents would value bet their hands.

5. **You remembered** the size of the bets on the flop and turn, and realized that an all-in opening bet on the river would give away the strength of your hand and cost you money.

You can see from this example how failing to think through a hand could lead you down the wrong path, even when you are holding a monster hand. There were a few spots where, if you chose to raise instead of call, or bet instead of check, you might not have stacked your opponents like you did. Never believe that holding a monster hand gives you an excuse to stop working and thinking. As you become better and better at thinking like you did in this hand, your chances of enjoying long term success in cash games will increase exponentially.

POSTFLOP HANDS IN ACTION

Now let's examine and analyze your options for playing ten postflop hands that you may face in the next no-limit hold'em cash game you play.

POSTFLOP ACTION HAND 1

In a ten-handed live $5/$5 no-limit game, the pot is limped around to you in the cutoff seat. You have almost met your profit objective for the session so you decide to look at one more flop before you leave, and you limp in with 7♥ 5♠. The button folds, the small blind checks, and then a weak-tight player in the big blind raises to $15. Four players call in front of you. While 7-5 offsuit is a hand with which you prefer to see a flop cheaply, it is only costing you another $10 and, assuming the small blind calls behind you, there would be seven players total and $95 in the pot. Since you think you will be getting 9.5 to 1 on your money, you call, as does the small blind. The flop comes 8♦ 6♦ 4♠. You have flopped the nut straight.

There is $105 in the pot. The small blind checks, the preflop raiser in the big blind bets $60, two players fold, and an average-loose player in middle position raises to $160. After another player folds, the action is on you. You started the hand with $720, the big blind started with $500, and the raiser started with $1,600.

SITUATION

You Have: 7♥ 5♠
The Board: 8♦ 6♦ 4♠
Money in the Pot: $325
Bet for You to Call: $160
Number of Players: Four

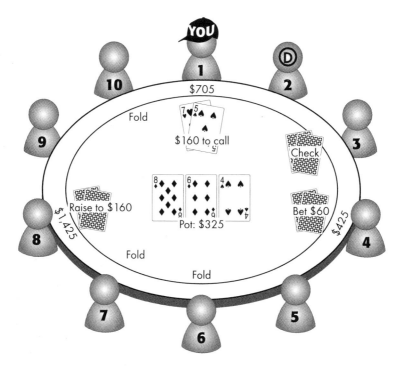

It isn't often that you hold the nuts and still feel concerned about the risks you are facing, but this is one of those times. The *Playing No-Limit Hold'em as a Business* method isn't merely about waiting for big hands, it also about how to intelligently manage risk. In this situation you need to think things through very carefully instead of just thoughtlessly moving in.

Seat 4 made only a small raise preflop, and his $60 bet feels like both a value bet and a probe bet on this low flop. It seems he could be holding an overpair such as 10-10 or 9-9, or perhaps he is holding two suited overcards such as K♦ Q♦ or J♦ 10♦. Unless he has flopped a set, you think he could be moved off his hand if you move in. Seat 8 really worries you because he's been playing fast and loose most of the session, and he's been winning. He is also playing a very deep stack and has you covered. You are concerned that if he has a big draw, he might be willing to gamble and call an all-in bet, which would put all your chips on the line with less than a 2 to 1 edge, a situation that you don't want to be in.

So, you look at the math to see if your concern about Seat 8 can be justified. If you move in, it would cost him another $545 to call into a pot of $1,030 (assuming Seats 3 and 4 fold). That would give him about 1.9 to 1 on his money, which might be good enough for him to call with a drawing hand. Could he be playing a hand that he thinks gives him the right odds to call?

You start to think through the specific hands he might be playing. If he only has a flush draw, he is about a 1.8 to 1 underdog, so he would be getting the right price to call. Considering the loose manner in which he's been playing, you think he might in fact call. Therefore, he would also call with any draw that is better than just a flush draw—a pair and a flush draw (A♦ 4♦, for example); a flush draw and a gutshot straight draw (5♦ 2♦, for example); or an open-ended straight flush draw (9♦ 7♦, for instance). If he is holding 9♦ 7♦, in addition to beating you with a flush, he could also leapfrog your straight if a 10 or 5 comes off on the turn or river. He would have 14 outs to beat you (remember you have one of the fives he needs to make a straight), which would actually put you slightly behind in the hand. Hands such as 10♦ 9♦, 10♦ 7♦ and 9♦ 5♦ would also give him a chance to leapfrog your straight if he hits his gutshot draw.

A set is another hand that Seat 8 could be holding that would leave him with a decent amount of outs to beat you. Although you would still be significantly ahead, he would have seven outs to pair the board on the turn, at which point your hand would be dead; and if he misses on the turn, he would have 10 outs to pair the board on the river. He would almost certainly call with a set if you move in on the flop. The only decent hands you would really feel comfortable with his holding are two pair, since he would only have four outs to beat you; and offsuit connectors such as 8-7, 8-5, 7-6, 6-5, 7-4 and 5-4, which would give him a pair with a draw to a straight that would only be good enough to chop the pot. He probably would fold just a pair and a gutshot straight draw if you move in.

It appears that if you move in, Seat 8 would either call with a hand that has a lot of outs to beat you with two cards to come, or he would fold. Therefore, your best play is to just call his $160 raise in order to look at the turn, even though you have another player to act behind you. You hope that the turn isn't a diamond, and you wouldn't want to see any of the following cards: 10, 9, 7 or 5. You also wouldn't want to see the board pair. If the turn card is a diamond, you would strongly have to consider mucking your hand if faced with a big bet, and if it is a 10, 9, 7 or 5, you would just have to feel out your opponents to find out if you are beaten. And if a 7 or 5 hit the board, you could very well still chop the pot.

If the turn is a safe card then you could feel more confident about getting the rest of your money in the pot. At that point, if your opponents check to you, an all-in bet would put them to a tough decision with only one card to come. Even with the biggest drawing hands such as 9♦ 7♦ and 5♦ 3♦ (flush draw and open-ended straight draw), Seat 8 would be priced out of the hand because he would need about 2.3 to 1 on his money to call at a time when he would only be getting about 1.9 to 1. By applying pressure on the turn, the chances of your opponents folding drawing hands would be much better, especially since your flat call of the $160 raise on the flop signals that you are holding a big hand.

Also notice that since you started the hand with $720, just calling the $160 raise doesn't commit you to automatically investing the rest of your chips to the pot. You will have spent $15 preflop plus $160, so $175 total is less than one-third of your live stack. One of the biggest mistakes players make is assuming that calling one large bet automatically commits them to the pot. They decide that if they call that bet, they might as well just push the rest of their chips in. This is precisely how staying aware of pot size and pot commitment can help you make better decisions. In this hand you have analyzed the dangers you could be facing, and you have realized that there is no need for you to risk all your chips with possibly just a small advantage against a very loose player, especially since you are not mathematically committed to doing so. That is smart and responsible decision-making.

You call the raise to $160, Seat 3 folds and Seat 4 also calls. The turn is the K♣.

SITUATION

You Have: 7♥ 5♠
The Board: 8♦ 6♦ 4♠ K♣
Money in the Pot: $585
Number of Players: Three

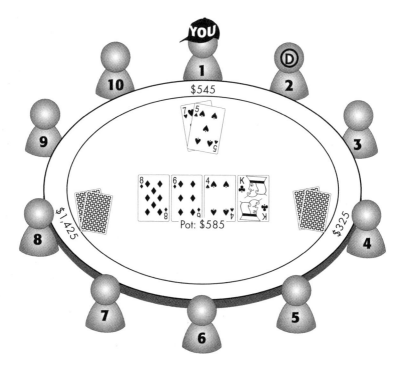

This is a great card for you, as you are still holding the nuts. It seems that Seat 4 is either on a draw or he is playing a medium pocket pair (poorly, I might add). If he had flopped a set, he would have moved in on the flop.

Seat 4 checks and Seat 8 moves in. You call. Seat 4 folds and shows Q♦ J♦. The river is the 7♠, which makes you nervous at first because Seat 8 could be playing 10♦ 9♦ or 9♦ 5♦ to make a higher straight. But he shakes his head, saying, "I missed." When you turn over your straight, he says, "You have no idea how many outs I had beat to you. I don't know how I missed." He throws his cards deep into the muck before you have a chance to ask the dealer to turn them over. You win a $1,675 pot.

It seems that he was playing a hand such as 9♦ 7♦ or 10♦ 7♦ where, in addition to his flush draw, he had a draw to a higher straight. If that is what he was playing, he probably would have called an all-in bet on the flop, especially with 9♦ 7♦. The difference is that you didn't throw caution to the wind and give him two chances to win with all your money on the line. You took that risk on the turn when there was only one more card to come. While your hand certainly was still vulnerable on the turn, you did a great job managing risk and showing restraint. You carefully considered the way your opponents play and the degree of risk they were capable of taking, and you acted accordingly. This degree of skill bodes very well for your long-term success in cash games.

POSTFLOP ACTION HAND 2

In an online $1/$2 no-limit game, you raise to $7 in early position with J♦ J♥ and get two callers. All three of you started with about $200. The flop is 2♣ 2♥ 2♠, so you have flopped a full house.

SITUATION

You Have: J♦ J♥
The Board: 2♣ 2♥ 2♠
Money in the Pot: $24
Number of Players: Three

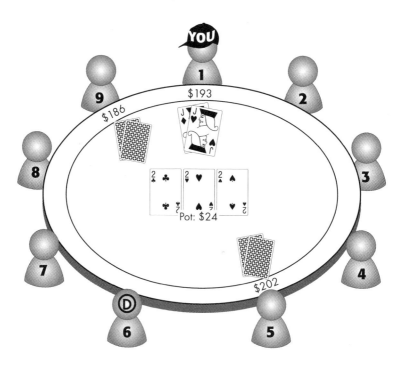

Since no one reraised preflop, you think you are winning on the flop. Still, you want to consider the types of hands that could beat you on the turn or river. If you think that an opponent is holding an overcard—an ace, king or queen—that will influence the course of action you choose. You also want to consider the possibility that an opponent is holding a 2. You start to think about the types of players that are in the hand and what they might be holding. The player in Seat 9 is weak-loose. Your notes on him say that you've seen him make some very poor calls, and he has a tendency to get his money in when he is way behind. You don't have any notes on Seat 5, but from what you've seen, he seems to be average-tight, a decent player who plays conventional hands preflop.

Does one of them have a deuce in the hole? Although a player in the cutoff could be playing a wide range of hands, it seems unlikely. Seat 5 would have had to call a raise with a highly speculative hand such as A-2 suited, K-2 suited or maybe 5-2 or 4-2 suited, which is improbable since it's not his style. Also, he isn't playing a deep stack, which might influence him to gamble more, so you put him on two overcards such as A-Q, A-J, A-10, K-Q or K-J, or possibly a low pocket pair. If anything, it's more likely that the weak-loose player in Seat 9 is holding a deuce because he is more capable of gambling preflop. Still, you are playing a three-way pot, and the fewer your opponents the less likely that anyone will hit the flop; therefore, it is highly unlikely that someone has flopped quads. You put Seat 9 on a wide range of hands: a low pocket pair, middle or low suited connectors, and possibly two medium-high overcards such as Q-10 or K-9. You decide to play the hand as though you are ahead. You are willing to play a big pot, but you will be willing to slow down mid-hand if overcards hit the board.

Seat 9 checks to you. With $24 in the pot, you bet $15 because you don't want someone with overcards to get a cheap look at the turn. Both players call. The turn is the 6♥.

SITUATION

You Have: J♦ J♥
The Board: 2♣ 2♥ 2♠ 6♥
Money in the Pot: $69
Number of Players: Three

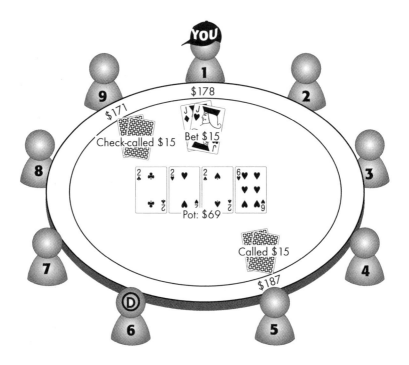

You don't think much has changed. The pot now contains $69. Seat 9 checks. You bet $35, Seat 5 folds, and Seat 9 raises to $80.

SITUATION

You Have: J♦ J♥
The Board: 2♣ 2♥ 2♠ 6♥
Money in the Pot: $184
Bet for You to Call: $45
Number of Players: Two

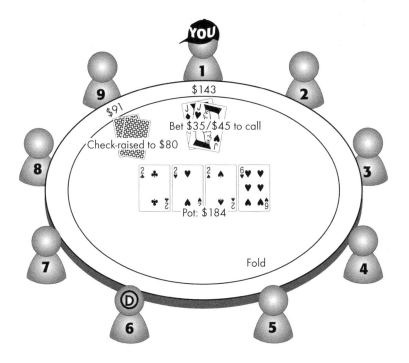

You should usually take check-raises seriously in no-limit hold'em because more often than not, they tell you that your opponent really likes his hand. However, against this opponent you could still be beating many hands that he likes. Still, you want to look at this possibility closely because you are involved in a big pot and you don't want to make a mistake. Other than his holding a deuce, your main concern is that he has just made a higher full house with pocket sixes. However, a really bad player will usually bet out when he holds just a decent made hand, meaning that if he had pocket sixes he probably would have bet the flop to protect his full house from getting outdrawn instead of check-calling like he did. Therefore, you are not convinced that he is holding pocket sixes. Although it is very unlikely, you consider that he could be playing pocket aces, kings or queens, the only other hands that are beating you. However, limp calling a raise with a big pocket pair preflop and then check-calling on the flop to trap you seems too crafty for him.

Given his style and caliber of play, you consider that he could have paired a 6 in the hole with A-6. That would be a weird hand with which to call a bet on the flop, but you wouldn't put it past him because you've seen him make some random calls; and he seems like the type of player that might get married to any ace in the hole. It is also possible that he is on a flush draw with two suited overcards such as A♥ X♥, K♥ X♥, or Q♥ X♥. He probably is not holding two big suited overcards like A-K, A-Q or even K-Q because he probably would have raised or reraised preflop instead of limp calling, so he could be holding hands such as A♥ 9♥, K♥ 10♥ or Q♥ 10♥. If so, then he has only three outs to beat you (three aces, three kings or three queens).

Since he already has more than half his chips in the pot, you think there is a good chance he will call an all-in bet right now when he is drawing very slim. In case he is on a flush draw, you don't want to just call and let him miss his draw on the river because he wouldn't pay you off. You decide to put the onus on him to make a bad call, so you move in. There is now $327 in the pot and he has $98 left. He takes extra time before he finally calls and types into the chat box, "Bad call but too much money in there." He turns over A♥ 8♥. The river is the 10♥, giving him a flush, but you win the $425 pot with your full house.

POSTFLOP ACTION HAND 3

In a ten-handed live $5/$5 no-limit game, you are holding Q♥ 10♥ in the big blind. You have $750 in chips. The pot is limped and checked around to you, so you also check. Six players are in the hand and $30 is in the pot. The flop comes A♣ 9♥ 8♥, giving you an inside straight flush draw. The small blind checks. Unlike other players, you don't get overly excited by the prospect of hitting a straight flush, since only one card in the deck can make that hand for you. You wouldn't mind drawing to a flush or a straight, so you make a blocking bet—that is, a bet intended to prevent a bet from opponents sitting in late position—of $20 and hope that you won't have to face a raise. Everyone folds around to the small blind. Alas, he raises to $80.

SITUATION

You Have: Q♥ 10♥
The Board: A♣ 9♥ 8♥
Money in the Pot: $130
Bet for You to Call: $60
Number of Players: Two

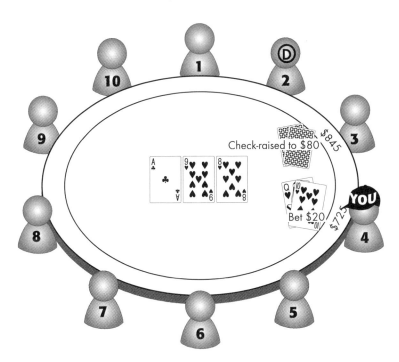

Your opponent is an average-loose player who usually has at least a playable if not decent hand when he is involved in a pot. However, he is certainly capable of check-raising with a big draw. You consider the range of hands you could be up against before you proceed:

1. **Higher flush draw.** It is possible that you are in big trouble against a higher flush draw. A♥ X♥ is a hand that your opponent will never let go of on that board because he would have top pair and a nut flush draw. He also could be holding K♥ X♥.

2. **Pair of aces.** He could have paired an offsuit ace with any type of kicker, even one as high as a jack. Since those hands are tough to play from the small blind, that would explain why he checked preflop.

3. **Set or two pair.** Even though he is a loose player, it is still reasonable to assume that he didn't want to raise out of position preflop with a medium pocket pair like nines or eights, or with a weak ace such as A-9 or A-8. Bottom two pair with 9-8 is another possibility.

4. **Pair of nines, eights or a low pocket pair.** Hands like these would induce him to make a move and try to take you off the pot. Perhaps he thinks you are drawing.

5. **Smaller flush draw.** He could be holding small suited cards, which would give you an opportunity to take his whole stack if another heart comes.

6. **Open-ended straight draw.** He could be holding J-10, 10-7 or 7-6.

Looking at these combinations of hands, you realize that you are only beating a smaller flush draw and an open-ended straight draw. Now you start thinking about how to proceed and the potential consequences of your actions. You know it can be very tempting to overplay a big draw, so thinking through the situation is very worthwhile.

a. **Call**. You are getting almost 2.2 to 1 on your money ($130/$60). If he is holding just a low pair and turning either a queen or a 10 wouldn't give him two pair, you would have 18 outs to beat him (nine hearts, three queens, three tens, three jacks). With one card to come you would only be behind by about 1.78 to 1 (36 percent/64 percent), so you would be getting the right price to call. Keep in mind this is only if a queen or 10 doesn't give him two pair.

However, there are still many hands he could be holding that give you far fewer than 18 outs. If he has a pair of aces, two pair, or a set, you would have 12 outs to hit a flush or straight to win. In that case you would be behind by about 3 to 1 (24 percent/76 percent), so you would not be getting the right price to call. Also, you can't really look at the implied odds because he probably wouldn't bet his whole stack with some of these hands if another heart comes out, although he probably would be willing to lose a big pot with a set.

If he is on a higher flush draw with K♥ X♥, you are behind. You would need to hit an offsuit jack for a straight or the J♥ for a straight flush, or possibly pair your queen or 10 to win, giving you a total of only 10 outs, which means that you wouldn't be getting the right price to call. Finally, if you call his raise but miss your card on the turn and he bets out, you will have wasted the extra $60 on the flop because you would not put any more money into the pot chasing a draw. It looks like calling isn't a great option.

b. Reraise. Many players would reraise in this situation believing they have enough outs to go to war. A reraise might win the hand right there if he is on a small flush draw, has an open-ended straight draw, or has a pair lower than top pair. However, reraising is a very high-risk play because it is difficult to know just how strong your opponent's hand is. Since he check-raised, he could have a set, two pair, top pair, or maybe top pair with a flush draw. He is also capable of check-raising with a king-high flush draw. He could call your reraise with this type of hand and force you to pay him off with your whole stack if another heart hits the board (unless it is the J♥).

In addition, if you reraise (let's say to $250), you would be pot committed, and your opponent could move in and put you in a position where it is mathematically correct to call off the rest of your stack on a draw. If he moved in, you would be getting 2.1 to 1 on your money ($1,025/$495 = 2.1), which is good enough to take the draw to beat a hand as big as a set or two pair with two cards to come. Still, would you really want all your chips on the line without a made hand, even if you were getting a good price to call? Worst of all would be calling his all-in bet and seeing him turn over A♥ X♥, rendering your hand almost dead with all your money already in the pot. Of course, you could decide to fold if he moved in, but that would make your reraise a complete waste of money. In short, it would be a terrible turn of events if he pushed after you reraised. Overall, the risk seems too high for you to reraise.

c. **Fold.** Quite a few hands are beating you. You don't need to get heavily involved with a draw that isn't even the nut draw except for the J♥ that would give you a straight flush. Folding ensures that you stick to your game plan by avoiding playing what could easily be a big pot with a losing hand.

You decide to fold. Your blocking bet wasn't a bad idea as it only cost you $20, but unfortunately you weren't able to see the turn cheaply. Perhaps the next time you consider making that play, you should bet with fewer opponents in the hand.

POSTFLOP ACTION HAND 4

In a ten-handed live $5/$5 no-limit game, everyone limps around to you on the button. You raise to $35 with A♣ A♦. Three people call. The flop comes 6♥ 8♥ 9♥. You started the hand with $600. There is $145 in the pot. The big blind checks, an average-loose player in Seat 1 bets $80, and a strong-loose player in Seat 3 raises to $180. The action is on you.

SITUATION

You Have: A♣ A♦
The Board: 6♥ 8♥ 9♥
Money in the Pot: $405
Bet for You to Call: $180
Number of Players: Four

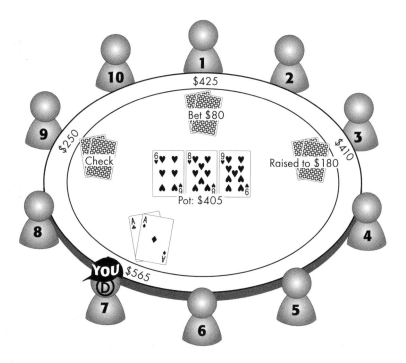

This is a terrible flop for you, especially against so much action—and you don't even have the A♥ in your hand. Either someone is on a big draw, meaning that your hand isn't a big favorite, or you are already beaten. If you try to win the pot by moving in, Seat 3 will probably call since he has already committed more than one-third of his stack to the pot. In that case, $970 would be in the pot (assuming Seats 9 and 1 fold), and he would have to call $385 more, so he would be getting about 2.5 to 1 on his money. With merely an ace-high flush draw, he would be behind by only about 1.8 to 1, so he probably would call. Of course, since you are holding two aces, it is less likely that he is on an ace-high flush draw, and a bit more likely that he is playing a made hand.

Even if he doesn't have a big made hand, you are still losing mathematically to hands like one pair with a flush draw (J♥ 9♣, for example), a pair with a flush draw and a gutshot draw (10♥ 10x, for example), or a flush draw with an open-ended straight draw (7♥ 7x or A♥ 7x, for instance). He might call with these types of hands if you move in because he would know that he has a good chance to crack your overpair. You also don't have any information about the strength of Seat 9's hand. Further, there is the other player to act behind him in Seat 1, who already showed interest in the flop, which further increases the risk for you in this situation.

You decide to fold. In the action that continues, Seat 9 folds, and Seat 1 calls the raise to $180, making $505 in the pot. When the turn comes with the A♥, both players check. The river is the 10♠, so the board is 6♥ 8♥ 9♥ A♥ 10♠. Seat 1 checks, Seat 3 bets $190, Seat 1 calls, and Seat 3 shows K♥ 10♥. Seat 1 shows Q♥ J♣ before throwing his cards into the muck.

What would you have done on the flop if your hand had been A♥ A♦? In a three-way pot like this, you would still have had a very risky hand. However, if you were heads-up, you would have been in a better spot.

Let's start by looking at the hand played out three-way when you have A♥ A♦. Your hand is obviously very tempting to play for all your chips because the A♥ gives you extra outs in case you are behind. Still, what you would prefer is a situation where your opponents don't show this much strength, so you could take the lead and apply the pressure on them to try to improve their hands. Then they would have to be concerned that you are holding an overpair with the A♥, K♥ or Q♥. This would at least give you folding equity, meaning that you would gain the option of winning the hand by making your opponents fold. Unfortunately, this situation is different since your opponents showed a lot of strength before you had a chance to act.

Although you could very well still be holding the best hand with A♥ A♦, you have to seriously consider that one of your opponents could be holding a better hand than just one pair. After all, you are holding the A♥, so it isn't possible that one of your opponents is on an ace-high flush draw, which many players are willing to play aggressively. Seat 3 is also committed to the pot, so moving in would be a little reckless because he would call you when you have possibly only a 44 percent chance to win the pot (nine hearts and two aces give you 11 outs to improve your hand). It would also be too expensive for you to just call the $180 and look for another heart or a safe card that doesn't make a straight. Since you would be committing more than one-third of your stack to the pot, calling would make more sense if you were very confident that you were holding the best, made hand. Also, Seat 3 is so invested in the hand that if you call, you couldn't expect the action to stop on the turn even if it is a safe card. Even if you don't improve on the turn, you would likely have to commit the rest of your chips after your opponents commit more of their own.

Here is the best way to think about what to do in this situation: If you think there is a good chance that you will need to use your A♥ to hit a flush to win (or another ace to win), you are getting your money in bad, and you never want to be in that position in a big pot. Therefore, you should fold. It is better to risk folding the best hand in a pot in which you have very little money committed (you have invested only $35) than to lose all your chips with a vulnerable hand like one pair.

Now let's look at how you would play it heads-up. Let's say that Seat 1 bets $80 and Seat 3 folds. There is less danger now, so you should be more willing to play this pot as most other people would play it three or four-way: In other words, you should be willing to play a big pot. While there is still some risk since three opponents have looked at the flop, there is still less danger than facing two players who are betting and raising into you. Only a few hands are beating you—a flush and a straight (and there is only a small chance that your sole opponent flopped those hands), a set, and two pair. Not only is there a small chance that your opponent hit the flop that big, but your opponent is a loose player who could easily be betting with a weak hand. With your A♥ A♦, you have beaten any pair and any big drawing hand, including a pair and a flush draw. Therefore, you can either call his bet hoping another heart hits, or you can feel free to get aggressive.

I prefer raising here. If you just call and he has a pair and an open-ended-straight draw with 9♣ 7♠ on the 6♥ 8♥ 9♥ flop, he has 10 outs to beat you, so you might want to make him pay for his big draw. The advantage of raising is that you may get him to commit the rest of his chips when he is behind with two cards to come; you may get him to call when he is way behind with one card to come; or you may get him to fold, and you would win a medium-sized pot. Also, by raising you make it harder for Seat 9 behind you to get involved and potentially hit a card that he might need on the turn. Of course, if Seat 1 has hit the flop really big, your hand would still be live (unless he has flopped a straight flush), as you would still have outs to hit the ace-high flush and win the pot.

POSTFLOP ACTION HAND 5

In a ten-handed live $5/$10 no-limit game, you are holding A♠ 10♠ on the button with $800 in chips. Everyone limps around to you. You call and the small blind calls. A weak-tight player in the big blind raises to $50. Three players call in front of you. The small blind is a very loose player who loves big pots, so you think he will call with this much action in front of him, which would make it $40 more for you to call into a pot of $250. Since you think you might get better than 6 to 1 on your money, you decide this could be a worthwhile gamble. You call, and the small blind calls behind you. Players at the table laugh at how quickly the pot has grown to $300 from a small limped pot, and they joke about the big blind getting so many callers looking to crack his big pair.

With six players in the hand, the flop comes 10♥ 6♠ 4♠. You have flopped top pair/top kicker with the nut flush draw. The small blind bets $80, a very small bet relative to the size of the pot. The big blind just calls. The action is folded around to you.

SITUATION

You Have: A♠ 10♠
The Board: 10♥ 6♠ 4♠
Money in the Pot: $460
Bet for You to Call: $80
Number of Players: Three

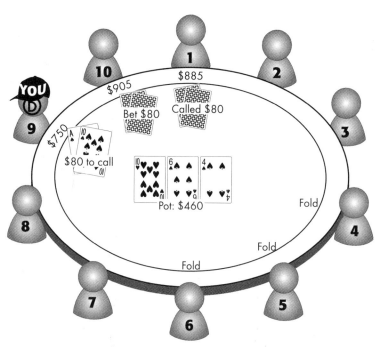

It is difficult to be sure just yet, but the small blind's opening bet feels like a blocking bet. You've seen him make strangely small bets like this when he is on a draw in order to prevent someone from leading with a larger bet. He might just want to see the next card cheaply. Still, a small bet like this sometimes signals that a player is holding a big hand, so you consider this possibility. You're not putting him on pocket tens because he probably would have raised preflop instead of initially calling in a limped pot. Perhaps even a player as loose as he is would not play 10-4 for $40 more in the small blind, and maybe the same can be said about 10-6, so there are at least some strong hands that you doubt he is holding. While he could have a hand as weak as a pair of tens or one as strong as a set of sixes or fours, it is also possible that he is on a spade draw, a straight draw, or some combination of the two. This means that if a spade comes or if a card comes that gives him a straight when you make your flush, there is a chance that you might win his whole stack.

By just calling the small blind's opening bet, the big blind seems to be playing an overpair very carefully because he knows that he could be in trouble in a six-way pot. If he has flopped a monster like top set, he would have raised in this spot to protect his hand. You know how he plays and you think that he just called to see if the turn looks like a safe card before committing more chips since there are four players yet to act behind him. He probably is holding pocket kings, queens or jacks and is trying to keep the pot small because he doesn't want to lose a huge pot by getting his big pair cracked.

You think that you probably are behind right now but if you hit your flush, or maybe if you turn an ace or another 10, you might take down a big pot. Still, you don't like to waste chips chasing draws, so you start thinking about the pot odds. With $460 in the pot, it is costing you only $80 to call, so you are getting about 5.8 to 1 on your money. You have 14 outs (nine spades, three aces to make top two pair, and two tens for trips), so with one card to come, the odds are about 2.6 to 1 against improving your hand. You are easily getting the right price. You call the $80.

The turn is the J♠. There is $540 in the pot, so you are now playing a big pot with the nuts. Both players check to you.

SITUATION

You Have: A♠ 10♠
The Board: 10♥ 6♠ 4♠ J♠
Money in the Pot: $540
Number of Players: Three

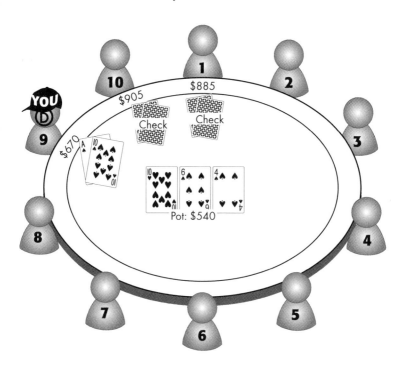

Instead of checking your big hand behind your opponents, you want to create action now because if Seat 10 has made a small flush, he might slow down if the river card is another spade. You bet $200 hoping for a raise from Seat 10. Indeed he raises to $450. The big blind folds, you move in, and Seat 10 calls your all-in bet, turning over 9♠ 7♠. You show your winning hand and he shrugs. The river card is the 9♦, and you win a $1,880 pot.

Notice that even though you were reading Seat 10 for a possible drawing hand, you still applied the Rule of Four and Two correctly by assuming that you had all your outs available in the deck. You didn't fabricate a number by reducing your outs when you calculated your pot odds. The reality is that you can never know for sure what your opponents are holding, so you should always apply the Rule of 4 and 2.

POSTFLOP ACTION HAND 6

In a ten-handed live $5/$5 no-limit game, a weak-loose player in early position raises to $35 and a strong-loose player reraises to $100 in middle position. You are holding J♣ J♥ in the cutoff seat. You started with $650.

SITUATION

You Have: J♣ J♥
Money in the Pot: $145
Bet for You to Call: $100
Number of Players: Six

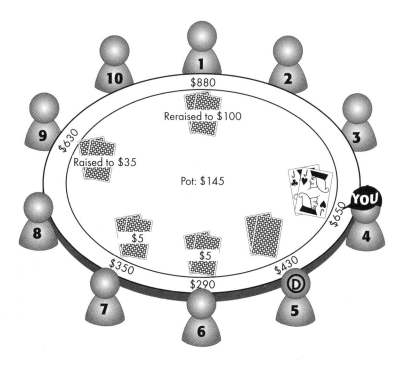

Seat 9 is having a losing night—he's stuck about $1,500—so he could be playing very loose at this point. Seat 1 knows this, which may be why he is raising him, but you don't have a strong read that tells you he is holding a weak hand. You think there's a chance that you are beating both Seats 9 and 1, but coming over the top is very risky, especially since Seat 1 has you covered and is a tricky player.

You decide to call. Seats 5, 6 and 7 fold, and the initial raiser in Seat 9 calls. The pot contains $310 and three players are in the hand. The flop comes 8♥ 7♠ 2♣. Seat 9 bets $120, and Seat 1 moves in.

SITUATION

You Have: J♣ J♥
The Board: 8♥ 7♠ 2♣
Money in the Pot: $1,310
Bet for you to call: $550
Number of Players: Three

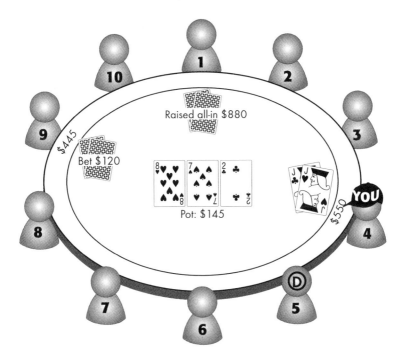

You are not sure whether Seat 1 is just representing a big hand or if he actually has A-A, K-K or Q-Q, but it will cost you all your chips to find out. This is too much action for your one pair, so you decide to fold. Seat 9 calls and opens up A♣ 8♦. Seat 1 is livid as he turns over A♠ K♣. When the turn and river don't improve either player's hand, Seat 9 wins a big pot with a pair of eights.

The strong-loose player in Seat 1 made a nice move and pushed you off the best hand, but he also was up against a weak-loose player who had been losing during the session and was on tilt. One of the key determinants of how successful a bluff will be is whether it is made against an opponent who is capable of folding. Seat 9 wasn't going to fold top pair/top kicker even to an all-in bet because that hand looked like a monster to him. While you would have won a huge pot if you had called, you should still be happy with your decision on the flop because you weren't sure whether you were ahead or were crushed.

In a cash game, when making a decision in a big pot feels like it could be a coin toss, you should make the conservative choice. Many players would have thrown their chips in the middle thinking, "Oh well, if I'm beat, it's just bad luck." While they might sometimes win a big pot like this one, they would lose quite often. It is too reckless to think "what the heck" and bet all your chips when you don't feel confident that you know where you are in a hand. That's pure gambling, a losing way to play poker over the long run.

> ### KEY TAKEAWAY
>
> When you are facing a big bet and a tough decision in a big pot, folding is usually the right play if you are not sure whether you are way ahead or way behind.

Also notice that the way you played your hand preflop was not on strategy. You should not have called a reraise with pocket jacks preflop. Your approach with J-J is to try to flop a set, and you want to do it relatively cheaply. You spent $100 in a $5/$5 no-limit game to try to flop a set, which cost you 15 percent of your stack, and that was too expensive.

POSTFLOP ACTION HAND 7

In a nine-handed online $1/$2 no-limit game, you are holding A♠ K♥ in middle position. An average-tight player sitting to your right raises to $6. You've only seen her play conventional starting hands, especially when she raises in early position, so you put her on hands such as Q-Q, J-J, 10-10, 9-9, A-Q, A-J or K-Q. It also is possible that she has A-K, though it usually isn't productive to consider that an opponent is holding the same hand as yours until you play the flop and see how the betting goes. The likelihood of an opponent holding A-A or K-K when you have A-K is very low (about 25 to 1) so you eliminate those hands for now.

You just call, opting not to build the pot by reraising and to make sure that she doesn't prevent you from seeing the flop by coming over the top with Q-Q or J-J. A weak-loose player on the button also calls. The blinds fold. The play is three-way and you each started with around $200.

The flop comes A♦ Q♣ 6♦. You have made top pair/top kicker. There is $21 in the pot. The preflop raiser checks, you bet $12, the weak-loose player calls on the button, and the preflop raiser folds.

SITUATION

You Have: A♠ K♥
The Board: A♦ Q♣ 6♦
Money in the Pot: $45
Number of Players: Two

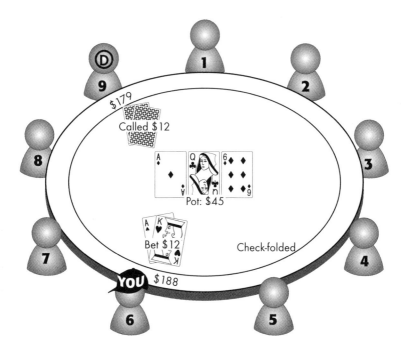

Before you even look at the turn, you think about the hands that the weak-loose player on the button could be holding. What hands would he only call with preflop on the button and only call with on this flop?

1. **A weaker ace like A-10 or lower.** He probably would have reraised preflop with A-Q, and he might have raised you on the flop with A-J.
2. **A pair of queens.** He could have paired a queen with a hand such as K-Q, Q-J, Q-10, Q-9 or Q-8.

3. **A pocket pair such as 8-8, 7-7 or 5-5.** Weak-loose players often have a tough time letting go of pocket pairs even when there are overcards on the board. They are somehow able to convince themselves that their opponents are bluffing, so they often think that their pair might still be good.

4. **A pair of sixes with 8-6, 7-6, 6-5 or 6-4.** Again, he might think you missed and has decided to stick around a little longer.

5. **A diamond draw.** There are many suited connectors and gappers he could be holding, and he would at least call if he had a chance to draw to a flush. He probably doesn't have a big draw like a pair and a flush draw, or a flush draw and a gutshot draw with hands such as K♦ J♦, K♦ 10♦, Q♦ 10♦ or J♦ 10♦ because he probably would have raised you on the flop, or even made a crazy play like pushing all in.

6. **A gutshot draw.** You wouldn't put it past him to be holding K-J, K-10 or J-10.

7. **A set or two pair.** He could have hit a big flop with A-6 or a set of sixes and is slowplaying (something any caliber of player is capable of doing on the flop). There is also a very remote possibility he has bottom two pair with Q-6 suited, as he may have called the preflop raise hoping to flop a flush draw.

Overall, there seems to be a strong likelihood that you are winning. There is only one scenario in which you are losing, and the range of hands that are beating you in this scenario is quite small. However, other than a pair of aces or a flush draw, there are very few hands he could be holding that he could pay you off with if you come out betting on every street.

The turn card is the 4♠. Despite the fact that you probably have him beat, you decide to check to keep the pot small. If he has a flush draw, he would probably call you anyway. And even though you would have a 4.5 to 1 advantage, you are willing to risk losing a small pot if he rivers a diamond. He checks behind you. Before you take a look at the river card, you again want to think about and evaluate what he is holding.

SITUATION

You Have: A♠ K♥
The Board: A♦ Q♣ 6♦ 4♠
Money in the Pot: $45
Number of Players: Two

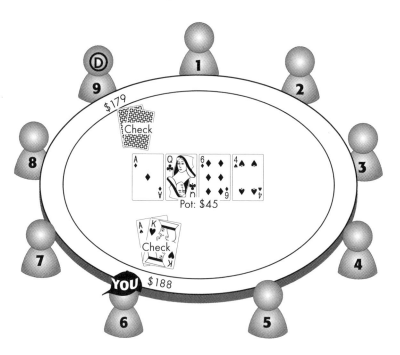

You pretty much eliminate his holding a set of sixes or A-6 (or even A-4) because you don't think he is capable of showing that much discipline with a strong hand. You have yet to see him do anything remotely tricky like smooth call on the flop, check behind on the turn, and then value bet the river with a strong hand. Unless he is holding pocket fours and has just turned a miracle card, you think he would have raised or bet out by now with a big hand on the flop.

The river is the J♦, so the board reads A♦ Q♣ 6♦ 4♠ J♦. There is still $45 in the pot. You check and he checks behind. He shows 5♦ 5♥. You win with your pair of aces.

Your decisions in this hand, while conservative and unconventional, were well thought out and you were aware of the potential consequences. If he had a flush draw and you got rivered, you would have been okay with that since the probability of it occurring was low. And since the pot was small, it wasn't going to be the one that made your night anyway. If you had made a solid bet like $30 into the $45 pot on the turn, the only hands he could have paid you with were a weaker ace or maybe a flush draw. Since a call would have led to your playing a big pot with only one pair on the river, there was nothing wrong with choosing the conservative route and checking.

Despite your preference for keeping the pot small with only one pair, betting the turn would also have been a solid option. Your opponent might have called a small bet of around $20 as a 9 to 1 underdog if he had a pair of queens, although he probably would have folded his low pocket pair. Also, you would have made him pay to draw to a flush if he in fact had a flush draw. There wasn't a strong chance that he would have raised you with a flush draw because raising on the turn instead of the flop is a tricky play that you usually see more skilled players make. By betting you also would have prevented him from getting very lucky on the river and hitting a card such as a gutshot. In short, betting the turn would have been as good a play as checking.

POSTFLOP ACTION HAND 8

You are almost one hour into playing a nine-handed online $1/$2 no-limit game with $170 in chips. You limp in with 4♠ 4♦ in middle position. In an unraised six-way pot, the flop comes K♥ 9♠ 5♦. Everyone checks the flop. The turn is the 4♣, giving you a set. With $12 in the pot, an average-tight player in the big blind bets $10, a strong-loose player raises to $30, and the action comes to you.

SITUATION

You Have: 4♠ 4♦
The Board: K♥ 9♠ 5♦ 4♣
Money in the Pot: $52
Bet for You to Call: $30
Number of Players: Six

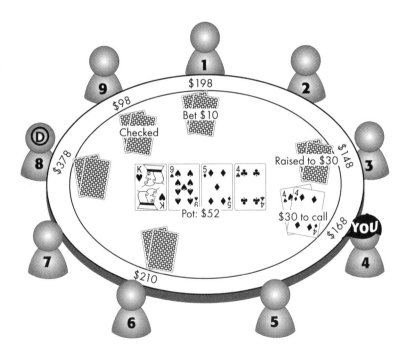

You are holding the fourth-best possible hand—only a higher set beats you at this point. You think that the big blind could have made a pair of kings on the flop, but didn't want to bet the flop with just one pair out of position, and with so many players yet to act behind him. You think that Seat 3 could have better than just a pair of kings. He probably would have bet his king on the flop if that was all he had, and he would know that just one pair is a vulnerable hand in this spot with a tight player betting in front of him. However, he is the sort of player who has the courage to raise with an open-ended straight draw, or to isolate the big blind and try to move him off his hand by representing an early-position limp with pocket kings or pocket nines.

Notice that it is difficult to put a strong-loose player on a hand, even on a rather harmless looking board like this. You aren't sure if Seat 3 checked a big hand on the flop, if he just improved to two pair on the turn, or if he is bluffing. Still, you decide that he is most likely holding a solid hand such as two pair; an open-ended straight draw is his next most likely holding. There is only an outside chance that he is holding a higher set.

Your hand is well disguised, as nobody can reasonably put you on a set of fours. This situation seems well suited for you to just call Seat 3's raise because, in case your opponents are holding either a pair of kings or a low two pair, you don't want to scare them away by reraising. You have a good chance to suck them in. There is also no flush draw out there to worry about, and even an open-ended straight draw is behind by about 5.3 to 1 to your set. Some players might consider moving in right here hoping an opponent with two pair calls them. That isn't a great play since you are still just piecing together the puzzle of what your opponents are holding. Unless one of them is holding K-9 or maybe K-5, you would force them to fold, eliminating any chance of getting paid off. In fact, one of the only hands that your opponents could call an all-in reraise with is a hand that is beating you.

You call. Seats 6, 8 and 9 fold. The big blind in Seat 1 also calls. The river is the J♥. You are now in a three-way hand with $102 in the pot. The big blind checks. Seat 3 bets $50.

SITUATION

You Have: 4♠ 4♦
The Board: K♥ 9♠ 5♦ 4♣ J♥
Money in the Pot: $152
Bet for You to Call: $50
Number of Players: Three

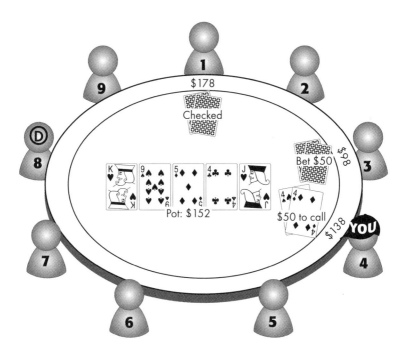

Seat 3 seems to be value betting two pair knowing that someone should have a king. Still, you play it safe and just call instead of raise. Calling accomplishes two things. First, it prevents you from losing all your chips in the unlikely event that you are beaten by a higher set or by Q-10, which would give an opponent the nut straight. Second, by just calling you could possibly suck in the big blind if he has a pair of kings.

The big blind also calls and shows K♣ Q♠. Seat 3 shows down 9♥ 5♥ for two pair. Your trips win a $202 pot. If you had moved all-in on the river, the big blind would have folded, and even Seat 3 might have opted to save the rest of his money by folding. Your decision to just call on the river probably earned you an extra $50.

POSTFLOP ACTION HAND 9

In a ten-handed live $5/$5 no-limit game, you are in the small blind holding 5♣ 2♥. Two players limp in and the action comes around to you. You check, as does the big blind. There are four players and $20 in the pot.

The flop comes J♣ 4♦ 3♠, giving you an open-ended straight draw. You check and everyone checks behind you. The turn is the A♦, so the board is J♣ 4♦ 3♠ A♦. You have made your straight. You are first to act. You bet $20 to make it look like you paired the ace, or that you have a jack but didn't want to bet it out of position on the flop. You are hoping to get some action from an opponent holding an ace or from someone who slowplayed a strong hand on the flop. The big blind folds. The weak-tight player in Seat 1 calls from a middle position. The average-loose player in Seat 5 raises to $80 from the cutoff position. The action comes to you. Each of you started with $600 in chips.

SITUATION

You Have: 5♣ 2♥
The Board: J♣ 4♦ 3♠ A♦
Money in the Pot: $140
Bet for You to Call: $60
Number of Players: Three

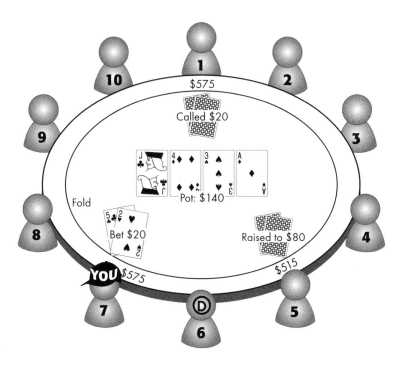

You first want to put Seat 5 on a hand before you decide whether you will raise or just call. You start thinking through the options. She limped in from late position preflop, and then checked on the flop. If she has a big ace, she probably would have raised preflop. If she has a weak ace, she might not have raised here knowing that she is up against two tight players who could have her top pair outkicked; instead, she might have just called with a weak ace. Maybe she flopped or turned two pair, but she probably doesn't have top two pair with A-J. Even

A-4 seems a little unlikely, as her style would be to bet the flop with second pair in late position after everyone checked to her. Perhaps she has A-3 or even 4-3. She could also have flopped a set of fours or threes, so you want to be careful if the board pairs on the river.

One type of hand you have to consider for her style of play is a big draw. When you consider this possibility, you see that she could be on a wide range of hands. Hands like K♦ 10♦, Q♦ 10♦, 7♦ 6♦, 7♦ 5♦, 6♦ 5♦ or 6♦ 2♦ give her a flush draw with a straight draw. She could have a suited king such as K♦ 2♦ and has turned a flush draw and a wheel draw. Or maybe she has a pair and a flush draw with a hand such as 6♦ 3♦. All these are hands that she could have limped in with preflop and then checked on the flop. As you think about these possibilities, it occurs to you that if she is playing low connecting cards, she could leapfrog your straight. You don't want to see any low cards on the river. Cards like a 7, 6, 5 or 2 could potentially give her a higher straight. Your worst-case scenario is that she is holding 6♦ 5♦ and has 14 outs to beat you—nine diamonds, the 2♣, the 2♠, the 7♠, the 7♣, and the 7♥.

While a reraise might scare away your other opponent if he is holding just a pair of aces or even a low two pair, you decide you need to avoid giving Seat 5 the opportunity to hit a draw in a big pot. You reraise to $220 to shut her out. Seat 1 folds, but Seat 5 calls. The river card is the 10♥.

SITUATION

You Have: 5♣ 2♥
The Board: J♣ 4♦ 3♠ A♦ 10♥
Money in the Pot: $480
Number of Players: Two

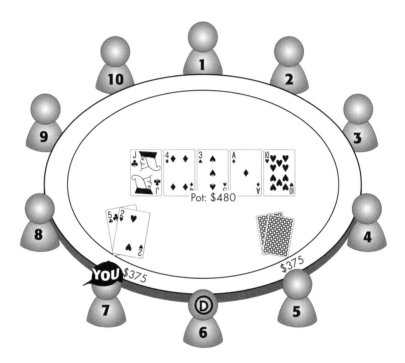

Pot: $480

You are no longer holding the nuts, but the only hand that beats you is K-Q for the nut straight. Your opponent probably would have raised preflop with K♦ Q♦, and if she had K-Q offsuit, she wouldn't have called your solid reraise on the turn with only a gutshot straight draw. You know you are winning, so you want to make a nice big value bet in case she has a low two pair. You figure that if she had a set, she probably would have pushed on the turn after you reraised.

You move in for $375. She instantly folds. It seems that she was on a big draw. Notice that since your objective was to push her off a big draw on the turn, you could have moved in. That play may not have worked, however, because it might have looked like you were on a semi-bluff with a drawing hand, which sometimes is an inherent downfall of going all-in. If she had a nut draw with a hand such as K♦ 10♦, considering that she called your reraise to $220 on the turn, she might have called an all-in bet anyway thinking that you could be on a lesser draw. Nevertheless, despite your objective of protecting your made hand from a draw, your play on the turn ensured that you got value for your hand, and that you made your loose opponent pay to see the river without making a silly all-in overbet.

POSTFLOP ACTION HAND 10

In a nine-handed online $2/$4 no-limit game, you are holding A♥ K♣ under the gun. You limp in, which leaves you with $327 in chips. Another player limps in, and then, an average-tight player two seats from the button raises to $12. The raiser has $392 in chips. It gets folded around to you, and you call the raise. The other limper folds, so you are heads-up with $34 in the pot. The flop comes 9♦ 6♠ 3♥.

You check and the preflop raiser checks behind you. Your notes on him say that he is an ABC type of player who raises with a conventional range of hands preflop, so you think that he would have bet an overpair in this spot if he had it. You put him on two weaker overcards like A-Q, A-J, A-10, K-Q or K-J. Although there is an outside chance that he flopped a set, you strongly believe that he is holding a hand that you are beating.

The turn is the 3♣ so the board reads 9♦ 6♠ 3♥ 3♣. You have no reason to believe the 3♣ helped him, so you bet $20 into the $34 pot and he folds.

While you may have been able to check the hand the rest of the way and win it, you decided to mix things up a bit and take a stab at the pot before he did to avoid giving him an opportunity to put you to a decision. Since you were confident in your read on your opponent, and you were playing a small heads-up pot, you decided to make a low-risk bluff.

Note that if your opponent had been a stronger player, you might have played the hand differently and been more willing to check it down. Because you checked, he could have figured out that you also didn't have a made hand worth protecting on the flop. He could have attempted to win the hand by raising you on the turn, or by bluff-calling and then trying to take it away from you on the river.

This hand is an example of how you can use knowledge of your opponents to win small pots with weak hands. While bluffing is not a key part of your strategy, it can help to mix up your game, conserve your chips, and continue building your credibility as a competent player. Just be sure not to start making this play every ten minutes. Many online players like to fire at pots before their opponents do, so you may be tempted to be the first one to bet when you have a weak hand. Making this type of play on a regular basis is a surefire way to lose money, so you must limit yourself to doing it only infrequently.

Now that we've discussed the best strategies for playing key hands from before the flop through the turn card, it's time to forge ahead to the river where your anticipated outcome can change in the blink of an eye.

PLAYING THE RIVER CORRECTLY

When you reach the river, you will be holding a very big hand in most of the pots you play, and you will likely have at least one player along for the ride to potentially make your session profitable. This section discusses some important events that can happen on the river. Understanding these points will help ensure that you make good decisions from before the flop all the way to the showdown.

FACING A RAISE

The river card has burned most hold'em players numerous times, yet it has saved them from certain disaster numerous other times. Many players fear facing a bet or a raise on the river because, with five community cards showing, a strong bet by an opponent could mean that he has made a strong hand. Since facing a raise on the river usually elicits an emotional reaction, guessing is the way that players often make decisions on the river. By failing to take the time to map out everything that has happened in the hand from before the flop up to the river, many poker players lose money in big pots by making poor decisions. One of the greatest benefits of implementing the *Playing No-Limit Hold'em as a Business* method is that you will hold hands that are strong enough to prevent your opponents from outplaying you. Nevertheless, you will always need to follow the action closely so that you can put the pieces of the puzzle together when you are faced with a tough decision on the river.

Let's say that you are holding A♠ A♥ in middle position in a ten-handed live $5/$5 no-limit game. You raise to $30 and two people call, the player on the button and the player in the big blind. You started the hand with $775 in chips. The player in the big blind started with less than $400, but the player on the button has almost $1,500. Your deep-stacked opponent is an average-loose player who has been involved in every hand when he's on the button and usually has not been afraid to get his chips in the pot. About an hour earlier, he took someone's entire stack when he pushed all-in with a flush draw and a gutshot draw, hit his flush, and beat his opponent's set.

The flop comes A♦ 8♣ 4♥. You have flopped top set, the stone cold nuts at this point. With $95 in the pot, the big blind checks to you.

SITUATION

You Have: A♠ A♥
The Board: A♦ 8♣ 4♥.
Money in the Pot: $95
Number of Players: Three

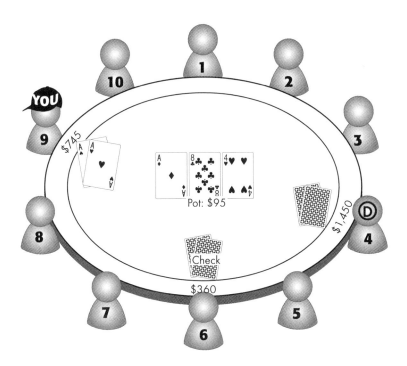

This is not at all a scary board for you, but you bet $50 to disguise the real strength of your hand. A bet here will probably make it look like you are holding A-K or A-Q, so if an opponent has hit two pair or a lower set, he might think he has you crushed. Also, your $50 bet is only about half the pot, so it's possible that it will be perceived as a weak continuation bet. Maybe an opponent will interpret it to mean that you are holding pocket kings or queens and are betting meekly because of the ace on board. This could open the door for an opponent to play back at you.

Right on cue, the average-loose player in Seat 4 on the button raises to $150. Seat 6 folds.

SITUATION

You Have: A♠ A♥
The Board: A♦ 8♣ 4♥
Money in the Pot: $295
Bet for You to Call: $100
Number of Players: Two

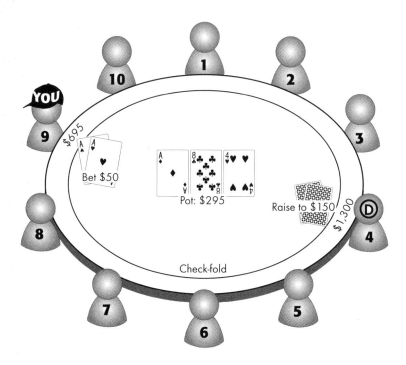

This is what you've been waiting for—you've hit a monster hand and a loose player is giving you action. You're not yet sure whether he actually flopped a big hand—maybe a set of eights or fours, or two pair with A-8 or A-4—or whether he's making a move. It's also possible, though unlikely, that he's holding a big ace like A-K or A-Q and chose to just call instead of reraise preflop. He could be trying to resteal the pot: He doesn't have a hand, he's testing you to see if you actually missed the flop or have pocket kings. You decide to continue disguising the strength of your hand by just calling his raise.

The turn is the Q♦, so the board reads A♦ 8♣ 4♥ Q♦. There is $395 in the pot. You are still holding the nuts, so you decide to continue disguising the strength of your hand this time by checking to him. You don't want him to fear that you have just improved to top two pair. He checks behind. You still don't have great information about his hand. If he checked the turn with a strong hand, he is trying to disguise the strength of his hand by representing that he was just trying to take it away from you on the flop. However, it's certainly possible that he had nothing on the flop and he simply tried to represent a pair of aces to resteal it. Since you called his raise on the flop, he has to know that you have a hand. Therefore, if he also has a big hand, betting the turn would have made sense.

The river is the 7♦ completing the board to A♦ 8♣ 4♥ Q♦ 7♦. You are no longer holding the nuts, as a straight or a flush beats you, but you decide to finally get some value for your hand, so you bet $200. He quickly raises to $650, which will virtually put you all-in if you call his raise.

SITUATION

You Have: A♠ A♥
The Board: A♦ 8♣ 4♥ Q♦ 7♦
Money in the Pot: $1,245
Bet for You to Call: $450
Number of Players: Two

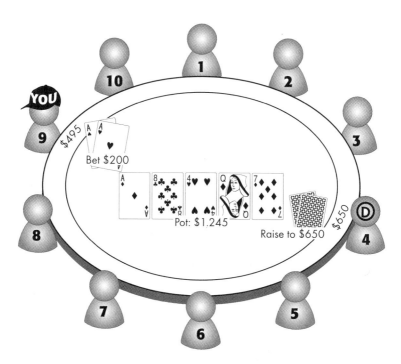

Now you have to decide whether he just got lucky and rivered you; flopped or turned a strong, albeit losing, hand and is choosing to get maximum value for it now; or is bluffing. Thinking very systematically about what he could be holding, you consider the possibilities:

    a. He flopped a set. It's possible he flopped a set and made a tricky check on the turn. If he is holding a set, he could raise you confidently, even though the river was a third diamond since there is no reasonable hand you can be holding with which to have picked up a flush. You can beat any set, so this is a good scenario for you.

b. **He has two pair.** He could be holding A-Q, A-8, A-7, A-4 or Q-8. He might be putting you on A-K, so if he turned or rivered two pair, he could raise. However, with any of these hands other than A-Q, he should be concerned that you have top two pair because you checked the turn when the queen came off, and then bet on the river. He should know that A-Q is a hand that you are capable of holding, so a raise on the river, as opposed to a call with a lower two pair, is pretty reckless even for him. In any case you can beat two pair, so this is a good scenario for you.

c. **He rivered a set of sevens.** This is unlikely to have occurred. However, if he is holding 7-7, it would make sense that he raised the flop to find out if you were really happy with it, and then checked on the turn and raised on the river. He might have tried to resteal on the flop, but eventually believed that you held A-K or A-Q. This is also a good scenario for you because you can beat a set of sevens.

d. **He made a flush.** This concerns you because you could lose a really big pot if you call and he has you beaten. However, as you think through this possibility logically, you realize that he would have had to catch runner-runner for a flush, which is uncommon. Also, he is the kind of player who is likely to have bet the turn if he picked up a flush draw, especially after you showed weakness by checking. You saw him play a big draw aggressively earlier in the session. Furthermore, if he is holding diamonds, he raised you on the flop with absolutely nothing, although you shouldn't put that past him (you did consider that he could have been restealing). Therefore, to be holding a flush, he would have had to:

1. Raise you on the flop with nothing.
2. Pick up a diamond draw on the turn.
3. Decide not to bet his draw after you showed weakness
4. Hit the flush on the river.

Since there are so many events that would have had to occur, it seems unlikely that he has a flush.

e. **He made a straight.** This also concerns you. He would have to be holding 6-5, which would be a weird hand to raise you with on the flop, although he could have tried to take the pot away from you while leaving himself four outs in case you called. It is unlikely that he has 6♦ 5♦ because the turn would have given him a flush draw to go along with his gutshot draw, and you've seen him bet out big with those types of hands. He really would have had to hit one of his miracle four outs to make a straight, so it's possible, although unlikely, that you are beaten.

f. **He is using the river as a scare card and is bluffing.** You have to consider this possibility because you have reviewed the hands that he might be trying to represent (a flush or a straight), and they don't add up very well. He might be trying to take advantage of the Minefield Effect here. If so, he is hoping that you remember the pot he took down with a flush an hour ago, and might be inclined to fold A-K or even two pair. He also has you covered, so he has the advantage of putting you to a decision for almost all your chips.

Now you have to sum up your analysis and articulate it concisely so that you can come to a decision. In four scenarios, you win. In only two, you lose, but the two losing scenarios are a bit unlikely. In addition, this is a big pot and you don't want to risk making a bad fold with a big hand when you are getting almost 3 to 1 on your money to call.

You call and he turns over 7♣ 6♣. He made a pair of sevens on the river, but missed a gutshot draw. You take down a pot of $1,695. He had in fact attempted to bluff you off your hand on the flop. He applied the brakes on the turn after you called his raise on the flop, and then he pounced on a scare card on the river.

Always keep your table image in mind when you are playing is the key lesson here. Your opponents will perceive you as a tight player who doesn't like to take a lot of chances, especially with only one pair, and some of them will try to take advantage of this. Sometimes an opponent will even notice that he is one of the players that you avoid. He might know that you don't want to lose a big pot to him, which will motivate him to bluff you. Your opponent will try to take advantage of the Minefield Effect by getting inside your head to make you convince yourself that folding is the right play. You have to be prepared for these situations, especially when you slowplay your big hands.

Remember that one of the reasons your strategy is so powerful is that the hands you play in big pots are deceptively strong, so your opponents might try to push you off what they think is a weaker hand than what you are actually holding. In this particular case, your check on the turn signaled that you were trying to keep the pot small with one pair, so your opponent probably thought he could move you off it with a scary raise on the river.

Also notice that the weaker bluffs are usually the ones that come from out of nowhere, especially on the river. Someone might make a panic move to try to win the pot because he knows his cards can't win it for him. The best kind of bluff is one where, during the entire hand from the flop to the river, it seems like the bluffer has a really strong hand. Sometimes a player might try to bluff beginning with preflop action and continuing all the way to the river. Those bluffs can seem a little fishy since most preflop raisers slow down when they keep getting action all the way to the river. If there are potential straights, flushes, or pairs on board, it would make more sense for a player who showed strength preflop to slow down in these situations and play more carefully.

KEY TAKEAWAY

A poor bluff often appears to have come out of nowhere. A good bluff usually is set up on the flop.

You may not always make the right decision when you face a tough decision. In the last example, if the river card had been a 5, your opponent would have made his straight and you would have paid him off by applying the same logic that induced you to call. In that case he simply would have been extremely lucky. However, you accounted for that in your thinking. You knew that if he hit that kind of card, even after attempting a steal on the flop with nothing, it simply would have been bad luck for you. You still would have made the best decision by calling his raise on the river because your overall scenario analysis had you ahead. The reality is that you will lose sometimes. Still, continually sticking to your game plan and always thoroughly evaluating the hands you play are the most important things you can do to increase the accuracy of your decisions. By doing so, you will no doubt come out on top in the long run.

BETTING FOR VALUE ON THE RIVER

The traditional definition of value betting is betting a medium-strength hand and getting paid off by a weaker hand, usually on the river. Since you won't often be betting with marginal hands on the river, you will define a value bet as one where you expect your big hand to get paid off by another strong hand. Making a good value bet is a skill that can help you surpass your profit objective. However, while you want to make sure you get maximum value for your big hands, you also want to make sure you don't get outplayed on the river or fall into a trap.

In the example you just read where you faced a bluff on the river, you had a tough decision after presumably making a value bet. Was that a real value bet that you made? Yes it was. Even before your opponent raised you on the river, you thought there was a chance that he had a strong hand even though you weren't sure. The key to value betting is knowing that there is at least a decent chance that your opponent has a strong enough hand to pay you off. If you are almost certain your opponent missed a draw, or he has a weak hand and he can't call a bet, then it's not really a value bet.

Let's say that you are on the button in a ten-handed live $5/$5 no-limit game. A player in an early position raises to $20, one player calls in front of you, and you call with A♠ 7♠ hoping to hit a big flop. The big blind in Seat 6 also calls, so you are playing four-way with $85 in the pot. The flop is A♣ 10♥ 7♥. You have hit a nice flop with two pair, and the chances are good that you are winning. However, you are not holding a big hand (top two pair or better), so you are not prepared to play a big pot just yet.

The big blind checks, the preflop raiser bets $60, the next player folds, and the action comes to you.

SITUATION

You Have: A♠ 7♠
The Board: A♣ 10♥ 7♥
Money in the Pot: $145
Bet for You to Call: $60
Number of Players: Three

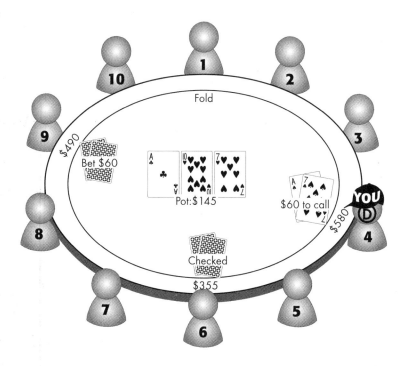

The bettor in Seat 9 is an average-tight player, but an exceptionally tight player preflop. You think he is probably holding A-K or A-Q. You have never seen him raise with a marginal hand such as A-10 at a full table, so you are not too worried about his holding top two pair. It's also possible that he has K-K or Q-Q and is taking one stab at the pot here on the flop. By just calling, you would give him the confidence to bet once more on the turn or river with A-K or A-Q, so you think you could win a big pot without raising and committing all your chips. Although by calling you might keep Seat 6 in the pot when he could be on a draw, you know that he's a weak-loose player who might not fold to a raise anyway if he is on a big draw.

You call and Seat 6 folds. You are now heads-up with $205 in the pot. The turn is the A♦, giving you a full house. Seat 9 bets $140.

SITUATION

You Have: A♠ 7♠
The Board: A♣ 10♥ 7♥ A♦
Money in the Pot: $345
Bet for You to Call: $140
Number of Players: Two

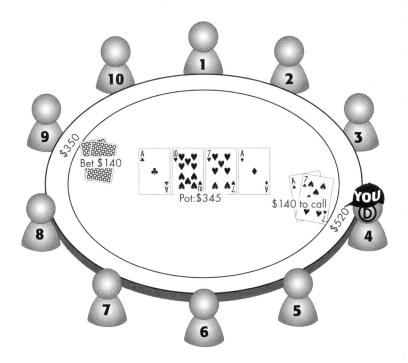

The A♦ is a terrific card for you, as it eliminates some of the hands that could have been beating you. Now you know that your opponent cannot have pocket aces and even if he is holding pocket tens, he has a lower full house. Although another ace on the turn could make it seem as though you don't have an ace in your hand, he probably still wouldn't have bet out again if he had K-K or Q-Q. Therefore, you think he might be holding trip aces with A-K or A-Q in the hole. He probably bet $140 because he doesn't want to give you the chance to hit a flush or straight in case you are drawing.

You start looking at the chips your opponent has bet and then at the amount of money in the pot. You call the $140 to make it look as though you were evaluating your pot odds for a drawing hand. The river is the 4♥, so the board reads A♣ 10♥ 7♥ A♦ 4♥. There is $485 in the pot, you have $380 left, and he has $350 left.

He checks to you. This could be a problem because the river may have scared him into thinking that you hit a flush. However, instead of choosing to make a very small bet just to ensure that you get some kind of action, you decide to stick to your read, which is that he probably has a hand that is very hard to lay down, especially since he is pot committed.

You mercilessly move in. He thinks for a minute before he finally calls. He turns over the A♥ K♠. You win a $1,245 pot.

You did a good job of understanding what your opponent could be holding, sticking to your read and playing accordingly. As a result, you got maximum value for your hand. A key learning here is that your opponent's check on the river didn't necessarily mean that he wouldn't call a big bet. Some players check good hands because they are hoping to keep the pot small and hoping their opponents will check behind them. Yet they will still call a big bet because they are holding a strong hand. Keep in mind that the key to your success in no-limit hold'em is hitting monster hands when your opponents also hit big hands. This goal should guide your thinking on the river because you need to get full value for your monster hands when you think that your opponents have a good hand. The prospect of getting a call in a huge pot makes it worth betting big, and is much better than taking the safe route by betting small.

KEY TAKEAWAY

Don't let an opportunity to win a huge pot slip by when the situation you've been patiently waiting for puts you in a highly favorable position.

Now that we've examined implementing your new strategy in full games, let's look at how you might play your hands to make a profit in shorthanded no-limit hold'em cash games.

10 PLAYING SHORTHANDED

In the action hand examples in the previous chapters, you were playing at a full nine or ten-handed table. But full online and live games are not always available; they tend to dwindle as the hour grows late. Once in a while, while you are still waiting to make your big score, only shorthanded games are in action. A full game has seven to ten players; a shorthanded game has four to six players. The style of play in a shorthanded game is significantly different from a full game. This section will prepare you with a moneymaking game plan for shorthanded games.

Shorthanded games often turn into what I call "two-card poker" games. This means that hitting just one pair usually is good enough for most players to play their hands confidently and aggressively. The likelihood of holding a monster hand decreases in a shorthanded game, and most players know this. As a result, players adjust their games and play looser. Even the conventional trouble hands increase a little in value since it becomes more likely that they can win pots. To illustrate this point, in a full ten-handed game, there is about a 75 percent chance that an opponent will be holding an ace in the hole when you are holding an ace in the hole. This means that when you play a weak ace in a full game, you must be wary that an opponent's bigger ace will beat you. However, in a five-handed game, the chance of someone else holding an ace when you have one is only about 41 percent. Therefore, in a shorthanded game it would make sense for someone to play a hand like A-7 or A-6 aggressively. The key question for you is, "Just how much do I want to loosen up my play?"

The answer is that you will not get too far off your game plan when the table is shorthanded. You will not put all your great work at risk by routinely playing big pots without big hands. However, if you don't loosen your play a little, you will end up folding too many made hands on the flop to the point that it will drain your chip stack and impede your ability to meet your profit objective. You will also lose money from the cost of the blinds since they come around more frequently. In addition, there probably will be a lot of raising preflop. Therefore, you need a strategy to guide you in how to dial down your starting hand requirements and how to better defend your made hands. While shorthanded play might not seem ideal for a player who has been trained to play patiently, rest assured that it is still a great way to get paid off on your big hands.

REDEFINING BIG HANDS

Your strategy at a full table is to win big pots with big hands. Your strategy in shorthanded games remains the same, but you need to redefine big hands as bottom two pair or better instead of top two pair or better. For example, suppose you're holding 8♥ 6♦ on a flop of A♠ 8♦ 6♠ in a five-handed game.

YOU

THE FLOP

You have a big hand, especially if you are playing the pot heads-up or three-way. If you get action on a board like this, you might be up against someone who has made a pair of aces, a pair of eights, has a low pocket pair, or perhaps has a drawing hand. If you hit bottom two pair, you can play a big pot if you think the circumstances call for it. The chances of your being beaten by a higher two pair or a set will be very low. Remember that if a hand is played out to the river, bottom two pair can still get beaten because your opponent's hand might improve by either hitting one of his outs or by counterfeiting your two pair. Just as you do in a full game, you want to be mindful of hands that can beat you and play accordingly.

In shorthanded play, while you should not be inclined to build a big pot when you are holding just top pair, you will need to play more pots and sometimes slightly bigger pots with top pair than you usually do. The reason is that if an opponent makes top pair with a weak kicker or second pair, or if he is holding a medium pocket pair with only one overcard on board, he may be willing to play the hand out to the river. In you bet the flop in a full game with top pair and get a couple of callers, you don't want to put too much more money in the pot after that. In a shorthanded game, making another bet on the turn with top pair is not a high-risk play. Also, you expect players to bet into you, and you shouldn't necessarily muck top pair if that happens. Unless the pot develops into a big one, you probably will need to play it out.

One last point: You should be less willing to pay a lot for speculative hands. A lot of the time you will need to fold middle or low suited connecting cards when an opponent raises preflop. It is less likely that you will get paid off when you make straights or flushes since there are fewer players at the table, which diminishes the probability that someone will catch a strong enough hand to get involved in a really big pot. Since there is less chance of receiving a big reward, you should curtail your upfront investment in these speculative hands and stick to more premium cards and pairs.

SHORTHANDED STARTING HANDS

Below is a list of your new starting hand requirements for shorthanded play. You will notice that compared to the list for a full game, some slightly weaker hands are higher on this list. The rationale is that these hands are good enough to beat many of the hands your opponents will play shorthanded, even in multiway pots. The weak hands your opponents will play are an ace with a kicker as low as a deuce; king high (K-Q, K-J, K-10, K-9, K-8 suited); queen high (Q-J, Q-10, Q-9, Q-8); jack high (J-10, J-9, J-8 suited, J-7 suited); many low connectors and gappers; and any low pocket pair.

1. A-A, K-K, Q-Q, J-J

Consider reraising, raising, calling a raise, or limping in on the button. You should see these hands as an opportunity to win a medium-sized pot. If you are first or second to act preflop, you will not limp in because you might end up playing a five-handed pot if you do, and if there is any kind of action on the flop you won't know where you stand unless you flop a set. Playing a raised pot ensures there are fewer players in the hand, which means less danger of your starting hand getting beat and a better chance of your taking the pot down with a bet on the flop or turn. The only time you can limp in with these hands is on the button when there are no callers in front of you, since there will be three of you playing the pot at most. This can be a strong play as you will be in a great position to win a medium-sized pot if someone flops a pair and you are holding an overpair. However, do not look to create a big pot by going all-in after the flop just in case someone has flopped two pair or better.

Feel free to reraise with J-J because, compared to full-handed play, there is a smaller chance you are up against a bigger pair, A-K, or A-Q. If someone holding a weak ace such as A-8 calls, you will be a big favorite when the flop comes out, so you should look to bet the flop even if it contains one overcard such as a king or queen. However, if an opponent calls your bet on the flop when there is an overcard, don't put any more money into the pot.

2. 10-10, 9-9, 8-8

Consider raising, calling a raise or limping in. You are primarily hoping to flop a set with these hands. However, you can also raise preflop and look to win a small pot by making one continuation bet on the flop if you are heads-up, even with one overcard on the board. If you can't take it down at that point, you shouldn't put any more money into the pot.

3. 7-7 OR LOWER

Consider calling a small raise or limping in. You are only looking to flop sets with these hands so you are not willing to call a big raise or a reraise with them preflop. At a full table you are more willing to pay a high price to try to flop a set because there is a better chance that you will be up against an opponent with a big pair. This means that the implied odds are much more in your favor in a full game. In a shorthanded game, you also don't want to get too heavily involved in feeling out whether your low pocket pair is the best hand after the flop.

Even when you are holding an overpair, it may be difficult to take pots down because a flop made up entirely of low cards could interest too many players. Do not call a bet in a multiway pot even if there is only one overcard on board, because you will have to guess whether your pair is good or whether an opponent is on a low straight draw. There is too much uncertainty when playing after the flop with low pairs, so you must not lose a lot of money with them.

A-K, A-Q, A-J, A-10

Consider raising, calling a raise, or limping in. A-J and A-10 have been added to the list of big aces because they can beat a variety of hands that people play in a shorthanded game, including weaker aces. Of course, if you hit a pair of aces with A-J or A-10 and you get heavy action, you will want to play carefully because there is still a chance you are beaten by A-K or A-Q.

HIGH AND MIDDLE SUITED CONNECTORS AND GAPPERS

(K♠ Q♠, K♥ J♥, K♦ 10♦, Q♣ J♣, Q♥ 10♥, Q♦ 9♦, J♠ 10♠, J♣ 9♣, 10♥ 9♥, 10♣ 8♣)

Consider limping in, and only calling a sizeable raise with K-Q suited or K-J suited. Most of these hands are speculative so you will want to play them as cheaply as possible preflop. Playing shorthanded doesn't give you a license to start overpaying for straight draws and flush draws after the flop. However, you can feel more confident that making a queen-high, jack-high, or 10-high flush (with two suited cards in the hole) will be the winning hand. You are also a bit less worried about making a straight and running into a higher straight, although always be very careful when you are holding the sucker straight (lowest end of a straight). Notice that playing very small flush cards is not recommended. Even shorthanded, baby flushes put you at risk of losing all your chips if you run into a higher flush.

If you make a pair, K-Q suited and K-J suited could be winning hands shorthanded, so you can call one raise with these hands preflop. Still, be sure not to play one-pair hands recklessly or play them in big pots, since getting outkicked is always possible. I do not recommend ever playing low unsuited connectors shorthanded. Hitting a flop you like with a highly speculative hand like 6-4 offsuit is rare, so you would need a lot of limpers in the pot to make it a worthwhile gamble. In a full game, it makes more sense to limp in or even call a small raise with low, unsuited connectors because if you hit a big flop, more players are involved and more money is in the pot to give you better implied odds.

A-X SUITED

Consider limping in or occasionally calling a small raise. You have less chance of receiving a big payoff with the nut flush than in a full game, so you want to play these hands cheaply. Although the lowest aces (A-5, A-4, A-3, A-2) give you the opportunity to draw to the wheel, they still do not offer as many opportunities to make a straight as middle or high connecting cards; once again, play them cheaply. Also be sure that you don't play low suited aces (an ace with a 9 kicker or lower) trying to pair your weak ace because of the danger in getting outkicked.

BULLYING IN
SHORTHANDED GAMES

Part of the elevated risk associated with playing in a shorthanded game is that players can more quickly figure out how their opponents play and can more effectively take advantage of them than in a full game. This means that there is a higher likelihood of at least one player detecting that you play a tight game, since he has noticed that you don't get involved in big pots unless you are holding a big hand. As a result some players might start raising you after the flop, regardless of what they are holding, in order to steal pots from you and lure you into a war, which is usually riskier for them to do at a full table. The danger is that you might be inclined to play with them when you are holding weak hands such as top pair with a low kicker or second pair.

A key component of your strategy is to avoid giving your opponents what they want, which is for you to significantly loosen your play, so you must not let this happen. In short, if you start to play the game the way they play it, you are at a disadvantage—and you put yourself at risk of losing all your chips, one pot at a time. If bullies are dominating your table and you are not able to win any small and medium-sized pots, consider leaving that table. You just have to chalk it up to one or two players controlling a game that is well suited to their style (it is more difficult to bully a full game). Look for another table where you will be able to more effectively implement your game plan.

HANDS IN ACTION AT SHORTHANDED TABLES

Now that we've redefined our standards for starting hands and learned how to handle bullies, let's examine five real situations you probably will face in shorthanded games.

SHORTHANDED ACTION HAND 1

In a five-handed live $2/$5 no-limit game, you are holding 10♦ 10♣ under the gun. You raise to $15 and get two callers. One is a strong-loose player on the button and the other an average-tight player in the big blind. You each started with $600 in chips. The pot contains $47. The flop comes Q♦ 9♥ 7♠.

The big blind checks, and you also check since an overcard is showing on the flop in a three-way pot. The button bets $25 and the big blind raises to $75. What is your play?

SITUATION

You Have: 10♦ 10♣
The Board: Q♦ 9♥ 7♠
Money in the Pot: $147
Bet for You to Call: $75
Number of Players: Three

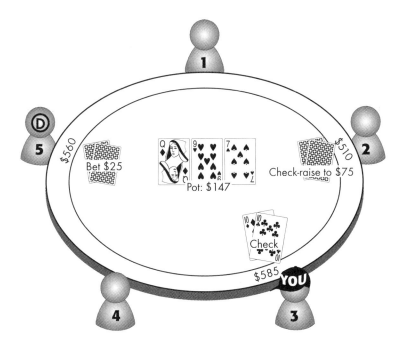

This is an easy fold because that is too much action with an overcard on board. Seat 5 might be making a position bet on the button, or perhaps he is playing a straight draw aggressively, but there is a good chance that Seat 2 in the big blind is playing at least a decent made hand. The pot was raised in front of him, so Seat 2 could be holding A-Q, K-Q or Q-J. Since you only have second pair, it is too risky and too expensive for you to find out. You probably would have folded even if Seat 2 had just called. The action continues after you fold.

The button calls. The turn is the 5♦, so the board reads Q♦ 9♥ 7♠ 5♦. There is $197 in the pot. The big blind bets $100 and the button calls. The river is the Q♥ so the board reads Q♦ 9♥ 7♠ 5♦ Q♥. There is $397 in the pot. The big blind bets $160 and the button moves in. The big blind calls, showing A♥ Q♣. The button turns over 8♣ 6♦ for a straight and wins a big pot.

This hand demonstrates that even in a shorthanded game, it can be wise to keep the pot small when danger is lurking. The big blind didn't even pause to think about why the button called his $100 bet on the turn. Since a straight and a full house could beat him on the river, he might have saved himself more than $200 if he had just checked-called on the river instead of carelessly getting all his money in.

SHORTHANDED ACTION HAND 2

In a five-handed live $5/$5 no-limit game that has been playing pretty loose, you are on the button with A♠ J♦. You raise to $20 and both blinds call. With $60 in the pot, the flop comes A♥ Q♣ 6♦. Your opponents check. This is a pretty good flop for you so you bet $35. After the small blind folds, the big blind calls. He is an average-loose player with $450 in chips to your $550.

SITUATION

You Have: A♠ J♦
The Board: A♥ Q♣ 6♦
Money in the Pot: $130
Number of Players: Two

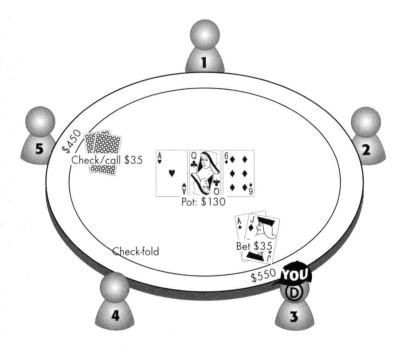

You think your opponent would have reraised preflop with A-A, Q-Q, A-K and maybe A-Q, so if he has you beaten, he probably is holding A-6 or a set of sixes. However, you think he might be sticking around with a very weak ace, a pair of queens, a pocket pair, or maybe even just a pair of sixes. Since you are on the button, he might not be buying the story that you're trying to sell, that you paired that ace on the flop.

The turn is the 7♥ so the board is A♥ Q♣ 6♦7♥. There is $130 in the pot. He checks again and you check behind. You think your opponent could be far enough behind in the hand that he might have folded if you bet, so you tried to get one more bet out of him on the river by showing weakness on the turn. The river is the K♠, and he bets $70.

SITUATION

You Have: A♠ J♦
The Board: A♥ Q♣ 6♦7♥ K♠
Money in the Pot: $200
Bet for You to Call: $70
Number of Players: Two

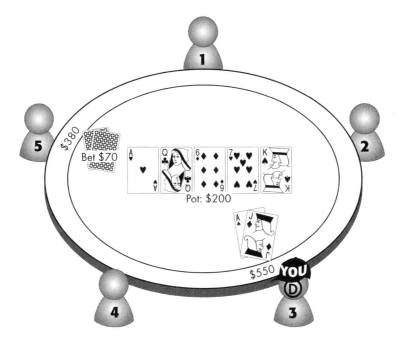

The king could be bad for you if he is playing K-Q or possibly K-6. He also may have hit two pair on the turn with A-7 or 7-6. Still, the game has been playing pretty loose and your check on the turn may have signaled to him that you made a continuation bet after missing the flop. When you consider this possibility, he could be playing a lot of hands that you are beating, including a pair of kings if he decided to call your bet on the flop on a gutshot draw with K-J or K-10. You call the $70. When he turns over Q♦ 10♠, you win a $270 pot.

By facing his bet on the river, the pot became a big one—more than half of a $500 starting stack if you called—yet all you had was one pair. Your play was correct since you had already limited the size of the pot by checking on the turn, and on the river, you decided that your read on your opponent trumped your rule of avoiding big pots with just one pair. You need to make this trade-off a little more often in shorthanded games.

SHORTHANDED ACTION HAND 3

In a five-handed live $5/$5 no-limit game, you are holding Q♠ 9♠ in the cutoff seat. One player limps in, you call, the button folds, and the blinds check. With $20 in the pot, four players look at the flop: A♠ 10♠ 9♦. You have bottom pair with a flush draw. Everyone checks around to you.

You just might have the best hand with a pair of nines, but you decide to take your free card and check because you are hoping to turn a big hand and then build the pot. Also, with an ace on the flop and no raise preflop, someone could get suspicious and start playing back at you. The turn is the Q♣, so you have made two pair in addition to having a flush draw. The small blind bets out $15 and the other two players fold around to you.

SITUATION

You Have: Q♠ 9♠
The Board: A♠ 10♠ 9♦ Q♣
Money in the Pot: $35
Bet for You to Call: $15
Number of Players: Two

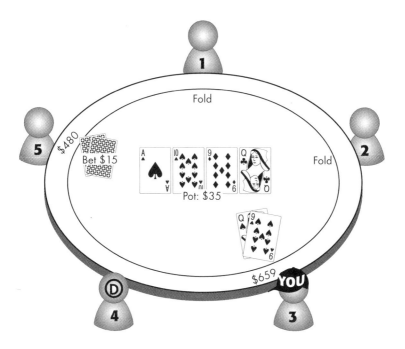

Seat 5 in the small blind is a strong-tight player. While you are holding a powerful hand, you want to get a read on your opponent by considering whether he could be playing some of the hands that are beating you. There is little chance he is holding A-A, Q-Q or even 10-10 because he would have raised preflop with those cards. You also doubt he is holding A-Q because he also might have raised preflop with that hand. While it's possible he has two pair with A-10 or A-9, you think he might have raised preflop, even out of position, with A-10; and since you also paired your 9, it is a little less likely that he has A-9. The fact that you paired your 9 also makes it unlikely that he is holding a set of nines. He could be holding a higher two pair with Q-10, although that would also be somewhat unlikely since you paired your queen. He also could have turned a straight if he is holding K-J or J-8.

Even if he has you beaten at this point, you still have nine outs to hit a spade on the river and another four outs to make a full house, which means you would be behind by about 3 to 1 and you are getting about 2.3 to 1 on your money to call. (Be aware, however, that if he has A-9, another 9 would give you a lesser full house, so a 9 may not be a viable out.) While the price you are getting isn't great, it's actually not terrible—and price is only an issue if he is in fact holding a hand that is beating you. In summary, numerous hands are beating you, but it is somewhat unlikely that he is holding a lot of those hands, and you have a lot of outs to improve on the river.

Now you should think about the hands you are beating. There is a decent chance that he flopped a weak pair of aces (A-7, A-6, A-5, and so on) and didn't want to bet the flop because he was first to act and he didn't want to risk getting raised before first seeing if his opponents were weak. You are also beating a pair of queens, which he may think is winning since nobody showed strength on the flop. He could also have a pair and a straight draw with K-Q, K-10, K-9, J-9 or 10-8. There is also an outside chance that he is holding a lower two pair with 10-9 which he slowplayed on the flop. Clearly, he could be holding many hands that you are beating.

Knowing that you shouldn't raise if you think you might have to rely on your spade draw (or full house draw) to win, you decide to just call and keep the pot small. The river is the 5♥. The board is A♠ 10♠ 9♦ Q♣ 5♥ and $50 is in the pot. He checks. Since he didn't show strength, you decide to get some value for your hand by betting $30. He calls. You show your Q♠ 9♠ and he mucks his hand. You win a $110 pot. You ask him if he had an ace and he nods his head. It appears that he thought you called his bet on the turn because you paired the queen.

SHORTHANDED ACTION HAND 4

In a five-handed live $2/$5 no-limit game, you are holding
K♥ 10♥ under the gun. You limp in hoping nobody raises. In
fact, nobody does. There is $20 in the pot, which is four-way.
The flop is 9♣ 8♥ 7♠. You have two overcards and an open-
ended straight draw.

The blinds check to you and you also check because you
don't want to bet and risk getting raised by the button or check-
raised by the blinds. The button also checks. The turn is the
K♠, giving you top pair to go along with your straight draw.
Again the blinds check to you.

SITUATION

You Have: K♥ 10♥
The Board: 9♣ 8♥ 7♠ K♠
Money in the Pot: $20
Number of Players: Four

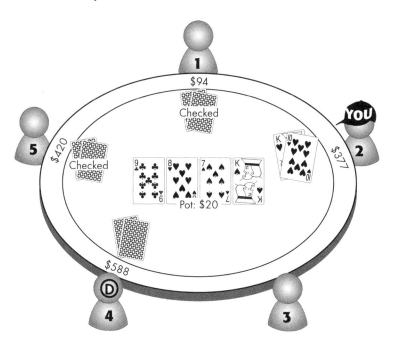

If one of your opponents has an open-ended straight draw, top pair, a pair and a straight draw, two pair, or a set, you think he would have bet it already. Therefore, you have less reason to fear a raise. You think there's a good chance your hand is winning, so you bet $15. The button folds, the small blind calls, and the big blind folds. Your opponent in the small blind is a strong-loose player. The river is the A♦. There is $50 in the pot and he bets $50.

SITUATION

You Have: K♥ 10♥
The Board: 9♣ 8♥ 7♠ K♠ A♦
Money in the Pot: $100
Bet for You to Call: $50
Number of Players: Two

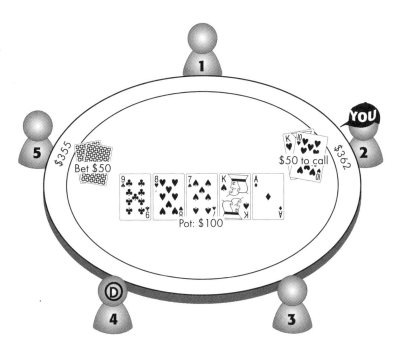

He could have flopped a straight and has been slowplaying it the whole way. The three hands he could be holding that give him a straight are J-10, 10-6 and 6-5, although he probably would have bet out with 6-5 before the river came to avoid getting leapfrogged. He could have turned two pair with a hand such as K-8 or K-7 and checked in the hope that someone would bet. He also could have made two pair on the river with a hand such as A-8 or A-7. If he had A-9, he probably would have tried to protect his hand by betting on the flop or he may have taken a stab at the pot on the turn, so he probably doesn't have that hand. If he had K-9, he probably would have bet the turn to get some value for his two pair and protect his hand from a straight draw.

He also could have hit a weak ace and was looking to call you on the turn to take the pot away from you on the river. After all, by checking the flop, you showed that you didn't have a hand that was good enough to protect. Perhaps he has A-6 and was hoping to hit an ace or a 5 for a straight. He didn't want to play the hand aggressively until now because he was only drawing to the low end of the straight.

You also have to consider that he could be bluffing. He might be thinking that unless you flopped the nuts with J-10, you would have bet the flop to protect a made hand. Then after you bet the turn, he might have put you on a king and he is now representing an ace or better. Also, he might think you bet the turn on a straight draw after the table showed weakness again and after taking a free card on the flop. So, perhaps he is betting with nothing because he believes you also have nothing.

This situation is a little confusing and it is exactly why strong-loose players are dangerous when you don't have a strong hand. It is reasonable to think he could be bluffing, but it is also reasonable to think he has an ace or two pair. You decide to fold because you don't have a strong hand or a great read on your opponent.

Many players would find it very reasonable to look him up and call. While it was certainly tempting to call since he didn't seem to have a hand worth protecting on the flop or turn, you cannot let yourself fall in love with making calls like that. I've seen players start making calls with weak hands (in many cases with ace high) just to look like a hero and catch a potential bluffer. The long-term result? They lose money. You played this hand well, but in the end you were only left with second pair against a tricky opponent who bet into you on the river.

SHORTHANDED ACTION HAND 5

In a six-handed live $5/$5 no-limit game, a strong-tight player raises to $15 in early position, the button calls and the small blind also calls. The action comes to you in the big blind. You are holding A♣ 9♣. It will cost you $10 more to call the $50 pot, so you call. You started the hand with $590.

The flop comes A♦ 8♣ 2♣. You have flopped top pair with a weak kicker and the nut flush draw. There is $60 in the pot. The small blind checks and the action is on you.

SITUATION

You Have: A♣ 9♣
The Board: A♦ 8♣ 2♣
Money in the Pot: $60
Number of Players: Four

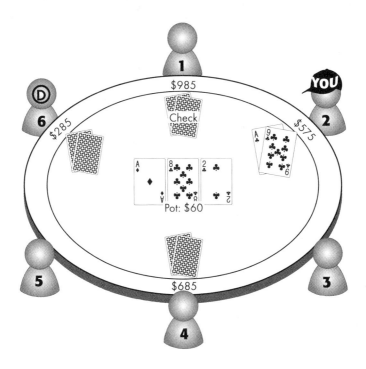

Since there is a chance the preflop raiser in Seat 4 has a bigger ace, you don't want to bet out and risk getting raised when you might be behind in the hand. You would like to see the turn and/or river with your hand if you can, so you check. If he bets a reasonable amount, you probably will call to see what he does on the turn. After all, he may have missed the flop with K-Q or K-J, or maybe he has K-K, Q-Q, J-J or 10-10. Your call will signal to him that you might be ahead, so you may get a free look at the river to improve your hand. Check-calling with top pair when you have outs to hit the nut flush or two pair can be a good play when you think there is at least a chance that your pair is winning; you want to avoid building a big pot when you're not sure where you're at in the hand.

Seat 4 bets $25, the other players fold, and the action comes to you.

SITUATION

You Have: A♣ 9♣
The Board: A♦ 8♣ 2♣
Money in the Pot: $85
Bet for You to Call: $25
Number of Players: Two

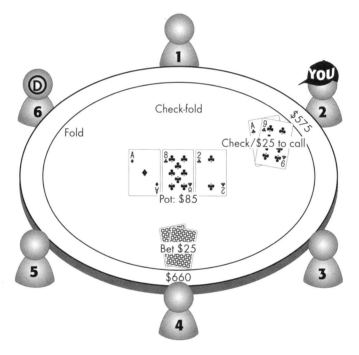

His bet seems oddly small. Usually when he has top pair, he bets larger to protect it and thin the field. Now you're not so sure that you are behind. Perhaps he has K-K, Q-Q, J-J or 10-10. You don't think he has a flush draw and a gutshot draw with 5♣ 4♣, 5♣ 3♣ or 4♣ 3♣ because he doesn't usually raise with those hands preflop. Still, maybe he is on a club draw with a hand like K♣ Q♣, K♣ J♣, Q♣ J♣ or J♣ 10♣. While there is an outside chance he flopped a set of eights or twos, or maybe hit two pair with A-8, you think you may have him beat. Of course, even if you are wrong, you have outs to hit the nut flush or two pair. You call.

The turn card comes 5♥, so the board reads A♦ 8♣ 2♣ 5♥. There is $110 in the pot. Since you are reading him as probably being weak, you might be able to win the pot with a bet right here. By check-calling on the flop and then betting the turn, your bet would signal that you have flopped a big hand (bigger than what you are actually holding), and that you don't want to give him a free look at the river in case he's on a draw. You decide to bet. You think it should be an amount that won't scare him away in case he's on a flush draw, and would entice him to call with a pocket pair like K-K or Q-Q.

You bet $45 into the $110 pot. He calls.

SITUATION

You Have: A♣ 9♣
The Board: A♦ 8♣ 2♣ 5♥
Money in the Pot: $200
Number of Players: Two

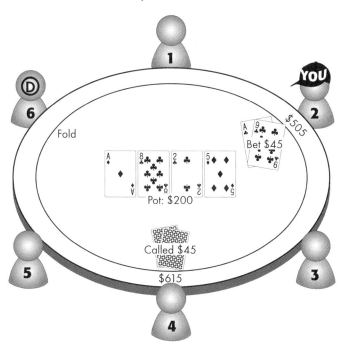

At this point you think he would have raised you if he were holding a big ace or maybe even a very strong hand such as a set or two pair. Your check-call-bet play might be scaring him a little, so while you think there is a small chance he could still be winning with a medium ace like A-10 or maybe A-J, your gut is telling you that he has a club draw or a pocket pair.

The river card is the J♥. The board reads A♦ 8♣ 2♣ 5♥ J♥. You're not crazy about the jack because he could be holding pocket jacks, so you check. He checks behind you. He looks at you and waits for you to show your hand, indicating that he has a made hand. You flash just your ace and he mucks his hand. He was probably holding a pocket pair and called your small bet on the turn just in case you were drawing.

The next chapter examines another important aspect of playing no-limit hold'em as a business: how to mix up your game to keep your opponents off guard.

11 MIXING UP YOUR GAME

When talking about a player who is mixing up his game, we usually say, "He's changing gears." Changing gears means playing fast, slowing down, speeding up again, and so on, to keep opponents guessing about the nature of your hole cards. Changing gears is not something you need to do on a regular basis because it often involves taking on extra risk in big pots by bluffing, semi-bluffing, chasing draws, raising with draws, and playing marginal hands aggressively preflop. As a proponent of the *Playing No-Limit Hold'em as a Business* cash game method, you can mix up your game and ensure that you maintain a healthy long-term profit by playing your hands differently from time to time. This doesn't mean that you should start chasing inside straight draws. It just means that you occasionally need to do something unexpected during a hand you're playing.

While you may find that mixing things up a little can be good for your game, you should never get away from the strategy you've learned in this book by starting to bluff in big pots. You will never need to play that way in cash games. However, doing things a little bit differently from time to time has some benefits.

FOUR BENEFITS OF MIXING UP YOUR GAME

The main benefits of mixing up your game are:

1. **Being less predictable.** Although a good player at the table will be able to figure out that you are still frugal and you still like to wait patiently for big hands, it will help to plant seeds of doubt in most of your opponents' minds. It can be valuable to show everyone that you are at least capable of making certain plays that appear out of the norm for you. That way, when someone is in a hand against you they won't feel like they know exactly how strong your hand is. Just a little bit of deception could cause your opponents to make mistakes.

2. **Getting paid off.** One outcome of being less predictable is that players might be a little more likely to pay you off on your monster hands. If they've seen you actually get your money in without a big hand or if they've seen you do a little speculating with a weak hand preflop, they might be more inclined to think they are winning when they are in fact up against one of your monster hands. Mixing up your game should be considered a small investment that could deliver a big pay off later on.

3. **Evaluating how players play against you.** For a reasonable 'cover charge' you get to observe your opponents in action against you. You can evaluate which players fear you and which players feel comfortable playing against you. The ones that know where they are at in a hand against you might be worth avoiding in the future. Also, these

players may be a little less inclined to pay you off on your big hands. This information can be invaluable because when you do hit a monster hand against them you may need to slowplay in order to extract chips from them. Conversely, a weaker player who carelessly throws money into the pot might only think about his own cards and not what you are holding. Hence, when you hit a big hand against one of these players you might feel the right play is to bet liberally and build a huge pot early on.

4. **Winning the pot.** Obviously, the purpose of mixing up your game isn't to lose money on purpose. Occasionally, you can take advantage of your tight image and win small or medium sized pots by bluffing when your opponents show weakness, by betting out with a big draw, or by playing top pair a little stronger than you usually do.

FIVE TYPES OF HANDS YOU CAN PLAY TO ADD VARIETY TO YOUR GAME

Here are some of the hands you can play to add a little variety to your game. Note that in most cases these plays should be made in small or medium pots and in three or four-way pots at the most. You must also try to avoid playing these hands for all your chips.

1. ANY PAIR IN AN UNRAISED POT.

You have already played small pots with only one pair. The difference here is you become willing to play any piece of the flop against as many as three opponents. When you fire at a pot in a situation where you usually play your hand more passively, you might take it down right there because your opponents will fear that you flopped a set or two pair. If you get one caller on the flop then you can even fire a second bet on the turn in order to continue representing a monster hand. Also, if someone bets on the flop you can consider raising or check-raising with a weak hand in order to represent a monster, especially if you sense that the bettor put out a probe bet. You can even show your weak pair to your opponents after they fold. Doing so will make you appear to be willing to play poker the way your opponents play it. It will keep them guessing about just how big your hand really is when they play a pot against you in the future, so it may help you trap them with one of your monster hands. Just be sure not to put any more money into the pot if someone calls one of your raises or if more than one player calls one of your bets, as the likelihood of winning the pot at that point will be much lower.

2. TOP PAIR/TOP KICKER IN A LARGER POT.

Once in a while you can play a big pot without a monster hand when you are confident you are winning heads-up. Let's say in a ten-handed live $5/$5 no-limit game, a few players limp in, you raise to $30 from the cutoff seat with A♣ Q♥, and only the button calls. He is an average-loose player. You started with $700 and he started with $500. While A-Q isn't an extremely strong hand preflop your opponent might have reraised with A-K, and on the button he could be playing a wide range of hands so you think you are ahead.

The flop comes Q♦ 3♠ 6♠. This is a nice looking flop for your hand. There is $85 in the pot. You bet $50 and the button calls. You take a moment to evaluate.

SITUATION

You Have: A♣ Q♥
The Board: Q♦ 3♠ 6♠
Money in the Pot: $185
Number of Players: Two

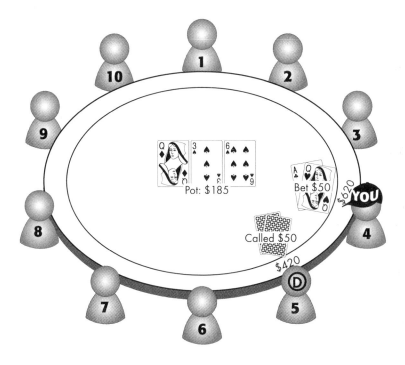

You would have him crushed if he is holding K-Q or Q-J, but he might have raised with those hands on the flop because your $50 bet wasn't large, and by raising he could have found out where he stood. He could have second pair with A-6 or a low suited connector with a 6, or perhaps a pocket pair like 9-9, 8-8 or 7-7, and he decided to call with these marginal hands because he didn't believe you hit the flop. He could also have a flush draw or perhaps an open-ended straight draw with 5-4. If he had a big draw like a pair of queens and a flush draw, a flush draw and a gutshot draw, or an open-ended straight flush draw with 5♠ 4♠, he might have raised so you don't put him on a big draw just yet. As for the hands that are beating you, he could have flopped two pair if he called with 6-3 suited, or he could have flopped a set of sixes or threes. Overall, you think there is a very good chance you are winning.

The turn is the J♣, so the board is Q♦ 3♠ 6♠ J♣. That card probably didn't help him unless he is playing Q-J, but you think he might have raised on the flop with it and he certainly would have raised with Q♠ J♠, which makes the chances of his holding Q-J a little lower. Also, he might have reraised preflop with pocket jacks. Instead of checking to keep the pot small you decide to take on some extra risk by betting out again, even though it will create a big pot. There aren't many hands that are beating you, and this time you decide not to give your opponent a free look at the river in case he is on a draw. If he is on a draw you will still be a big favorite with one card to come so you have a good chance of winning a big pot instead of just a small pot with top pair/top kicker.

Still, you don't want to bet too big and put yourself in a position where you are playing for all your chips, so you bet $90 into the $185 pot. Your opponent takes longer to think and calls the $90.

SITUATION

You Have: A♣ Q♥
The Board: Q♦ 3♠ 6♠ J♣
Money in the Pot: $365
Number of Players: Two

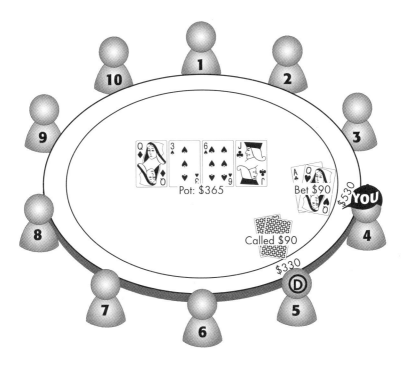

You are starting to get the feeling that he knows he's beat. You now know he is not playing a marginal made hand like a low pocket pair or a pair of sixes. You think his range of holdings is a draw, maybe a weaker queen, and maybe a set or top two pair, but you are still not convinced he has you beat. The river is 10♥, so the board is Q♦ 3♠ 6♠ J♣ 10♥. Your opponent isn't a bad player and even though he is loose you think he would have the sense to have folded Q-10 by now (or to have raised with it on the flop to see where he was at), so you doubt he rivered two pair. He doesn't have two pair with J-10 offsuit because he wouldn't have called your bet on the flop with that hand, and you doubt he has J♠ 10♠ because he might have played the turn more aggressively and more confidently with that hand. To make a straight he would have to be holding A-K, which is unlikely, and for him to be holding

K♠ 9♠ or 9♠ 8♠ (he wouldn't call with those hands on the flop unless he had spades) means he would have had a flush draw and gutshot draw on the turn, and he usually plays those big drawing hands more confidently and aggressively. It also means he would have had to catch perfect-perfect for a straight.

You really think he missed a straight draw or flush draw, with an outside chance of him holding two pair or a set. However, since you doubt there is an opportunity to make a value bet, you decide to check. Checking also prevents you from committing yourself to the pot; betting a total of $234 would commit you to the pot but you have only spent $170 so far. Your opponent bets $140.

SITUATION

You Have: A♣ Q♥
The Board: Q♦ 3♠ 6♠ J♣ 10♥
Money in the Pot: $505
Bet for You to Call: $140
Number of Players: Two

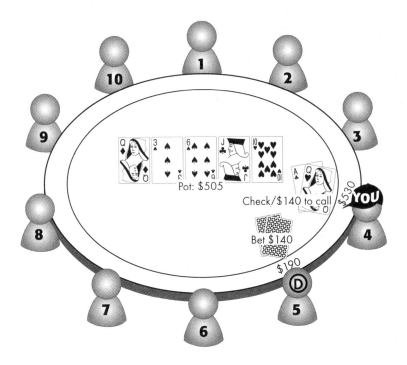

Your gut is telling you that he missed a draw, and you know he is capable of bluffing on the river. The only hands that are beating you are ones with which he would have had to get lucky. With $505 in the pot you are getting about 3.6 to 1 on your money so, at this price, you don't want to risk folding the best hand when your gut tells you that your opponent might be bluffing.

You call and he shows 10♠ 7♠. You win a $645 pot. This hand shows that you can end up taking on significant risk when you keep betting and building the pot with only one pair. However, you were confident in your read on your opponent. Therefore, you had decided that in this hand you were willing to risk losing a bigger pot than you are normally willing to lose in order to mix up your game, and to show your opponents that you are a quality player who isn't easily beat.

3. ATTACKING A CONTINUATION BET.

You just read a good example of picking off a bluff. As long as it doesn't cost a lot if you make a bad call, you can consider bending the rules of your game plan by calling or raising with a weak hand when you are confident your opponent has a weaker hand. Here is another example. In a nine-handed live $1/$2 no-limit game, a weak-loose player raises to $8 and you are the only player who calls. You are on the button holding K♥ Q♥. You each have about $250 in chips. The flop is 10♣ 8♥ 5♠ and there is $19 in the pot. You only have two overcards.

YOU

THE FLOP

Your opponent comes out betting $9, which feels like a weak continuation bet. He has been doing a lot of betting in most pots he has played, and almost always makes continuation bets on the flop. On a 10-high flop, you are inclined to think he doesn't have much this time around. While a raise could certainly be justified here, you decide to bluff-call hoping that he slows down and you can bet him off the hand on a later street. You choose not to raise because you want to wait and see if he shows weakness on the turn before you commit more than $9 to this pot with only king high. Notice that this is a stronger play when you have position because you get to act last. If you had to act first, a check-raise probably would be an effective play.

The turn is the 3♦ so the board reads 10♣ 8♥ 5♠ 3♦. There is $37 in the pot.

YOU

OPPONENT

THE BOARD

Your opponent checks and you decide that it's time to convince him that you have outflopped him. You bet $20. He folds, shows K♠ Q♣, and says, "Here, just so you know I don't raise with bad hands."

If he had called your bet on the turn, you would not have put any more money into the pot because it would be possible that he was on to you and suspected you were trying to steal the pot. Also, if he had called your bet on the turn and then checked the river, you would have checked behind him, and taken the chance that he missed a draw with a hand such as Q-9, 7-4 and so on. After all, if he could sense a steal on the turn, there's a pretty good chance that he could sense the same thing on the river, so he might have check-called even if he had just a pair of eights or sixes.

Keep in mind that you don't want to make this play every time someone makes what you think is a continuation bet. Don't try to play the role of hero by constantly trying to pick off bluffs—you don't need to do that to win in cash games.

4. THE SEMI-BLUFF CALL WITH A DRAW.

This play is similar to the previous play except that in this case, you are willing to pay a reasonable price to find out if your opponent has hit the flop while leaving yourself some outs to make a big hand. This play gives you the opportunity to try to hit a draw, assuming the price isn't terribly high, while also preparing to bluff your opponent off the pot in case you miss your draw. While calling with a draw is usually a bad play because you rarely get the right price to call, this play becomes more valuable when you use your tight image to steal a pot on a later street if you miss your draw, assuming that you believe your opponent has a weak hand. It is very important that you only make this play against weak or average players, not against strong players with whom you should rarely get involved when you are holding a weak hand.

Let's say you are in the big blind in a nine-handed live $5/$5 no-limit game holding 8♥ 7♥. A weak-loose player on the button raises to $15. The small blind calls, you call, and two other limpers behind you call making the pot five-way. The flop comes 5♥ 6♠ 10♣, so you have an open-ended straight draw. You all check to the preflop raiser who bets $30 into a pot of $75. The small blind folds, and the action is on you.

YOU

THE FLOP

THE BET FOR YOU TO CALL: $30
SIZE OF THE POT: $75

You need better than 5 to 1 odds on your money to see the turn, but you are only getting 2.5 to 1 assuming that nobody calls behind you. You decide to mix things up and call. Since players often give you respect when you call bets after the flop, especially in multiway pots, you just might prevent someone from raising or even calling behind you if they have hit a piece of the flop. More importantly, you might earn a free look at the river because the bettor might not want to bet into you on the turn if he has a weak hand.

The other players fold behind you, so you are heads-up with the preflop raiser. The turn is the A♣, so the board reads 5♥ 6♠ 10♣ A♣. You check and the preflop raiser bets $80 into the $145 pot.

YOU

THE FLOP

THE BET FOR YOU TO CALL: $80
SIZE OF THE POT: $145

Obviously, you missed your straight and now it feels like he had hit his weak ace, which you don't think he is capable of folding. You decide to fold. While it didn't work out this time, and while you certainly shouldn't be in a rush to make this play again just for the sake of executing it successfully, you still had a well thought out plan that perhaps you will be able to carry out some other time.

Notice that even though you might have been able to take the pot away from your opponent by raising on the flop, you didn't want to invest as much as another $80 or $90 merely because your opponent may have made a weak continuation bet. For all you knew, he had A-K or A-Q and would have called you, at which point you probably would have given up the pot after the turn unless you made your straight. You were willing to invest only $30 to see if your opponent gave you a free look at the river or an opportunity to bet him off his hand on the river, assuming you gained more information about the strength of his hand on the turn.

5. REPRESENT A-A, K-K OR A-K.

Another effective way to take advantage of your tight image is to raise preflop with any two cards and then follow up with a strong continuation bet on the flop almost regardless of what comes out on the flop. You are looking to build a small pot preflop that you can take down with one solid bet on the flop that convinces your opponents you are holding a big overpair. Of course, if the flop comes ace-high, you would be representing A-K. This is obviously a high-risk play that you should only make in late position when no more than one or two limpers are in front of you preflop. Position is important because you want to see your opponents check the flop before you bet. Also, you don't want to face an opponent who feels more confident about playing the hand out simply because he has position on you. If you get three or more callers preflop, you shouldn't make the continuation bet since there will be too many players to push out of the hand on the flop. Regardless of whether this play works, you should not try it more than once in a session.

While it can be useful to mix up your play, you must remember that it is not a fundamental component of your strategy in cash games. You do not want to start playing a lot of pots, making fancy plays and gambling on draws on a regular basis even if these plays sometimes work. You should view mixing up your game as merely a small part of your overall strategy and as a way to create a little more deception in your play.

12 MANAGING YOUR MONEY FOR MAXIMUM PROFIT

Bankroll management is the conventional term for making sure a poker player doesn't run out of money. It means managing the money that you set aside specifically for poker games. While proper bankroll management is important and will help you sustain yourself as a poker player in the long run, I think the term is too limited.

Bankroll management primarily refers to ensuring that you sit in the right game ($1/$2 no-limit versus $5/$10 no-limit, for example), and knowing how much you should be willing to lose in one session (the convention is roughly 10 to 15 percent of your bankroll). I prefer to use the term money management because it refers more broadly to any decision you make that could impact your ability to make money or save money. While playing in the right game and risking the right proportion of your bankroll are both important considerations, there are other factors that influence your ability to make money.

SETTING AN OBJECTIVE

One of the most discouraging things that can happen to you as a poker player is losing money after a long session in which you were winning earlier on. The best way to avoid this dilemma is to set a profit objective and stick to it. This is one of the most important money management decisions you can make.

When I talk about profit objective, understand from the get-go that I'm not trying to encourage you to set new records for consecutive wins across sessions, because thinking about consecutive wins can mislead you into playing under less than optimal conditions. You will be so focused on trying to turn a losing session into a winning session that you will try to force the results by chasing cards and making poor decisions. If you start doing this when you are tired or playing at tables filled with strong opponents, you will risk losing even more money.

So, instead of thinking about long winning streaks, think about your profit objective as a way to responsibly manage your money over the long run. In the short term, you will certainly have some losing sessions and you must accept them as a part of the big picture in poker.

To summarize, long-term profitability from playing poker can be attained by:

1. Not getting greedy during a profitable session by sticking around in less than optimal playing conditions to try to make more profit;
2. Only continuing to play when you are losing for as long as you feel alert and capable of playing your best game, and when you know that weaker players are at the table.

It's okay to finish a session below your profit objective to avoid playing tired and potentially walking out a loser late at night after making one big mistake. Of course, in some of your sessions you will take down a few big pots and double or triple your buy-in. And if your playing conditions are optimal, such as playing with a lot of weak players when you are still feeling alert, your best choice might be to keep playing even after surpassing your profit objective.

However, during sessions in which you aren't able to achieve spectacular results, or when the playing conditions are not optimal, you will need some guidelines for when you should pocket your profits and stop playing.

Keeping these points in mind, I suggest targeting a profit of roughly 50 percent of your original buy-in in medium and large games such as $5/$10 no-limit, $10/$20 no-limit and higher. If you sit down with $2,000 in a $10/$20 no-limit game, you should be happy to leave with $1,000 in profit, and even $700-$800 profit is fine. Undershooting your objective is a lot better than taking on more risk and potentially leaving a loser. When you look at $800 profit per session prorated over a year, assuming you play five times a week, that is an income of $208,000 in cash ($800 x 5 x 52 = $208,000). Even after factoring in some losses, vacation time and averaging less than five sessions per week, it is still a fantastic six-digit cash income. Therefore, once you meet a reasonable profit objective in a session you shouldn't risk losing it by continuing to play in an effort to earn more, especially if you are feeling tired.

If you are playing in a smaller game, especially in a game that has a low cap on the buy-in, setting your objective a little higher than 50 percent is reasonable. Pots tend to grow quickly in short-stacked games because players move in more often to defend top pair, or sometimes when they pick up a drawing hand. In a $2/$5 no-limit game that limits the buy-in to $300, one preflop raise to $40 is 13 percent of a starting stack, and that percentage could be higher if the raiser has less than $300 in chips. If the raiser gets some action after the flop, there is a good chance he will be all-in. This makes it more likely that you can win an opponent's entire chip stack if you hit a big hand, and sometimes you can win more than just one opponent's chip stack in one hand. Another reason you can set your profit objective higher is that sometimes, smaller games have weaker players. If you are sitting at a table with players who make a lot of mistakes and are virtually giving their money away, it is reasonable to expect more return on your buy-in.

In a $1/$2 no-limit game where most players start with $200, a $150 to $175 profit objective seems reasonable. In a $5/$5 no-limit game where players start with $500, a $300-$400 profit objective seems about right. You might think that is low, that you can make a lot more in a $5/$5 no-limit game. This may be true if you like to play very long sessions, but generally, if you expect to win $600 or more in each session, you probably are taking on a lot of risk in your play. If you play a few times per week, your $600 goal will be difficult to keep up. You probably will also be setting yourself up for larger than normal losses in some sessions. The style of play that you have learned in this book requires a lot of patience and waiting for big hands. Therefore, it stands to reason that you should take your profits and leave a session pretty soon after hitting a big hand and meeting a reasonable objective, assuming the playing conditions are not optimal.

When you're playing multiple tables online, it can be very tempting to stick around and try to muscle a table after you have built a large chip stack. While that type of play can be effective, I don't recommend that you alter your style of play dramatically just because you have a large stack. Keep your overall profit objective in mind. While you might be winning big on one table, perhaps you are losing at another. You should use the 50 percent profit objective as a guideline for your total profit across all the tables you are playing to ensure that you leave your session a winner.

For example, if you are playing three tables at $.50/$1.00 no-limit where the maximum buy-in is $100, you should shoot for about $150 total profit, assuming you start with a full buy-in of $100 at each table. Reaching a chip count of $350 at one table doesn't mean that you should expect to see that same result at your other tables. If you are down by $50 to $100 at your two other tables, and you are up by a total of $190 across all three tables, you should consider ending your session since it is already a profitable one. Of course, your profit objective is just a guideline, so you might make an exception when you are certain that the playing conditions are optimal at all three tables and you feel strongly that your results will turn around at the other two tables.

TRACKING YOUR RESULTS

Tracking your results will help you gain a sense of focus and control that will empower you to handle your money responsibly, and stick to your game plan at the tables. Here are more specific reasons why keeping track of your winnings can be helpful.

1. **You feel more in control of your poker playing**. Playing poker isn't only about what happens at the table, it is about decisions you make away from the table. For example, looking at your recent results might shed some light on whether moving to a new live cardroom or to a new format (online versus live) has worked out for you. A serious player should not keep playing poker without any idea of how it is affecting his or her finances.

2. **Invest your winnings.** Knowing how much you have been winning is helpful in making the right decisions about what to do with your money. A later section in this chapter discusses ways to invest your winnings.

3. **Reevaluate the size of the game.** Tracking your results will help you decide if the time is right to step up to a larger game. This may involve increasing your profit objective, so you should get a handle on

this information before you jump into a new game. Tracking your results also may reveal that you have been playing in games that are too big, so you may need to consider moving to smaller games.

4. **Control losing streaks.** Keeping track of your results will help you evaluate just how bad things have been if you have lost during a few sessions. You may find that you are so far up in the profit column over the last couple of months that some recent losses you've sustained do not require you to make any changes. Attitude is everything, so some perspective can help prevent you from losing your composure when faced with a potential losing streak.

5. **Enjoy your results.** There is no shame in celebrating your victories, and if it adds an element of fun to the game, then by all means take pleasure in your great results.

A good way to keep track of your results is to simply write things down in a notebook or keep them in an Excel spreadsheet on your computer. After each session you play, record the result and the date so that you can go back and track your results over long periods of time. It is likely that after reading this book, you will notice some strong results.

PLAYING THE RIGHT SIZE OF GAME

If you employ a solid and effective game plan like the one I have outlined, you will be able to play in a number of different sized games, not just the smallest levels in no-limit hold'em. However, one constraint is whether you have the bankroll to sit in a big game. In a $5/$10 or $10/$20 no-limit game, you could potentially lose $5,000 or more in one day if you get very unlucky. This number can become big because most players start with over $1,000 and sometimes $2,000 or more in chips. If you are just starting out, you should not sit in large games even if you can afford to lose that much.

Why?

Because the strategies you have learned in this book require playing against some weaker opponents, and if you're a relative beginner, you may not yet be able to recognize the weaklings at your table. Instead, start out playing a smaller game that is more likely to include players closer to your level of experience. These levels could be 25¢/50¢ no-limit, 50¢/$1.00 no-limit, or $1/$2 no-limit games. Keep in mind that live games smaller than $1/$2 no-limit are hard to find, so you will likely need to play online for those limits.

Starting small can be important to build your poker bankroll. Just in case you experience an extended streak of bad luck, make sure you can cover the losses if you want to keep playing. You should be covering those losses from your poker bankroll, not from your personal savings. You never want to have to start cashing in investments and retirement funds to keep playing poker, even if you play full time. I know players that have had to do this and some that even had to sell their houses because they got in so deep playing in big games, although playing badly and taking on too much risk, not bad luck, was the main reason these players struggled. These players should have simply moved to a smaller game where a few losses wouldn't have significantly diminished their bankrolls. Choose the right size of game so that you don't run out of cash and become tempted to look at your personal savings as a way to finance your poker playing.

A good rule of thumb to help you judge how much money you need to play poker without tapping into your personal savings is to have a bankroll of about twenty times the maximum buy-in at the game you choose. For example, if you want to play in a $2/$4 no-limit game on a regular basis where the maximum buy-in is $400, you should be working with a bankroll of about $8,000. You might think this amount is excessively large, but $8,000 is only twenty buy-ins. Understand that strange variances in the way you earn or lose money are possible in no-limit hold'em.

The reality is that few players sufficiently bankroll themselves for their games—that is why so many of them get broke. If a player begins playing in a $2/$4 no-limit game with only a $4,000 bankroll, which is only ten buy-ins, he can get cleaned out if he experiences an inordinate amount of bad luck in a short period of time. When you think about how many players you've seen rebuy into a game three or four times on an off night, you can understand how quickly a player's bankroll can disappear. Of course, most of the time other players let bad luck affect their play, which in turn negatively affects their results. While the strategy in this book provides you with an inherent defense against losing streaks, you should still adhere to the twenty-buy-in rule so that you never have to feel any pressure on your bankroll or start thinking about drawing cash from your personal savings.

If you don't play poker for a living, you might feel that it isn't necessary to come up with all the cash for a full bankroll since you earn paychecks from your day job. I'm not crazy about this approach because it could interfere with your ability to separate your poker bankroll from your personal wealth. Here is the way I believe that you should look at things: Your paycheck should be used to pay rent, mortgage and other bills, as well as for disposable income and personal savings. Your poker bankroll should be used only to finance your poker playing. When you earn money from your games, you should either invest it to build your personal wealth or use it to build your bankroll so that you can play in bigger games.

Another potential problem with relying on your paychecks to finance your poker playing is that you might become afraid to put money in the pot feeling that you are playing with money that you can't afford to lose. This can be especially troublesome if you are constantly waiting for your next paycheck to be able to buy into a game again. If you think about your bets as money that you can't afford to lose, you will be unable to think clearly when you play your hands. If that happens, the *Playing No-Limit Hold'em as a Business* method will be of little use to you, even though it espouses a conservative approach to playing poker. To play in no-limit hold'em cash games regularly, you should prepare to build the appropriate bankroll and consider this bankroll as a separate source of cash from your paychecks.

It is especially important that inexperienced players adhere to the twenty-buy-in rule and sit in small games where they can afford an extended losing streak. Even experienced players shouldn't feel like they have to swallow their pride to sit in a very small game.

Remember that your objective is to make money, not to brag about how big the games are that you play.

One more key factor to be aware of when it comes to the size of game you play is the quality of players, which I mentioned earlier. If you find that bigger games are filled with really good players, you should probably find smaller games to play in. One very important part of managing your money is finding and playing with players who are less experienced or are mistake-prone. The game plan you have learned in this book arms you for success, even against the sharks, but you should still look to sit in games with weaker players. If you find weaker players at bigger games and can only moderately afford a streak of bad luck should that ever happen, feel free to play in those bigger games once in a while.

TOPPING UP: WHEN AND WHY

Topping up means buying more chips to add to your stack so that you always have a lot of chips in front of you. It will become necessary to do this if you have to surrender a few small pots or if you get unlucky and lose a large pot. You should top up fairly regularly, assuming you are playing well and following your game plan to a tee. Having a lot of chips in front of you when you hit a big hand is critical. Since the basic tenet of the *Playing No-Limit Hold'em as a Business* strategy is playing fewer pots but very large pots when you hit a big hand, it follows that you need to have a substantial chip stack with which to reap the rewards.

You might hear someone say that it is bad luck or just a bad idea to top up. This advice usually comes from players whose experience has taught them that when they are losing or running bad, they should either stop playing or just hope their luck turns around before they reach back into their pockets to risk more money. What this type of thinking fails to consider is that you need to have enough money in front of you to do some damage when your luck does change. Meeting your profit objective in a session could be difficult if you have very few chips when you flop a set against someone with pocket aces. If you get unlucky in a session, ride it out, stick to your game plan, and trust that your fortunes will reverse.

I have played many sessions where I started out losing because someone hit a lucky card against me in a big pot, and sometimes more than once. On many occasions I waited for a big hand, took down a monster pot at the end of the session, and left with a good profit when I had been in the hole earlier. It may seem as though I am trivializing what it feels like to experience multiple bad beats, but I assure you I have been there, done that, and I know how losing can mess with your head. However, what I have learned is that as long as you continue to play under optimal playing conditions and still feel like you are playing well, you should get right back down to business after a beat and wait for a big hand with which to make a good score.

If you don't think you are playing your best—and certainly, if you think your bankroll cannot withstand another loss in that session—you should pack it in, and either take a break from the game or get back on the horse the next day after clearing your head and getting some rest.

Another reason you don't want to take advice from other players when it comes to topping up is that they probably played poorly after experiencing some bad luck. Many players let bad luck mess with their heads and affect their game. You will not do that because your game plan ensures that you don't start getting involved in a lot of pots, a mistake that many players make when they get stuck early or get unlucky. Ignore what others tell you and make sure you have enough ammunition in front of you to win a big pot when you get a big hand.

Throughout this book, you have discovered many examples of how you will think and act differently than almost all other players you know. Trust and embrace this divergence between yourself and other players. After all, you will be winning and most of them will be losing.

SAVING YOUR WINNINGS

While you are free to do anything you want with your money, I believe that if you play cash games regularly, you should handle the money you make like anyone else who has a regular job. After you have built up a sufficient poker bankroll, think about saving some of the money you earn playing poker. These savings should be considered separate from your poker bankroll. Some of this money you may want to keep in a regular savings account and some of it you might use to buy savings bonds, stocks or retirement funds. You probably will want to talk to your accountant about how to handle gambling income, whether it is a primary or secondary source of income for you.

The key to growing your personal savings by playing poker is avoiding long stretches of time without setting aside any money. You can even set a light investment schedule where you deposit a specific amount of money into your bank account every two weeks or every month. Every few months you can then invest some of this money so that it truly becomes separate from your poker bankroll. If you ever have to start withdrawing this money or cashing in these investments due to a losing streak, it probably means that you haven't done a great job of sticking to your game plan or you got unlucky while playing in games that were too large. Learn from this experience and make the necessary adjustments. Investments should become a part of your personal wealth, so always try to avoid tapping into your personal wealth to play poker. Remember that you don't need to fall behind the rest of the investing public simply because you are a "gambler."

No matter how solid your money management skills are, you are likely to suffer losing streaks from time to time. The next chapter outlines how to handle those dreaded times when nothing seems to go right.

13 THE NATURE OF LOSING STREAKS

No matter how well you play you can't avoid an occasional losing session. Since your hands will not always be 12 to 1 favorites, you can sometimes lose a big pot if an opponent gets lucky. Sometimes you can even lose a big pot when you are ahead by 12 to 1. These things happen from time to time—and they occasionally happen before you have a chance to recover financially or emotionally. When this happens, you may be headed for a losing streak.

This book's game plan provides you with a two-point defense against suffering extended losing streaks. First, you will be playing big pots with hands that often have large mathematical edges over your opponents' hands. Second, you will play fewer pots altogether. When you don't overplay your starting hands or become involved in too many hands, you aren't exposed to a lot of risk. Still, nobody is impervious to losing, so it is important that you understand the nature of losing streaks in cash games.

THE THREE STAGES OF A LOSING STREAK

The three common stages of a losing streak are bad luck, more bad luck, followed by bad play.

STAGE 1: BAD LUCK.

In stage one, you lose a big pot unexpectedly because an opponent gets lucky and hits a three or four-outer on you, or because you were the victim of a set-up hand such as set over set on the flop. Nothing is overly new or surprising about this stage, as it mostly involves the usual bad beats that you frequently hear poker players talking about. In stage one, you will have lost one or two big pots.

STAGE 2: MORE BAD LUCK.

You have reached the second stage when you are not able to mount a comeback after one or two sessions. This can happen if you go card dead, if you continue to experience bad beats, or if you run into set-up hands soon after enduring stage one. When you are deep into the throes of stage two, you begin to marvel at how bad your luck has been, if for no other reason than simply the mathematical odds of getting unlucky so many times. If you have gotten paid off on a few big hands and have walked away with a few profitable sessions, you have not reached stage two. Your losing has stopped at stage one, thankfully, and you can chalk it up to getting unlucky in one or two big pots during one or two sessions.

If you reach stage two playing online, you will usually have lost most or all of your bankroll. Many players don't sufficiently bankroll themselves, which is why they can get cleaned out in stage two. The main point is that in stage two you are starting to feel it in the pocketbook.

You also are in stage two when you find yourself "on the sheet" in a home game, which means that the host has lent you money to continue playing the session. The host expects you to repay the loan by either continuing to play and winning, or by repaying your loan the next time you play.

STAGE 3: BAD PLAY.

In this stage, you are so distraught about the bad luck you've experienced that you start changing the way you play, making poor decisions, and becoming more willing to gamble. Consequently, stage three becomes the true defining stage of a losing streak, and potentially the most damaging. Emotions begin to take over your style of play and your decisions. You begin playing more pots and taking more chances, ironically spending your money more liberally when you should be sitting tight waiting to get paid off on a big hand. At this stage, your poor play gives you no chance to bust out of your losing streak and start winning again.

You start chasing draws in big pots hoping to get lucky. You might pick up eight or nine outs in a hand and think that it has so much potential that you become willing to overpay for your draw. You fail to realize that chasing draws puts you even deeper in the hole. Even worse, you might make a play with your draw and move all-in. The really sad part about this play is that it will be transparent to most players at the table: They know you've been losing and they recognize your all-in bet as a play often made by players on tilt. So, they are more willing to call you at a time when you have all your chips on the line as a probable 2 to 1 underdog.

In stage three, you might also fail to see warning signs that you are beaten when you make a hand. For example, let's say you call a raise preflop with K♥ Q♠, a weak hand you're likely to pay any price to play in this stage. Another player has also called, so you're in a three-way pot. The flop comes Q♣ 9♦ 8♦.

YOU

THE FLOP

The preflop raiser, an average-tight player, bets three-fourths of the pot, the next player raises, and then the action comes to you. You will be more likely to throw caution to the wind and reraise, possibly moving all-in. The preflop raiser could have A-A, K-K or A-Q, and while the other caller could be on a draw, he may be the one holding A-Q or better. Further, if he is a loose player, he might even have made the nut straight with a draw to the straight flush with the J♦ 10♦. Also, if either of your opponents has a big draw, you are not a strong favorite and shouldn't risk all your chips with two cards to come. While you usually know to at least consider folding K-Q in this spot, when you are in stage three of a losing streak, you're a lot less likely to think through the hand and evaluate your risk. In other words, you are more likely to play the hand poorly.

The third stage is when you start overextending yourself financially. If you play online, you might continue to deposit money into your online account without any real sense of how it is affecting your finances. Live players might withdraw a lot of money from their personal bank accounts or even take out cash advances on their credit cards to come up with extra cash. Sometimes players in stage three even cash in some of their investments like stocks, bonds or 401k's.

Obviously, this is a very dangerous stage to be in. The key learning for you as a player who implements this method is to fight the urge to change the way you play if you get unlucky and lose some pots. You must never enter the third stage by playing overly emotionally or by playing long hours when you are weary and are playing badly. Why get yourself into even deeper trouble? Sometimes it is best to just walk away from the poker table or from your computer for a few days, few weeks, or even longer if you need to.

Always make sure that you play under optimal playing conditions, which consist not only of the right opponents, but your own physical and psychological state. In short, if you feel frustrated and angry about your luck and your results to the extent that you aren't able to approach the game with a level head, you need to take a break. Playing poker should be an enjoyable experience that you look forward to. If ever you start to lose those feelings, it is probably best that you take a break.

Now let's discuss how to analyze why you are losing and how to keep your game sharp during a losing streak.

ANALYZING WHY YOU ARE LOSING

There are some very important factors other than bad luck that can influence your results and determine whether or not you enter a losing streak. When you notice you have been losing you will also need to keep these other factors in mind.

1. **Different players have entered your regular games.** When the players at your games change, the texture of the table changes. Perhaps you started losing at one of your live games because the quality of play increased. Maybe one of the loosest players stopped showing up, which changed the dynamics at the table, and you lost one of your best customers. Maybe you haven't been able to find some of your better customers online, or maybe you've become lazy and stopped looking for them. Playing against weaker players is an important part of your strategy, so not having them in your games could pose problems for your bottom line.

2. **You have stepped up to a bigger game.** By moving to a bigger game, you may have opened yourself up to more risk. Maybe the size of your losses and bad beats have been affecting you more than you think, causing you to play badly. It is also possible that you haven't yet properly adjusted to the new game and are taking on too much risk in making your decisions. If so, there may be better players in this game who know how to take advantage of your poor decisions. You may need to analyze your play to ensure that you have been properly executing your strategy. You might even consider the possibility that you have quite simply been

getting outclassed. In addition, you may also need to rethink whether this bigger game is right for you from a financial standpoint, since you should only be playing in games where you can afford to withstand an extended losing streak.

3. **You are getting involved in hands too early.** Another cause for your struggles could be that you're playing too many medium-sized pots before you have a chance to observe and group opponents. Consequently, you might not be playing as well as you should be, and may be digging a hole for yourself early in games. Getting involved too early could also mean getting bluffed off one of your big hands because you don't know how your opponents play. Remember, using an effective strategy doesn't necessarily mean that winning will come easy. You always need an understanding of how your opponents play to make the right decisions and enjoy good results.

4. **You are playing off strategy.** In some cases, a losing streak can begin because you purposely play off strategy. When we looked at playing against good players, we discussed how a tight player might emulate a strong-loose player. This is something you don't want to do because it exposes you to too much risk. Another example of playing off strategy is making too many tough calls by trying a little too hard to pick off bluffs, which usually happens because you want to feel like a great player, a hero. You must avoid the trappings of vanity that seem alluring to many poker players. Perhaps you started mixing up your game a little too much by playing too many large pots with only one pair or by betting out with drawing hands. Just know that anytime

you get off your game plan, you become vulnerable to losing streaks. To get great results you must stick to your game plan and be willing to surrender some small pots so that you can avoid losing big pots with weak hands.

5. You've begun to gamble with your profits. This is somewhat related to number four. A player who has been making money might think that he can afford to lose in an effort to try some new things or to have fun making plays. While there is some logic to this thinking, you have to think about the hours you have put in to make that money. Are you really willing to give back money you made with your patience, hard work and discipline by making plays that probably won't be an integral part of your cash game strategy in the future? Your best answer is no. Before buying this book, maybe you have lost money at poker. If so, you now have put in the time to read, study and apply all the learning here, so you really might not want to throw it away by getting off your new game plan just for fun.

Why not set aside some of your profits to buy into tournaments and try out some new plays there instead? In fact, I recommend using a looser style of play in tournaments where you should be willing to embrace more risk. Then you won't be at risk of beginning an extended losing streak by getting off your game plan in cash games. Just be sure to remain aware of your play in cash games so that your tournament play doesn't carry over to them. You are learning how to use a powerful weapon for cash games in this book, so to borrow a cliché, don't fix what isn't broken.

Doing just one or two little things wrong in no-limit hold'em could lead to an extended losing streak, during which it is possible to lose more money than you've ever lost before. That is why it is so important to be aware of a losing streak when you are experiencing one. While your game plan may be simple, you should continually analyze your play, the play of your opponents, and the poker environment in which you play. If you do this, at the very least you will prevent yourself from ever entering the third stage of a losing streak.

Of course we all want to win all the time. The next chapter addresses some things you can do to ensure that you become a winner and stay a winner throughout your poker career.

14 BECOMING A WINNER, STAYING A WINNER

Playing your cards right is an important part of the game—but there is much more to winning at poker than just that. Poker not only requires executing the right strategy at the table but also considering other elements that come into play when you are not in a hand. Only after mastering all these variables, in addition to consistently and successfully applying your game plan, will you truly become a winner.

DEVELOPING AWARENESS

Focusing only on playing your hands and tuning out everything else that is going on around you can be very tempting. However, there are many important things to be aware of that can directly or indirectly influence your results:

PAYING ATTENTION TO PEOPLE

You can always pick up valuable pieces of information just by watching and listening to players around you. Here are a few:

LOSING STREAKS

Even before you start playing, you might overhear someone talking about what bad luck he's been having, which might be a sign that he's in a losing streak and possibly playing poorly, as losing streaks tend to mess with a player's head and bring down his quality of play. As a result, you might find that an average-tight player plays a little more like a weak-tight player or maybe even like a weak-loose player. Although player groupings usually remain stable after a certain amount of time has passed in a player's career, a losing streak can create an emotional reaction that causes a player to play differently.

PLAYERS IMPROVING

You might notice that certain players are trying to improve their game. You may overhear someone talking about poker books he is reading when you never thought he would consider studying the game seriously. Perhaps after his first six months of playing poker, he is ready to graduate from weak-loose to average-loose. Most players go through a learning curve toward the beginning of their poker-playing career, so you may notice some changes in a player's game. When playing online, you might need to update your notes on a player if you think his game has changed permanently. No matter where you play, pay attention to how players are developing or whether they seem to be trying to improve their game.

PLAYERS LEAVING

A nifty little piece of information is finding out that a player needs to leave the game shortly. Players who fall into the "loose" player groupings might be motivated to play more hands. They might also be inclined to make a move in a big pot on a draw in a last ditch effort to take down a pot before they leave. Don't allow this tell to override your hand analysis, but incorporating it into your thinking might be beneficial when you consider the types of hands this opponent might be playing.

PAYING ATTENTION TO THE TABLE

You will not only want to think about your opponents on an individual basis, but also as a collective. Here are some key questions you can ask yourself to ensure that you are always playing in the best possible environment for you to win:

BECOMING A WINNER, STAYING A WINNER

ARE YOUR BEST CUSTOMERS STILL THERE?

If the players who routinely pay you off are gone, it may be a little harder for you to hit or surpass your profit objective. If you are playing online, you can switch tables or run a search to find your good customers. In one of your live games, perhaps you will notice that a good customer of yours hasn't shown up for a while. Inquire to find out where he has gone, or whether he is just on vacation. If he has started playing elsewhere, consider visiting the other game to keep playing with him.

HAS THE TABLE BECOME TOUGHER?

If stronger players have just joined the game and your best customers are gone, it may be harder for you to get paid off on big hands or win smaller pots. Consider switching tables or even going home if you're in a live game.

HAS THE MOOD OF THE TABLE CHANGED?

If your table goes from talkative to less talkative and more serious, it could mean that players are focusing more on the game, making it a tougher table. When playing online, you sometimes can learn a lot about a player from his chat, so playing at a chatty table can be very helpful. For starters, you can find out if a player is steaming after a bad beat. Even more informative is finding out how sophisticated a player's thinking is by seeing how he analyzes some of the hands at the table. Consider leaving a live game if the mood at the table changes for the worse (for example, people start talking trash) and these changes are distracting and unpleasant to you. You usually need to feel upbeat to play good poker, so you shouldn't spend hours at a table when you are dreading the experience.

HAS PLAY SPED UP OR TIGHTENED UP?

It can be very important to scrutinize how quickly pots build up. If there are a lot of large raises preflop and pots build up quickly, it will affect how you decide to play your hands. When you are first to act, you might decide to speculate less often (either preflop or postflop) because playing your hand probably will cost you more than you would like. At a very fast table, you might have to play only pairs preflop and try to flop sets. If you do pick up a monster hand at a fast table, you might bet more liberally because you are likely to get action, but be sure to play it right so that a loose opponent doesn't draw out on you in a big pot. At a table that is playing slowly, you will be able to see more flops cheaply so you can open up your range of starting hands. Also, you will be able to play medium-strength hands such as top pair with more confidence because there is less chance of the pot becoming large.

HAVE A FEW PLAYERS STARTED GOING TO WAR?

A war that breaks out between a couple of players sometimes drives fast play at a table. You might pick up a big hand and trap them by letting them bet or raise for you. As they try to outwit each other, you may be able to suck in the two adversaries. Also, when the two warring players are not in a particular hand, you might find that the table plays pretty tight, and you need to adjust accordingly.

IS A NEW TABLE OPENING UP?

It is possible to be stuck at a strong table in a live game or at a table full of people whose company you don't enjoy. At a casino, ask the floor for a table change if you're not happy. At a home game, if a new table is opening up you might be able to see if some weaker players that you know are sitting there, so you may want to consider moving. Sometimes a casino or home game implements a must-move policy. This means that tables will constantly be moving players to one or two main tables when seats open up. Consequently, if you are already sitting at a main table you may not get an opportunity to move. This is not a problem you run into online, as you can switch to any table that has an open seat.

UNDERSTANDING THAT YOU CANNOT ALWAYS REACH YOUR PROFIT OBJECTIVE

Although you always keep your profit objective in your mind during a game, you sometimes need to ask yourself whether you should leave short of your goal or continue playing. For example, let's say that you're playing a live $5/$5 no-limit game with a $250 profit objective and your profit is currently at $190. You are feeling a little tired, one of your best customers has just left, and the table seems a little tougher now. Maybe it's a good idea to pack it in. When the downside of continuing to play is losing money, there's nothing wrong with leaving short of your objective if the playing environment isn't ideal. It is also okay to leave with a smaller than expected profit before you hit a monster hand and win a big pot. If that happens, be pleased that you were able to turn a profit by winning small or medium-sized pots.

BEING SELF-AWARE

Since we can often become our own worst enemy, we need to make sure that we are thinking, doing and feeling the right things in order to set ourselves up for success. Here are some things to consider.

PLAYING TIRED

Be sure you are in the right mental and physical state to play well. Playing tired will negatively affect the quality of your decisions. Sometimes, regardless of how far away you are from your profit objective, you probably need to stop playing if you are very tired.

KEEPING YOUR EMOTIONS IN CHECK

Armed with the game plan outlined in this book, one challenge will be to avoid letting your great results affect you emotionally. Sure, you feel good about your results and you enjoy the game even more knowing that you a have a great game plan, but you must harness those good feelings rather than getting cocky. Feeling like a superstar at the table might make you try to play like one, and then you might start playing more pots and making moves when you never did before. Instead, you need to keep playing the way you have been playing. Learn to take your success in stride. Recognize that you aren't necessarily the best poker player in the world, you have simply found the best way to make money in cash games. Showing humility will go a long way toward keeping your play sound.

Another aspect of the emotional spectrum is anger. Anger can lead you to start headhunting an opponent who has gotten lucky against you, or someone who just rubs you the wrong way. Anger can tempt you to play more pots with weaker hands. Don't let the game or your opponents get the better of you. By stubbornly sticking to your game plan, you will no doubt get the better of them in the long run.

RECOGNIZING YOUR MOOD

Do you really feel like playing? Sometimes you simply may not be in the mood to play even though you are not mentally or physically fatigued. Your game plan requires patience and mental acuity, so you need to be sure that you feel up to the challenge, as we are all prone to making mistakes when we aren't feeling up to playing. There is absolutely nothing wrong with finding something else to do if you have been playing a lot of poker and feel that you need a break.

PLAYING WHILE INTOXICATED

While drinking might be more about being in control than being aware, it is still an important factor in awareness. Enjoying one or two drinks is fine, but you never want to do anything that gets you off your game plan. When you see a player drinking too much, you can usually expect that player to make a mistake, and you just have to hope it's against you. Cash games reward thinking and intelligent decision-making much more than thoughtless, reckless gambling.

IMPROVING YOUR GAME

To become a winner and remain a winner, always try to improve your game. Reading this book will not automatically transform you into a new player, no matter how simple the game plan is. You still need to take what you've learned here, apply it properly, and hone all the poker skills that are required to turn your game plan into a success. Here are some suggestions for how to take your game to the next level after you've learned to implement the *Playing No-Limit Hold'em as a Business* method.

TRAIN YOURSELF TO THINK THROUGH A HAND

Poker is a thinking game in which continuing to develop your hand reading and analytical skills is critical. When you are holding a monster hand, it is tempting to continue acting (betting or checking) without thinking. When you do that, you miss out on an opportunity to learn.

Stay focused on the action and the decisions being made during a hand you're playing. Try not to act without having a plan and some idea of what your opponents are holding. Working on these skills will enable you to more quickly and accurately surmise what is happening when you are involved in hands. This clarity is crucial in poker—it gives you an edge over your opponents. You should also watch hands closely even when you are not involved in a hand. The more you learn about how other players think through a hand, the more you will be able to do it well yourself.

REVIEW THE KEY HANDS
FROM YOUR SESSIONS

Reviewing key hands is an important form of training. After a session, think about what you learned in the hands you played. Whether you are lying peacefully in bed, driving your car, or relaxing in front of your TV, reviewing the hands you played or the hands you watched others play is great practice. Doing this will help develop your analytical skills.

READ BOOKS

You don't have to stop with this book. There are a number of books that offer you different perspectives on how to play many types of hands, especially on how to play them aggressively. If you overhear some of your opponents talking about books they've read, why not read those books to learn what your opponents know? Perhaps you will find opportunities to capitalize on this knowledge later on. Also, a lot of books are geared for tournament play and most players don't make proper transitions from tournaments to cash games. These books can open you up to some of the plays you might be up against, and give you an advantage when you're trying to get into your opponents' heads.

EMBRACE CRITICISM

Even though you have learned a winning game plan in this book, there is still plenty of opportunity to learn from others who have a more objective view of your play. Ask your poker buddies for a critique of your play. Even though you will play differently from most players, always be willing to listen to the constructive criticism of other experienced players. In almost every hand you play, you face numerous risks and threats, and you always have multiple options when considering how to deal with these risks. Since there is rarely only one correct way to play a hand, you can benefit by hearing how your friends think you should have played it.

GAIN EXPERIENCE

In poker the more you watch, play and think, the more you learn. Therefore, it is important to put in time at the tables. If you only play once or twice a month, it will be hard to develop your game at a rapid pace because many things happen at the tables that books cannot teach you. Among other things, you need to understand in real time the particular tendencies and decisions of your opponents. While player groupings certainly help (and I don't recommend getting away from using them), players are still people who can do idiosyncratic things. In general, no matter how many books you read, they still won't cover all the types of situations and plays you will see at the tables, so try to take advantage of seeing them first hand by playing regularly.

OPEN UP YOUR GAME

Playing in tournaments, in small home games, or in any other poker game where the risk to your bankroll is minimal will allow you to practice. You want a playing environment in which you can feel comfortable taking more risks in the hands you play without significantly impacting your poker profits. That way, you can work on evaluating opponents, reading hands, and honing your analytical skills to become a better competitor in the cash game arena.

Many variables influence your long-term results at the poker tables. Always think about these additional key aspects of the game, factors that too many players ignore. You want to be a player who controls the game, not someone who allows the game to control you.

15 SUMMING UP

The influence of tournament poker on television has created a generation of poker players who embrace too much risk. Using the skills and strategy in this book, you will be able to confidently compete against these players. While many poker players struggle to understand why they fail in online cash games, you will leverage your new game plan and succeed by counterbalancing the aggressiveness of online players.

Too many players blame their poor results on bad luck when it is flawed strategy and a lack of careful and deliberate decision making that cause them to lose money. The risk management techniques that you've learned in this book will enable you to generate steady profit growth. They will limit your exposure to those terrible poker sessions in which you can lose four or even more buy-ins. Instead of experiencing large swings in your bankroll, you will enjoy seeing your profits grow far more steadily than most poker players—which should make your poker career enjoyable and long lasting.

Play well! And play no-limit hold'em like a business.

APPENDIX

ODDS AND PROBABILITIES CHARTS

Knowing the odds of making your hand is an integral part of winning at no-limit hold'em. Using the statistical odds and probabilities on the following charts, you can better determine your best course of action preflop and on the flop, as well as know the odds of seeing an overcard hit the flop when you are holding a pocket pair.

PROBABILITIES & ODDS OF HANDS WINNING PREFLOP		
TYPE OF HAND	PROBABILITY	ODDS
Severely Dominated Hand		
A♦ A♣	93%	13.3 to 1
A♠ K♥	7&	
Dominating Pocket Pair vs Lower Pocket Pair		
Q♦ Q♣	82%	4.5 to 1
9♥ 9♠	18%	
Overpair vs Low Suited Connector		
K♠ K♣	77%	3.3 to 1
7♦ 6♦	23%	
Dominating Unpaired Hand		
A♦ K♣ (5% chance of tie vs any other unpaired Ace)	71%	3 to 1
A♥ J♠	24%	
Overcards vs Undercards (Unsuited)		
K♥ Q♦	67%	2 to 1
7♣ 2♥	33%	

(continued)

PROBABILITIES & ODDS OF HANDS WINNING PREFLOP

TYPE OF HAND	PROBABILITY	ODDS
A♣ K♠	63%	1.7 to 1
10♦ 9♥	37%	
Winning Hand Unpaired (opponent's high card beats your kicker)		
A♠ J♥	63%	1.7 to 1
K♦ 10♣	37%	
Winning Hand Unpaired (opponent's two cards beat your kicker)		
A♠ 9♥	58%	1.4 to 1
K♦ J♣	42%	
Pocket Pair vs Overcards (Unsuited)		
8♣ 8♦	53%	1.1 to 1
A♥ K♠	47%	

Notes:
Suited cards increase in probability by +3%
1% chance of tie is rounded out

FLOP ODDS & PROBABILITIES

HAND	PROBABILITY	ODDS
1 Pair, 2 Pair, Trips or Quads with 2 Unpaired Cards		
K♦ Q♠ on K♣ 8♦ 4♦ flop	33%	2 to 1
Set or Quads When Holding a Pocked Pair		
7♣ 7♦ on J♥ 7♠ 2♥ flop	12%	7.5 to 1
A Flush Draw When Holding 2 Suited Cards		
A♣ 4♣ on Q♥ 10♣ 7♣ flop	11%	8.1 to 1
2 Pair Using Both Unpaired Hole Cards		
J♦ 9♠ on J♣ 3♦ 9♦ flop	2%	48 to 1
Trips Using 1 Unpaired Hole Card		
A♦ 6♣ on 10♠ 6♦ 6♠ flop	1%	73 to 1

FLOP ODDS & PROBABILITIES

HAND	PROBABILITY NO OVERCARD ON FLOP	ODDS NO OVERCARD ON FLOP
K K	77%	0.3 to 1
Q Q	59%	0.7 to 1
J J	43%	1.3 to 1
10 10	31%	2.3 to 1
9 9	21%	3.8 to 1
8 8	13%	6.5 to 1
7 7	8%	11.7 to 1
6 6	4%	23 to 1
5 5	2%	53 to 1
4 4	<1%	162 to 1
3 3	<1%	979 to 1

GREAT CARDOZA POKER BOOKS
ADD THESE TO YOUR LIBRARY - ORDER NOW!

DANIEL NEGREANU'S POWER HOLD'EM STRATEGY by Daniel Negreanu. This power-packed book on beating no-limit hold'em is one of the three most influential poker books ever written. Negreanu headlines a collection of young great players—Todd Brunson, David Williams. Erick Lindgren, Evelyn Ng and Paul Wasicka—who share their insider professional moves and winning secrets. You'll learn about short-handed and heads-up play, high-limit cash games, a powerful beginner's strategy to neutralize pro players, and how to mix up your play, bluff and win big pots. The centerpiece, however, is Negreanu's powerful and revolutionary small ball strategy. You'll learn how to play hold'em with cards you never would have played before—and with fantastic results. The preflop, flop, turn and river will never look the same again. A must-have! 520 pages, $34.95.

POKER WIZARDS by Warwick Dunnett. In the tradition of Super System, an exclusive collection of champions and superstars have been brought together to share their strategies, insights, and tactics for winning big money at poker, specifically no-limit hold'em tournaments. This is priceless advice from players who individually have each made millions of dollars in tournaments, and collectively, have won more than 20 WSOP bracelets, two WSOP main events, 100 major tournaments and $50 million in tournament winnings! Featuring Daniel Negreanu, Dan Harrington, Marcel Luske, Kathy Liebert, Mike Sexton, Mel Judah, Marc Salem, T.J Cloutier and Chris "Jesus" Ferguson. This must-read book is a goldmine for all serious players, aspiring pros, and future champions! 352 pgs, $19.95.

SUPER SYSTEM by Doyle Brunson. This classic book is considered by the pros to be the best book ever written on poker! Jam-packed with advanced strategies, theories, tactics and money-making techniques, no serious poker player can afford to be without this hard-hitting information. Includes fifty pages of the most precise poker statistics ever published. Features chapters written by poker's biggest superstars, such as Dave Sklansky, Mike Caro, Chip Reese, Joey Hawthorne, Bobby Baldwin, and Doyle. Essential strategies, advanced play, and no-nonsense winning advice on making money at 7-card stud (razz, high-low split, cards speak, and declare), draw poker, lowball, and hold'em (limit and no-limit).This is a must-read for any serious poker player. 628 pages, $29.95.

SUPER SYSTEM 2 by Doyle Brunson. SS2 expands upon the original with more games and professional secrets from the best in the world. New revision includes Phil Hellmuth Jr. along with superstar contributors Daniel Negreanu, winner of multiple WSOP gold bracelets and 2004 Poker Player of the Year; Lyle Berman, 3-time WSOP gold bracelet winner, founder of the World Poker Tour, and super-high stakes cash player; Bobby Baldwin, 1978 World Champion; Johnny Chan, 2-time World Champion and 10-time WSOP bracelet winner; Mike Caro, poker's greatest researcher, theorist, and instructor; Jennifer Harman, the world's top female player and one of ten best overall; Todd Brunson, winner of more than 20 tournaments; and Crandell Addington, no-limit hold'em legend. 704 pgs, $29.95.

CARO'S BOOK OF POKER TELLS by Mike Caro. One of the ten greatest books written on poker, this must-have book should be in every player's library. If you're serious about winning, you'll realize that most of the profit comes from being able to read your opponents. Caro reveals the secrets of interpreting *tells*—physical reactions that reveal information about a player's cards—such as shrugs, sighs, shaky hands, eye contact, and many more. Learn when opponents are bluffing, when they aren't and why—based solely on their mannerisms. Over 170 photos of players in action and play-by-play examples show the actual tells. These powerful ideas will give you the decisive edge. 320 pages, $24.95.

GREAT CARDOZA POKER BOOKS
ADD THESE TO YOUR LIBRARY - ORDER NOW!

THE POKER TOURNAMENT FORMULA *by Arnold Snyder.* Start making money now in fast no-limit hold'em tournaments with these radical and never-before-published concepts and secrets for beating tournaments. You'll learn why cards don't matter as much as the dynamics of a tournament—your position, the size of your chip stack, who your opponents are, and above all, the structure. Poker tournaments offer one of the richest opportunities to come along in decades. Every so often, a book comes along that changes the way players attack a game and provides them with a big advantage over opponents. Gambling legend Arnold Snyder has written such a book. 368 pages, $19.95.

POKER TOURNAMENT FORMULA 2: Advanced Strategies for Big Money Tournaments *by Arnold Snyder.* Probably the greatest tournament poker book ever written, and the most controversial in the last decade, Snyder's revolutionary work debunks commonly (and falsely) held beliefs. Snyder reveals the power of chip utility—the real secret behind winning tournaments—and covers utility ranks, tournament structures, small- and long-ball strategies, patience factors, the impact of structures, crushing the Harringbots and other player types, tournament phases, and much more. Includes big sections on Tools, Strategies, and Tournament Phases. A must buy! 496 pages, $24.95.

CHAMPIONSHIP NO-LIMIT & POT-LIMIT HOLD'EM *by T. J. Cloutier & Tom McEvoy.* New edition! The bible for winning pot-limit and no-limit hold'em gives you the answers to your most important questions: How do you get inside your opponents' heads and learn how to beat them at their own game? How can you tell how much to bet, raise, and reraise in no-limit hold'em? When can you bluff? How do you set up your opponents in pot-limit hold'em so that you can win a monster pot? What are the best strategies for winning no-limit and pot-limit tournaments, satellites, and supersatellites? Inspired advice you can bank on from two of the most recognizable figures in poker. 304 pages, $19.95.

CHAMPIONSHIP HOLD'EM *by T. J. Cloutier & Tom McEvoy.* New edition! Hard-hitting hold'em the way it's played *today* in limit cash games and tournaments. Get killer advice on how to win more money in rammin'-jammin', kill-pot, jackpot, shorthanded, and full table cash games. You'll learn the thinking process for preflop, flop, turn, and river play with specific suggestions for what to do when good or bad things happen. Includes play-by-play analyses, advice on how to maximize profits against rocks in tight games, weaklings in loose games, experts in solid games, plus tournament strategies for small buy-in, big buy-in, rebuy, satellite and big-field major tournaments. Wow! 392 pages, $19.95.

OMAHA HIGH-LOW: Play to Win with the Odds *by Bill Boston.* Selecting the right hands to play is the most important decision to make in Omaha. This is the *only* book that shows you the chances that every one of the 5,278 Omaha high-low hands has of winning the high end of the pot, the low end of it, and how often it is expected to scoop all the chips. You get all the vital tools needed to make critical preflop decisions based on the results of more than 500 million computerized hand simulations. You'll learn the 100 most profitable starting cards, trap hands to avoid, 49 worst hands, 30 ace-less hands you can play for profit, and the three bandit cards you must know to avoid losing hands. 248 pages, $19.95.

HOW TO BEAT SIT-AND-GO POKER TOURNAMENTS by Neil Timothy. There is a lot of dead money up for grabs in the lower limit sit-and-gos and Neil Timothy shows you how to go and get it. The author, a professional player, shows you how to reach the last six places of lower limit sit-and-go tournaments four out of five times and then how to get in the money 25-35 percent of the time using his powerful, proven strategies. This book can turn a losing sit-and-go player into a winner, and a winner into a bigger winner. Also effective for the early and middle stages of one-table satellites. 176 pages, $14.95.

Order now at 1-800-577-WINS or go online to: www.cardozabooks.com